Your Road Map to Lifelong Happiness

A Guide To The Life You Want

Other Books by Ken Keyes, Jr.

Handbook to Higher Consciousness
The Power of Unconditional Love
Gathering Power Through Insight and Love
   (Penny Gillespie, coauthor)
How to Enjoy Your Life in Spite of It All
Your Life Is a Gift
Prescriptions for Happiness
Your Heart's Desire: A Loving Relationship
Handbook to Higher Consciousness:
   The Workbook   (Penny Gillespie, coauthor)
Discovering the Secrets of Happiness:
   My Intimate Story
Planethood   (Ben Ferencz, coauthor)

OUT OF PRINT
The Hundreth Monkey
Taming Your Mind
Loving Your Body
Looking Forward
   (Jacques Fresco, coauthor)

Your Road Map to Lifelong Happiness

A GUIDE TO THE LIFE YOU WANT

Ken Keyes, Jr.

Love Line Books
Coos Bay, Oregon

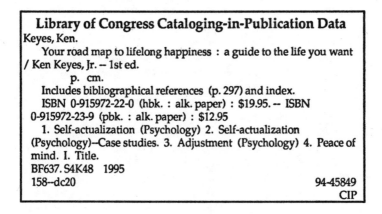

Library of Congress Cataloging-in-Publication Data
Keyes, Ken.
   Your road map to lifelong happiness : a guide to the life you want
/ Ken Keyes, Jr. -- 1st ed.
     p. cm.
  Includes bibliographical references (p. 297) and index.
  ISBN 0-915972-22-0 (hbk. : alk. paper) : $19.95. -- ISBN
0-915972-23-9 (pbk. : alk. paper) : $12.95
  1. Self-actualization (Psychology) 2. Self-actualization
(Psychology)--Case studies. 3. Adjustment (Psychology) 4. Peace of
mind. I. Title.
BF637.S4K48 1995
158--dc20   94-45849
                                           CIP

Love Line Books
**1620 Thompson Road
Coos Bay, Oregon 97420**

*To the precious wounded child
in all of us—who had to survive the
unexpressed pains of childhood by
twisting itself in ways that paradoxically
undermine our adult lives today.*

Contents

Introduction
Getting the Quirks Out of Your Happiness

Every chapter in this book is focused on how we destroy our happiness—and how we can nourish it. We are remarkably adaptable and intelligent. So why are stress and unhappiness at such an epidemic level? It seems that a structural problem in our brains is doing us in.

In 1969, Dr. Paul D. MacLean announced that humans have a three-part brain consisting of a reptilian base with mammalian and human brains piled on top. We will lump the reptilian and mammalian parts together and call them the "old brain." The old brain is also known as the unconscious (or subconscious) mind—and metaphorically as the "inner child." Most of its activities are usually below the threshold of our awareness. After integrating for the last 250 million years, the reptilian and mammalian parts of our "triune" brain work well together.

Our uniquely human new brain is only about 40 thousand years old. Our new brain (the conscious, thinking neocortex) is not wired into the old brain with the monitoring, feedback, and control circuits we need. The poor communication between our old and new brains can create enormous problems in our everyday lives. It's like we tried to leap out of the jungle—but haven't quite made it yet!

Our rational new brain often doesn't know what's really going on down there in the old brain. The two sometimes work at cross purposes. They use entirely different "languages." The old brain produces feelings. The new brain specializes in thinking. It boils the world down to words and symbols. And all of this goes over the head of the old brain, which evolved to get us through primordial jungles.

Let's look at an example of how our old and new brains are at odds with each other because of the inadequate wiring between them. The rage of a severely abused four-year-old toward its mother or father can be bottled up in the unconscious old brain. When triggered, this repressed time bomb can be *projected* 30 years later onto one's spouse—or ex-spouse, children, friends, or anybody. The repressed anger from pain inflicted three decades ago may be triggered today by a superficial similarity between the past and the present. This is why we often make "mountains out of molehills," unexpectedly "fly off the handle," rashly "hit the ceiling," or simply "run amok."

The old brain can *by-pass the thinking brain's control systems* and project a verbally violent or even murderous energy onto an innocent person! Fifty percent of female murders in the U.S. are by husbands or ex-husbands! Two thousand children in the U.S. are killed yearly by a parent whose unconscious old brain is dumbly crucifying an innocent child for the parent's childhood pain that was not safe to express.

And the new, thinking brain really doesn't understand "what came over me." If it were properly integrated through adequate circuitry, in a few milliseconds the new brain could come up with a more appropriate response than murder. In an intelligently designed brain, the wisdom of our new brain could not be bypassed by our reptilian-mammalian brain which evolved for animal survival in eons past. This lack of coordination makes our lives vulnerable to "quirks" that harm our relationships, upset our marriages, and create horrors from family murders to international wars.

> **We define a quirk as a life-damaging illusion produced by our unconscious mind.**

Compensating for the Quirks

So the bad news is that every day we live, in one way or another, our lives are harmed by pervasive quirks in our old brain. The good news is that our new brain today can learn how to effectively *compensate* for this unfinished part of the evolution of our species. As you and I do this "inner work," our lives can go into new dimensions of love, health, fun, inner peace, enjoyment, and happiness.

This ground-breaking book will show how the quirks between our two brains are an overlooked root cause behind most of our social and individual problems: war, crime, divorce, depression, compulsions, psychosomatic illness, drug addiction, murder, insanity, and suicide—to mention only a few. Society has taken each of these sicknesses and attacked them in isolation—with pitiful results. They only seem to get worse. That's because we've been working on *symptoms*—and ignoring a primary *cause.*

This book explains how the faulty integration between our old and new brains is a neglected factor that continuously harms our lives. Our verbal attacks on each other, as well as physical aggression, are basically due to the quirks of our old brain. *The quirks in the parent's unconscious mind* damage the child by making it develop a protective false-self—and thus numb a part of their authentic, true-self. And the torn or ruined lives caused by the illusions of our quirks continue to pile up. . . .

We will discuss the skills we need to *compensate* for the poor communication between our old reptilian-mammalian brain and our new, thinking neocortex. As we develop these skills, many of our unsolvable personal problems may dissolve like an iceberg in warm equatorial waters. I believe the greatest thing we can do to improve our own lives, and also contribute to society, is to nullify our quirks by mastering the techniques for creating a *partnership* between our two brains.

The Life You've Wanted

Both your conscious and unconscious minds have their own wisdom. And each has enormous power in controlling your life. As you learn the skills needed to help your two brains work in harmony, you will be greatly rewarded. You will find increased aliveness and energy in your life. Instead of an endless chain of problems to be solved, life can become a challenging adventure.

You will find that although your ship of happiness may rock with the waves, it will not be overturned by life events. There will always be "problems" or "challenges"—depending on how you look at it. Almost everyone experiences the death of loved ones, job loss, financial reverses, divorce, sickness, hostility, misunderstandings, disagreements, criticism, judgmentalness, disappointments, diminished abilities in old age—and inevitable death and taxes. And yet when you learn how, you can keep on living in relaxed enjoyment—even on the day you die.

Skillful parents will not only nurture their child's *conscious mind*—they will also learn how to effectively nurture their child's *unconscious mind*. And this enormously enhances the aliveness and happiness in their own lives—as well as their children's. But first, they must learn how to compensate for the quirks between their own two brains in order to nurture their child's unconscious mind.

This book is practical. It shows you how to begin attaining the enormous benefits it describes. When you take the Inventory of Childhood Survival Strategies (Chapter 7), you can develop a deeper understanding of your personal growth targets.

As you notice, I'm making great claims for the new horizons this book can show you—*if you do your part*. I've found these promises have been wonderfully fulfilled in my own life. I'm glad I can sincerely offer them to you for your lifetime journey of personal growth. I send you my loving best wishes for increasing your skill in opening the doors to happiness in your life.

Ken Keyes, Jr.
Coos Bay, Oregon

A Grammatical Note

I want to continue the style I adopted in *The Power of Unconditional Love*. In this book I wrote:

English today lacks singular third person common gender pronouns. I'm not willing to bog down the reader with, "When you hide your real feelings from your partner, you're depriving him or her of the realities of life she or he needs to work on himself or herself to go beyond her or his demanding programming." Since third person plural pronouns in English are not gender-specific, we've decided to use "them," "they," "themselves," and "their" for both singular and plural. Thus it will come out, "When you hide your real feelings from your partner, you're depriving them of the realities of life they need to work on themselves to go beyond their demanding programming." We hope it reads smoothly for you.

Merriam Webster's Collegiate Dictionary (10th Edition) states:

The use of *they, their, them,* and *themselves* as pronouns of indefinite gender and indefinite number is well established in speech and writing, even in literary and formal contexts. This gives you the option of using the plural pronouns where you think they sound best, and of using the singular pronouns (as *he, she, he or she,* and their inflected forms) where you think they sound best.[1]

PART I

YOUR MENTAL EQUIPMENT

1

The Dawn of Humanity

To operate your car, it's useful to know something about how it works. To create a happy life it is essential to understand the way your mental equipment was put together in the distant past—and how it works today. This is a first step in compensating for its limitations—and empowering you to live the life you want.

Our planet Earth came together from cosmic dust and gasses about 4.8 billion years ago. Life began to evolve about 3.5 billion years ago.

As we developed beyond single-celled organisms in a primordial slime pool, our distant relatives included marine organisms, amphibians, reptiles, and finally mammals. About 250 million years ago, descendants of Paleozoic reptiles branched off into dinosaurs, snakes, turtles, alligators, lizards, and birds on one side of the family—and various mammals and humans on the other side!

About four million years ago, our ape-like *Australopithecus* ancestors increasingly walked erect. About two million years ago, their *Homo habilis* descendants developed a distinctly larger brain and were probably the first to make stone tools. About 1.6 million years ago, *Homo erectus* developed an even larger brain. The brain kept expanding as *erectus* spread through Europe and Asia, learned how to control fire, and survived under dramatic climatic changes. "They probably looked much like us—a clean-shaven, well-dressed *Homo erectus* male might prompt little comment if he wandered down a busy street today," according to biologists Robert Ornstein and Paul Ehrlich.[1]

Erectus tramped the Earth for over a million years. About 300,000 years ago, evolutionary changes began that spawned the early forms of our species, *Homo sapiens*—i.e., thinking man! Ornstein and Ehrlich in *New World New Mind* help us get a perspective on our ancestry:

3

Reptiles, Mammals, and Us

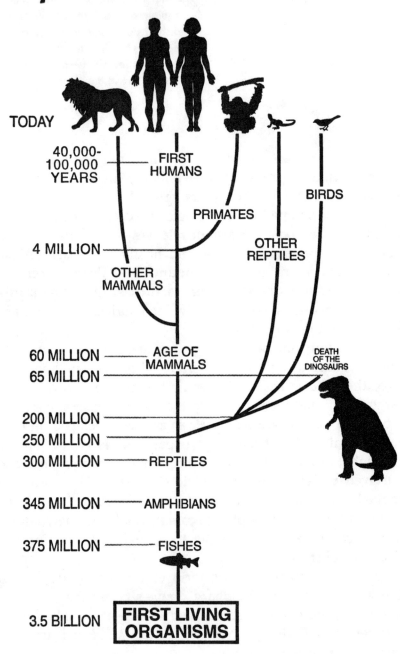

TODAY

40,000-100,000 YEARS — FIRST HUMANS

PRIMATES

BIRDS

4 MILLION —

OTHER REPTILES

OTHER MAMMALS

60 MILLION — AGE OF MAMMALS

DEATH OF THE DINOSAURS

65 MILLION

200 MILLION

250 MILLION

300 MILLION — REPTILES

345 MILLION — AMPHIBIANS

375 MILLION — FISHES

3.5 BILLION — **FIRST LIVING ORGANISMS**

Suppose Earth's history were charted on a single year's calendar, with midnight January 1 representing the origin of the Earth and midnight December 31 the present. Then each day of Earth's "year" would represent 12 million years of actual history. On that scale, the first form of life, a simple bacterium, would arise sometime in February. More complex life-forms, however, come much later; the first fishes appear about November 20. The dinosaurs arrive around December 10 and disappear on Christmas Day. The first of our ancestors recognizable as human would not show up until the *afternoon of December 31.* *Homo sapiens*—our species—would emerge at about 11:45 P.M. All that has happened in recorded history would occur in the final *minute* of the year.[2]

Developing Our Thinking Brain

So you and I had a reptilian ancestor that lived about 250 million years ago from whom we mammals branched off. As mammals evolved, the medulla oblongata or reptilian brain was topped by the addition of an egg-shaped limbic area that generates emotions in mammals. We will call this combination reptilian and mammalian brain the "old brain." It is the seat of our unconscious mind. It's a very simple brain. The old brain is mainly attuned to the "Four F's:" feeding, fighting, fleeing, and sexual behavior—as biologists humorously put it.

The reptilian brain orchestrates actions for safety and satisfaction of biological needs. The mammalian limbic brain provides vivid emotions such as fear, grief, jealousy, and anger. By surgically stimulating the limbic area, brain scientists can produce outbursts of fear or anger in a mammalian brain.

The reptile brain has the sensation of pain when its body is injured. However, it does not create emotions. A rattlesnake may bite you, but I'm sure you'll be glad to know that it's really not angry with you! However, the limbic area of the mammalian brain of a tiger probably will feel angry if you invade its territory. The combined reptilian and mammalian brains have integrated over the last quarter billion years. They work great together as our "old brain."

5

Our Old and New Brains

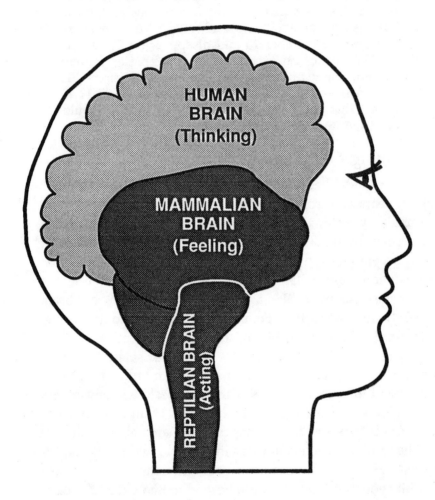

HUMAN
BRAIN
(Thinking)

MAMMALIAN
BRAIN
(Feeling)

REPTILIAN BRAIN
(Acting)

 New Thinking Brain
40 thousand years old

Old Acting and Feeling Brain
250 million years old

When ape-like mammals began walking on two legs, some of them began a four-million-year journey to humanhood. The outside front cover of the brain of our erect ancestors began to add more neurons, which required a larger skull. Billions upon billions of added neurons, connecting circuits, and new neurochemicals (permitting more retrievable information) were being constantly added to the mental machinery of these walk-abouts.

These changes in this jelly-like ball we call our brain added new abilities. Our wandering ancestors continued developing a more elaborate use of tools and utensils—and language skills. Millennium by millennium, our ancient relatives passed on more effective lifestyles to their young. Their rapidly growing ability to transmit more information to the next generation was crucial. Once something was invented, it could be passed on and improved.

About 100,000 years ago, some of our ancestors began an enormous proliferation of cells on the eighth-inch outside covering (neocortex) of their brains. Other mammals have a cortex. But in the quantity of neurons, our cortex is like a mountain compared to a small hill. When we broke the ten-billion cortical neuron level, it appears that the added *quantity* of neurons gave us a new *qualitative* dimension—the ability to think abstractly or symbolically. This explosion of neocortical cells aided the survival of our tool-and-language using relatives.

The multiplication of cortical cells continued for the next 60,000 years until about 40,000 years ago. Thus, it was perhaps about 8,000 generations ago (five generations per century) that our species was equipped with a "biocomputer." These billions of neocortical neurons enable us to reason, analyze, achieve insights, philosophize, play checkers, and discuss quirks in our brains.

Throughout this book we will refer to our cerebral cortex as the "new brain" or "thinking brain." It is the seat of the conscious mind. In later chapters we will also refer to it as the "inner adult" or "inner parent" part of our brain. In contrast, the old brain or feeling brain in the medulla-limbic area is the seat of the "unconscious mind" or "inner child" mind.

Our Factory Defects

Unfortunately we have built-in "factory" defects. Our wonderful biocomputer is not yet wired in a way that permits fully effective cooperation between our old and new brains. We refer to the resulting problems as "quirks." As mentioned before, a quirk is a life-damaging illusion produced by our unconscious mind.

Day by day these quirks greatly diminish the quality of our lives unless we compensate for them. Their ravaging effects on our lives will be discussed in the next chapter. Sometime in the future, *Homo sapiens* may evolve the missing wiring, and get rid of the quirks. You and I have to live with what we have. But it's great to know that if we develop the skills described in this book, we can vastly improve the integration between our two brains. We can help them communicate and cooperate so that we may have the benefit *today* of some possible evolutionary improvements in the future. Chapter 2 tells how we can begin to do this.

Our Three-Pound Universe

So it was about 40,000 to 100,000 years ago that the first human beings stood upon the Earth. In terms of mental and physical equipment, they were the equal of you and me today. Of course, they lacked our accumulation of knowledge and skills. They didn't know how to fire missiles at each other, nor could they cure pneumonia with antibiotics.

Judith Hooper and Dick Teresi in their excellent book *The Three-Pound Universe* wrote that although our brain is about the size of a grapefruit:

> Everything we know—from subatomic particles to distant galaxies—everything we feel—from love for our children to fear of enemy nations—is experienced and modeled in our brains. Without the brain, nothing—not quarks, not black holes, nor love, nor hatred—would exist for us. The universe exists for us only in so far as it exists in our brains. The brain is our three-pound universe.[3]

The electrical nerve currents of the brain travel between 100 and 200 miles per hour. Our cerebral cortex has perhaps up to 100 billion neurons, and each neuron makes between 5,000 and 50,000 contacts with its neighbors. We have more "bits" in our heads than any computer ever built. "A computer with the same number of 'bits'," Hooper and Teresi point out, "would be a hundred stories tall and cover the state of Texas."[4] We have more possible interconnections between our neurons than there are grains of sand on all the beaches of the world![5] And we have over 50,000 thoughts each day—most of which are reruns from the day before!

Our brain—this three-pound universe—produced the Declaration of Independence, has sent machines to photograph the planets of our solar system, erected the Statue of Liberty, painted the frescoes of the Sistine Chapel, wrote countless volumes that make the truths and trances of one generation available to the next—and has designed nuclear killing machines that can wipe out all human life on earth.

You and I are pioneers in the saga of civilization. As we pointed out, *Homo sapiens* is only about 8,000 generations old! Only 100 billion people have ever lived on Earth—and over five percent of them are alive today![6]

Welcome to the Trailblazer Club!

Happiness Is the Relaxed Enjoyment of Our Lives

We can learn how to operate our biocomputers in ways that provide us with our birthright: *a relaxed enjoyment of our lives.* We can savor the fun and adventure life offers us. We can learn to deal with threats and pain so we don't remain in constant reptilian attack and defense.

This book can point us toward the skills we need to amplify our lives. In the next chapter, we will learn more about how our old and new brains are at odds with each other and continually damage our personal lives, our relationships, and our society. When we begin to understand how our brains work—or don't work—we can use our *insightful*, rational mind to compensate for the quirks that are eroding our lives.

> *Many people today are learning to actually talk with their old brain through inner child work, voice dialogue, etc. And directly reprogramming out-of-date "lifetraps" of the old brain to harmonize with the new brain is routinely done by leading-edge therapists today!*

As we harmonize our two brains, our lives can enter into a new dimension. *We can increase our happiness and ensure the survival of humanity when our conscious and unconscious minds can routinely communicate and work together.* As we bring our two brains into increasing harmony, we may enjoy a creativity and power we've never experienced before. We can have physical energy and health that turns our age clock back by decades. We can transform both ourselves and our society in ways that seem miraculous.

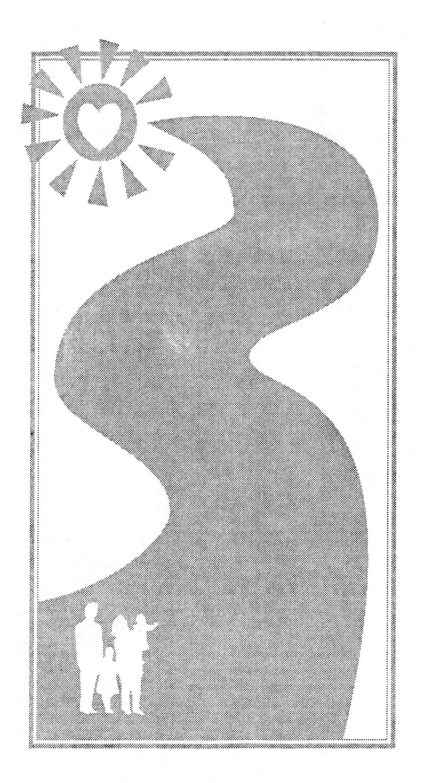

2

The Quirks in Our Brains

Our conscious and unconscious minds have factory defects—with no warranty. This chapter tells us what to be aware of so we can compensate for the life-impairing illusions caused by the built-in quirks between our two brains.

Most of our individual and social problems appear to be fundamentally created by the missing feedback and monitoring circuits between our new "biocomputer" brain and our old jungle-survival brain. This may be a shocking statement to most people. We are accustomed to blaming problems on individual or group character deficiencies. So, let's look at the brain flaws that hurt the relaxed enjoyment of our lives—and see what you and I can do about it.

"The mind is a squadron of simpletons. It is not unified, it is not rational, it is not well designed—or designed at all. It just happened, an accumulation of innovations of the organisms that lived before us. The mind evolved, through countless animals and through countless worlds," Ornstein states in *The Evolution of Consciousness*.[1] Suppose you built a comfortable, two-bedroom house. After living there for a while, you want a quiet study and a hobby room. So you get a builder to add on new rooms. Later, you want a second-story bedroom with a deck outside. This will mean cutting in steps to join the first and second floors. By the time you've built these two additions to the original house, it can look a bit odd from the outside—with some dysfunctional arrangements on the inside.

It's like that with our brains. "The brain was 'built' upward from the brain stem," explain Ornstein and Richards, "each layer of this 'ramshackle house' having been placed over the previous one."[2] You and I are limping along on ancient reptilian and mammalian brains with a new human brain (the neo-cortex) added as a third story. This does not mean that the reptilian part of our brain is today identical with an alligator brain any more than your leg is identical with an alligator leg. However, both the alligator and human parts today have functional and structural similarities. Both evolved from a common reptilian ancestor that lived 250 million years ago.

"We often lose sight of the fact that the brains we carry in our heads are not the last word in nervous systems," muses Georgetown University neurophysiologist Daniel Robinson in *The Enlightened Machine*.[3] In many ways, our old and new brains are out of phase with each other—*since neither brain is fully aware of what's really happening in the other brain.* They don't even speak the same "language." The new brain thinks; the old brain cannot. The old brain doesn't find meaning in logical thought. It specializes in picking up emotions and classifying what's happening in our lives as safe or unsafe—and satisfying or unsatisfying.

Until we learn *how to compensate* for the quirks in our reptilian-mammalian and human brains, we will continue to pay an unnecessary price in shortened, unhappy lives. Our bodies and minds will be torn by stress. We will endure a confusing life with conflicting parts inside us. We'll feel separated from other people—and even ourselves. We'll continue thrashing and trashing the environment in a futile hunt for happiness in ways that can't work.

The Dawn of Emotions

Let's review briefly. Our reptilian brain is geared for life-saving action—but not emotions. And certainly not empathy and love. The dawn of emotions had to await the development of the limbic area in the brain of mammals—animals that have hair and give milk to their young. Our mammalian brain produces emotional feelings, and plays a key part in creating fun, energy, and health in our lives. The mammalian limbic brain also controls your heart rate, breathing, temperature, and energy level. If you are bored, it can make you dead tired in a few minutes. If there is something that strongly interests you, it can give you a big shot of energy, even though you were previously tired.

Although the reptilian brain developed before the mammal brain came along, both brains have been evolving together in mammals for a long time. These two old brains today seem to be wired to work well together, given this quarter billion years of "product development." The "lemons" have been eliminated. This lets us simplify things by referring to them as the "old brain." It has brought our ancestors through millennia of jungle life. If the old brain hadn't worked well, we wouldn't be here today.

To sum up, our neocortex is the new kid on the old block (40,000 years old vs. 250 million years old). Neurologists tell us that in many ways our old brain and the rational, new brain that developed on top of it are not effectively coordinated. They unfortunately don't have the integrated circuitry needed to best serve us.

Five Major Quirks

In the last chapter, we briefly mentioned quirks between our old and new brains. You'll recall a quirk is a life-damaging illusion produced by our unconscious mind. Here is a summary of these quirks:

1. **OBJECT QUIRK: The old brain confuses different people and things.**
2. **TIME QUIRK: The old brain merges past, present, and future into a "now" experience.**
3. **UNSAFE-STRANGER QUIRK: The old brain feels threatened by strangers.**
4. **UNCHANGING-ENTITY QUIRK: The old brain is not attuned to the way people and things are constantly changing.**
5. **ADAPTABLE-MEMORY QUIRK: The old brain adapts or creates memories to support current interests.**

Let's explore how these quirks damage us in daily life—so we can learn to counteract them.

The Object Quirk

The unconscious mind does not distinguish well between different people and things. Because of inadequate connections, poor computing "hardware," or limited storage and retrieval capacity, the unconscious mind tends to hazily merge everything and everybody. Its main interest is to quickly pick up a pattern similar to anything that has been painful—and to attack, run, submit, or hide. Secondarily, it moves toward anything that has a similarity to what it liked in the past. That's why cheese-baited rat traps are effective.

The illusions of our Object Quirk may make us verbally or physically violent—or silently judgmental and disdainful. In our everyday adult life, our *repressed* childhood anger, jealousy, resentment, irritation, hate, rage, and fury are continually projected onto innocent mates or acquaintances without our being aware of it. Verbal and physical aggression, as well as critical thoughts, are based on the repressed emotions that were not safe to express with a power-based parent. Our anger and resentment toward a parent may be hidden by an obedient-conforming strategy adopted by the child to feel safe with its caregivers. A child may be abused or beaten to death when a parent's bottled-up childhood fury is projected decades later by the Object Quirk of the parent's unconscious mind. This quirk seems to create the illusion in the unconscious mind that it is responding appropriately *to one's original abuser or perpetrator.*

> We are naturally self-healing. However bad the abuse, if a hurt child can express its pain to an empathetic ear, it can heal itself.

"It is not *experienced* hatred that leads to acts of violence and destructiveness," advises Alice Miller, "but hatred that must be warded off and bottled up. . . ."[4] Children in a plane crash may experience great fear and pain—many times what they may get from a power-based parent. However, a child in a severe accident feels safe to cry, and it has lots of sympathy. ("You poor dear. Where does it hurt? What can I do? You've been through a lot.") And the child does not carry fear and rage

16

from this terrible event as a hidden time bomb for the rest of its life.

To help counteract the Object-Quirk, we can give our unconscious mind the experience that we *now* have the freedom to feel our feelings—and express them. We can also learn to immediately sense these quirks when they are about to trigger—and consciously avoid acting them out. Or we can learn to consciously withdraw our energy when the time bomb explodes on us. (See Chapter 10 for an example.)

The Time Quirk Causes Stress

Our rational mind can vividly experience the past, present, and future. To the unconscious mind, past and future are confused and dimmed. They are merged into a unified *now* experience. Whatever is experienced as *now* is FELT to be *forever* or *eternal*. To our unconscious mind, it's all *here and now*. While our conscious mind can correct such "time" illusions, the quirky interconnections between our two minds may bypass our analytical, conscious mind. However, we can learn to observe or witness our minds as we react to what's happening. We can learn to consciously intervene whenever the illusions of the quirks are noticed by our thinking brain.

Suppose you are attacked by a bear. Your body will respond by giving you a shot of adrenaline that jet-powers your muscles. Your emotions of anger or fear will focus your attention on saving yourself. An instant jump in your heart rate and blood pressure provides more oxygen and glucose to your muscles by increasing the flow of blood. These survival mechanisms are needed when your life depends on running faster or fighting harder *in the next few minutes*.

In most jungle threats to life, the animal engages in fight or flight, and in a few minutes relaxes—or is eaten! If it escapes from becoming dinner for another animal, the heart slows down, blood pressure drops, and the adrenaline that powered its muscles is used up. The survival mechanisms have done their job.

Now suppose your conscious, thinking mind is worrying about your job future. Your unconscious will pick up this *imagined* threat. In its hazy, merging way, your unconscious mind cannot distinguish between the present and the future. It will keep you hyped up for fight or flight by increasing your heart rate and blood pressure. This emergency readiness of the old brain to an imagined threat may even continue through the night. Your thinking brain *knows* that a good night's sleep will best prepare you for any future challenges. But the simpleton old brain doesn't connect well with the new brain. This stress-causing quirk that evolved perhaps a billion years ago to help an animal escape from danger ensures today that the makers of tranquillizers are prosperous!

> *Our old brain evolved to handle situations in which our lives are threatened for only a few seconds or minutes. However, the IMAGINED threats that our new brain can concoct today are endless. The simpleton reptilian-mammalian brain can't tell the difference between a real, immediate threat (a bear on your tail) and an imagined, long-term concern (such as your house losing value because the neighborhood is deteriorating).*

Our old brain can hazily sense the new brain's concern. It may then inappropriately jump up our heartbeat and blood pressure for days, months, or years—even though the tension it creates may impede rather than help us solve the problem! This unneeded stress puts us at risk for heart attacks, strokes, and ulcers, weakens our immune system—and destroys our relaxed enjoyment of life.

When we worry, or are impatient, irritated, or resentful, the old brain can dumbly keep us on "lifesaving emergency." It can keep us ready to fight or run by triggering adrenaline, and increasing heartbeat, and blood pressure. We get this "jungle emergency" when we interview for a new job, ask the boss for a raise, watch a horror movie, or have nightmares about unresolved problems in our lives. This ongoing tension is as useful as a flat tire in the Indy 500 race.

To sum up, for the old brain, there is no past or future. *It lives in the now moment.* Emergency reactions were evolved in our wildlife past to key us up *right now* to save our life *right now* from a *here-and-now* physical danger. Since our emotions are wired with circuitry that may bypass conscious control, we need to learn ways to keep the Time Quirk from tearing us apart psychosomatically. Meditation may be helpful in dealing with this quirk.

Combining Time and Object Quirks

The combined Time and Object Quirks can lead us into projecting our past pain onto innocent people who were not responsible for our childhood pain. This treacherous combination of quirks harms or ruins countless lives. Suppose we project the pent-up anger and hostility that we could not express to a punishing parent onto a policeman who triggers our bottled-up "authority figure" rage. This is not an effective way to respond to a law enforcement officer!

> *"Projection" is a psychological term used to refer to the spewing of the old brain's unexpressed emotions from the past onto an innocent person in the present. Everyone's life is damaged by this "stupidity" of the old brain.*

Let's suppose the missing wiring were available today. If your mate says, "You are terrible," your old brain might flash on a similar situation at age four when you felt fear and anger toward a punishing parent. The physical danger from an angry parent about to whip you was "real." The danger from your mate probably is not. Ideally, your intelligent cerebral cortex would signal the limbic area that there is no danger from your mate. Cancel, cancel. With improved wiring, your new brain could use your *adult capabilities* to respond to your wife or husband in this situation. Having reassured the old brain that there is no danger, the new brain could choose from many options. It could change your perception of criticism from a personal threat to a helpful source of information. Or perhaps it might lovingly respond, "I know you feel that I have not heard what you said. I really want to understand you."

Projection in Everyday Life

We often see a mother in a supermarket with a young child who wants to explore and touch things. The mother wants the child to stay close to her so she can keep it from pulling out the bottom can on a shelf. The mother may threateningly say, "I've told you to stay near me. If you don't obey me, your father's going to spank you tonight. Now come here right now!" She is trying to control the child with fear, guilt, and shame. This power-parenting seldom controls the child for more than a minute or so—and then has to be repeated. The brain of a four year old is aware of what's *now*—the *future* is hazy.

To the conscious mind of the mother, there is a quarter century between the present moment in the supermarket with her son—and the times when she was a little girl who was severely scolded and struck by a parent. But the mother's unconscious mind acts *as if* she were "paying back" her power-based parent. The "adult-child" now finds herself more powerful physically. To reclaim some of her lost self-esteem and power from childhood, her unconscious mind will "project" her past anger and desire for revenge upon her young son today. This is the bottled-up anger it could not safely vent twenty-five years ago with her parent.

If her repressed emotions were not misdirected by the combined Time and Object Quirks, the mother's new brain could find more effective ways of handling her child in the supermarket. To make a child obey from fear, guilt, and shame may have catastrophic effects later on. It is interesting to note that dog trainers use patience, love, and rewards to train a dog *in very complex and unnatural behaviors for dogs.* Any animal trainer that uses fear, guilt, and shame to teach will not be successful.

It's too bad our caregivers were not as skilled as animal trainers!

The Unsafe-Stranger Quirk

Our unconscious mind evolved in the wild, where animals ate other animals. It instantly polarized an animal into *me vs. you* or *us vs. them*. This feeling of "otherness" or "enemy" helped our animal ancestors survive. Since our human survival is based more on clear perception, analysis, communication, and cooperation, this Unsafe-Stranger Quirk often misleads us. This quirk makes our unconscious perceive a newcomer through a paranoid "Unsafe-Stranger" filter. It can cloud the emergence of a friendly, cooperative relationship that we need to get the most out of life.

This primal, unconscious instinct of "otherness" can hurt our human lives today by interfering with our conscious mind's curiosity, and checking out new people with open-mindedness. Our human mind and "heart" can create friendliness, appreciation, compassion, caring, and unconditional love—our highest and most noble goals. ("A stranger is a friend I haven't met." Christ advised "Love one another.") Our Unsafe-Stranger Quirk can bias our minds toward personal, racial, religious, social, and political prejudices. It fosters aggression in school playgrounds, murderous gangs, and civil and international wars. By using the techniques described in this book, we can avoid the ravages of the Unsafe-Stranger Quirk.

The Unchanging-Entity Quirk

A beaver trap lying flat on the ground seems harmless to the old brain of a beaver. But this apparently static object can be quite dynamic—even deadly.

Our old brain seems to operate with the illusion that things are non-changing "entities." The reality is that we do not live in a world of *static* people and things. Instead we live in a world where *everything is constantly changing*. Changes in a rock are slow; changes in a young infant are rapid. But on the atomic level, even the rock is a whirling group of atoms and

21

electrons. Every *thing* we can see is a dynamic, ever-changing process—not a solid, "permanent," unchanging entity. The unconscious mind's illusion of a static world (often shared by the conscious mind) can keep us from opening our eyes to perceive changes.

The Unchanging-Entity Quirk may lead us to perceive a person's character, the reliability of a car brand, or ourselves as permanent entities. This can blunt our awareness of changes we could notice to make more-effective decisions. Our human minds solve problems better when we view ourselves (and everything else around us) as dynamic, ever-changing processes instead of fixed, unchanging entities. We must constantly keep our eyes, ears, and minds open. We constantly change—slowly or rapidly. If someone asks you, "Can you play the violin?" you might answer, "I don't know. I've never tried!"

"Knowledge," said Alfred North Whitehead, "keeps no better than fish." In our fast-moving world, we need to stay on our toes to alert ourselves to changed conditions. It is helpful to remember that our heads are crammed full of what Robert Hutchins called "rapidly aging facts." Reality is constantly washing its face. "Many a man fails to become a thinker," declared Nietzsche, "for the sole reason that his memory is too good." We must not let our old memories block new learning. By just understanding this quirk, our human mind can begin to counteract it by observing carefully—and noticing what's new.

The Adaptable-Memory Quirk

Over the past hundreds of millions of years, animal survival was based on *adapting* to life in the wild. Accurate photographic memories were not needed for survival in the jungle. Instead, the old brain mixed perceptions of time, space, and objects into hazy blurs that it re-assembled to meet its current interests. This continuous falsification of memories to reflect our here-and-now interests is anti-survival for humans. Today we need accurate re-collection to find more-effective ways to create a better future.

Ornstein studied the accuracy of human memories and concluded, "Memories are a dream." We have the illusion of accurate recall. But whenever we are emotionally involved, our memories may be "adapted." Our unconscious mind can change memories by blanking out, in whole or in part, inflating some things, or actually adding pieces to a memory. This well-meant (quirk-based) violation of "the truth" can distort our thinking. It can destroy mutual trust between people—a trust that is an essential component of human cooperativeness, appreciation, generosity, and love.

Consistency in our point of view is an illusion. The mind evolved to help us constantly adapt. *It is not designed to help us objectively know ourselves—or the world.* So even events we think we remember perfectly can be just a re-semblance, the mind's re-creation to meet our interests right now. We constantly change our minds: recounting how someone harmed us, the predictions we made last year, or the weight of the fish we caught last summer. *And we usually don't know we're doing it!*

Transforming Our Lives

> *Our lives will be transformed when our old and new brains work harmoniously. We'll be enlightened when the power of both brains synchronize. Until we learn how to coordinate the reptilian-mammalian brain with "nature's crowning achievement" of our rational neocortex, we'll continue to trash our lives—and our planet.*

To summarize, we have a conscious mind and an unconscious mind—and we need them both. *Each gives us important functions not performed by the other.* But you and I lack certain feedback and control mechanisms that enable them to work well together. We have enormous abilities and powers. And there's a "screw" loose.

23

The human mind was never designed. It is a collection of remnants and mechanisms that helped us survive in the antediluvian jungles. There's no way we can get our brains rewired today. However, we can begin to notice when we are caught in the dysfunctional quirks between our old and new brains. We can learn to quickly recognize and compensate when this happens. *And these skills can rapidly begin to harmonize both brains.*

In the next chapter, we will further describe the structure and operation of our old and new brains—the unconscious and the conscious minds. We need to fully understand our dysfunctional mental mechanisms so we can compensate for them. Fortunately the thinking ability of our new brain enables us to develop the skills we need. Then we can have our birthright of relaxed enjoyment—with appreciation and love for ourselves and others.

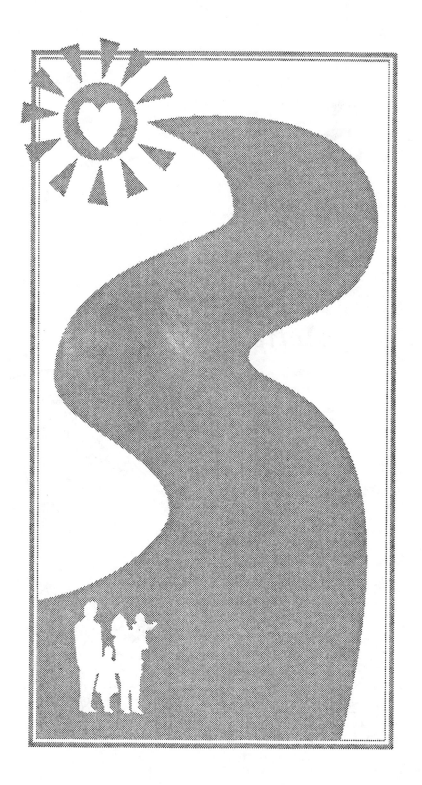

3

Our Brains in Action

When we understand how our mental equipment works, our thinking brain can interact more effectively with our feeling brain to offset our built-in booby-traps. Knowing this, we can develop the skills we need to create more fulfilling, happier lives.

A *brain* is a thing—a jello-like hunk of matter. You can touch it or photograph it. The *mind* is a process. It's the old and new brains in action. If you try to photograph the mind, all you get is a picture of the brain.

Suppose you're driving along in heavy traffic. Someone quickly cuts in front of you—and you have to slam on your brakes. Here's what may be happening inside your skull:

Reptilian Brain Reaction: Under attack! Danger! Action alert! Hit the brakes!

Mammalian Brain Emotions: Fear! Terror! Anger! Your autonomic nervous system gives you a wrenching feeling in your heart. Adrenaline squirts into your blood to prepare your body for fight or flight.

Human Brain Thoughts: "You damn idiot! You want to get us both killed?"

Dr. Harville Hendrix, author of the popular *Getting the Love You Want*, pointed out that when we go to bed at night with our mate, we are lying down with a reptile, a mammal, and a computer!

Each of us has programming in our old and new brains that is different in some ways from that of any other person who has ever lived. As with an iceberg, we can observe only the small part on the surface of our conscious-awareness. The bulk of our motivations, interests, fears, and desires are programmed into the unconscious mind below the level of our awareness. Yet our thinking brain upstairs arrogantly tells itself that it knows what's happening!

The term "unconscious mind" (also called the "subconscious mind") refers to programming we are not aware of. Our unconscious programs cannot be readily changed by the logic of the conscious thinking mind. For instance, the anxious feelings of a traumatized Vietnam War veteran cannot be eliminated by the new brain thinking, "How silly it is to respond with anxiety to a loud sound today when I'm thousands of miles and many years away from Vietnam."

Our unconscious mind creates many quandaries for us humans. You'll recall that Paul MacLean first brought attention to our "triune" brain. MacLean told Hooper and Teresi when they were researching *The Three-Pound-Universe*:

> "You know what bugs me most about the brain?" MacLean says suddenly. "It's that the limbic system, this primitive brain that can neither read nor write, provides us with the feeling of what is real, true, and important. And this disturbs me, because this inarticulate brain sits like a jury and tells this glorified computer up there, the neocortex, 'Yes, you can believe this.' This is fine if it happens to be a bit of food or if it happens to be someone I'm courting—'Yes, it's a female, or yes, it's a male.' But if it's saying 'Yes, it's a good idea. Go out and peddle this one,' how can we believe anything? Logically I've never been able to see around this impasse. As long as I'm alive and breathing and have a brain to think with, I will never forgive the Creator for keeping me in this state of ignorance."[1]

So we had better beware of our newfangled brain. Our mental equipment doesn't come with a money-back guarantee!

Bypassing the New Brain

Probably the most life-damaging dysfunction of the old brain is that it can act out intense emotions such as jealousy, fury, rage, etc., without control by the intelligence of our new brain. Ornstein tells us:

> Emotional information fed to the brain enters via a different neural network than other, perhaps more ordinary,

information. Most of our brain science has until recently assumed that all signals to the cortex travel over the same routes, but this seems not to be so. New research shows that emotions have a separate system of nerve pathways, through the limbic system to the cortex, allowing emotional signals to avoid conscious control.[2]

Suppose you come home early from a trip and your old brain sees "your" mate in "your" bed making love in "your" home to your next-door neighbor. This can trigger repressed childhood wounds such as the fear of abandonment, murderous rage, and jealousy when someone takes what's yours. An enormous wave of intense emotions and energy for action surges from the old brain. You feel like hurting or killing. And big trouble may lie ahead because the wires from the limbic area to the cerebral neocortex *allow emotional signals to avoid conscious control!* (You'll recall that one-half of the female murders in the U.S. are by husbands or ex-husbands.)

This is the type of situation in which we most need the wisdom of the new brain. If the new brain were wired so it could mediate this "jungle" energy, it would most likely counsel that killing a human being is so final, so shameful, so guilt-producing, so morally wrong, so unloving, and so fraught with legal consequences that alternatives should be found. But since the strong blast of emotions from the limbic area of the old brain manages to bypass the conscious control centers of the new brain, we can be at the mercy of a primeval style of brain function in this type of situation. No doubt it was helpful to animals a quarter billion years ago—or even today. But humans are paying a heavy price for this quirk.

The Brains in Action

As our old brain receives information, it instantly compares the incoming stimuli with instincts (such as fear of a sudden loud noise) and what we've experienced that has yielded pain or pleasure. ("That dog bites" or "Granny buys us ice cream.") The old brain then takes immediate action to avoid pain—or go for pleasure. To observe how the old brain works, watch the behavior of puppies, kittens, or a toddler. They want what they

How They Work

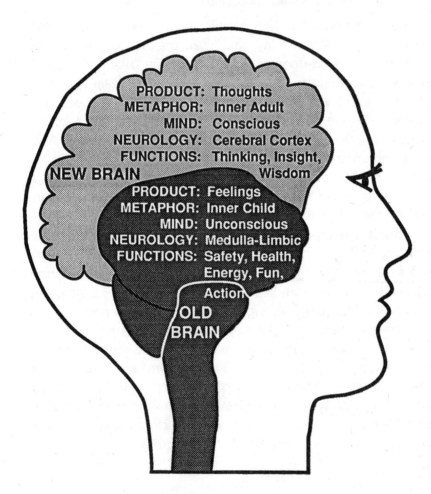

PRODUCT: Thoughts
METAPHOR: Inner Adult
MIND: Conscious
NEUROLOGY: Cerebral Cortex
FUNCTIONS: Thinking, Insight, Wisdom

NEW BRAIN

PRODUCT: Feelings
METAPHOR: Inner Child
MIND: Unconscious
NEUROLOGY: Medulla-Limbic
FUNCTIONS: Safety, Health, Energy, Fun, Action

OLD BRAIN

New Thinking Brain
40 thousand years old

Old Acting and Feeling Brain
250 million years old

want when they want it. There is no future. There is no past. They live in the *continuous now moment*—avoiding pain and seeking pleasure or satisfaction.

The old brain does not think—it feels and acts. The new brain does not feel—it deals with life by thinking. The new brain is emotionally dumb and intellectually smart. It perceives problems and tries to solve them. The old brain is intellectually dumb—and very perceptive in picking up on the emotions of others in its environment. As we discussed in Chapter 2, the old brain cannot distinguish clearly between people and places, or even between past, present, and future. It feels danger when it recognizes an *element* of a situation about which it has generalized "This situation is painful." Our old brain worked great for animal survival of the fittest in the wild. With our fantastic neocortex, we can do better today.

Old Brain Processing

Harville Hendrix in *Getting the Love You Want* helps us understand how the old brain operates:

As it goes about its job of ensuring your safety, your old brain operates in a fundamentally different manner from your new brain. One of the crucial differences is that the old brain appears to have only a hazy awareness of the external world. Unlike the new brain, which relies on direct perception of outside phenomena, the old brain derives its incoming data from the images, symbols, and thoughts produced by the new brain. This reduces its data to very broad categories. For example, while your new brain easily distinguishes John from Suzy from Margaret, your old brain summarily lumps these people into six basic categories. The only thing your old brain seems to care about is whether a particular person is someone to: 1) nurture, 2) be nurtured by, 3) have sex with, 4) run away from, 5) submit to, or 6) attack. Subtleties such as "this is my neighbor," "my cousin," "my mother," or "my wife" slide right on by.

The old brain and the new brain, different in so many ways, are constantly exchanging and interpreting information. Here is how this takes place. Let's suppose that you are alone in your house, and all of a sudden, person A walks through the door. Your new brain automatically creates an image of this creature and sends it to your old brain for scrutiny. The old brain receives the image and compares it with other, stored images. Instantly there is a first observation: "This humanoid is not a stranger." Apparently encounters with this creature have been recorded before. A millisecond later there is a second observation: "There are no dangerous episodes associated with this image." Out of all the interactions you have had with this mystery guest, none of them has been life-threatening. Then, rapidly, a third observation: "There have been numerous *pleasurable* episodes associated with this image." In fact, the records seem to suggest that A is someone who is nurturing. Having reached this conclusion, the limbic system sends an all-clear signal to the reptilian brain, and you find yourself walking toward the intruder with open arms. Operating out of your new brain, you say, "Aunt Mary! What a pleasure to see you!"

All of this has taken place outside your awareness in only a fraction of a second. To your conscious mind, all that has happened is that your beloved Aunt Mary has walked in the door. Meanwhile, as you visit with your aunt, the data-gathering process continues. This latest encounter produces more thoughts, emotions, and images, which are sent to the limbic system to be stored in the part of the brain reserved for Aunt Mary. These new data will be a part of the information scanned by the old brain the next time she comes to visit.[3]

A Tale of Two Brothers

For the first few years of our lives, we navigated our way through childhood primarily relying on our reptilian-mammalian brain—the "old brain." All of the hurts and injuries—and pleasures and delights—of the first few years of our life are mainly encoded in the unconscious old brain. "Unconscious" does not mean this mind is asleep. "Unconscious" means that our new brain (with which we identify) is not consciously aware of what's happening in our "unconscious" old brain.

The neocortex of the new brain matures slowly. During the first seven years, it's engaged in developing language skills, learning to think, dealing with "time," etc. To develop our uniquely human capacity for *abstract thinking*, the billions of neurons in the neocortex have to extend their dendrites to make over a trillion connections with other dendrites. These countless "fingers" of each neuron, reaching out to touch the "fingers" of other neurons, largely become functional for symbolic thinking during our sixth or seventh year. It is not an accident that the first grade usually begins around age seven. Of course, extending dendrites to acquire new skills, and pruning them when not used, is a lifelong process.

To observe firsthand the "thinking" or generalizing limitations of a young neocortex, find a family that has two sons, one about four years old and the other around ten. Ask the four-year-old if he has a brother. Since his mother has said things like "Don't tease your big brother," the four-year-old has associated the word "brother" with a specific person in his family. He will answer, "Yes, I have a brother." Next ask him, "Does your brother have a brother?" You'll find that he'll say, "No."

Now let's get a second opinion from the ten-year-old. If you ask him if he has a brother, he will say "Yes." If you ask if his brother has a brother, he may say something like, "Silly, it's me." He will make this *abstract* mental connection quickly. He may even look at you disdainfully because you asked such a stupid question!

Healing Your Unconscious

Memories of the first two or so years are usually not available for conscious recall by the new brain. When we've been beaten by a parent who unskillfully tries to teach us obedience, we probably won't remember. These painful memories are buried in our unconscious mind—the old brain. To the new thinking brain, it's almost as though they had never happened.

But not so with the unconscious mind. Pain and terror from childhood are alive and well in the old brain! Time bomb repression, inhibition, and false-self survival strategies will act like sand in the gears of our mental and physical machinery in our adult life—unless they are healed. And perhaps the greatest tragedy is that our thinking brain doesn't know what the problem is. It took a genius like Freud to point out that we do have a problem with what's bottled up in the unconscious mind—and we had better do something about it.

As avant-garde parents learn how to nurture *both* the conscious and unconscious minds of their children, it is important for them to avoid feeling guilty or ashamed of any power-based caregiving they have done in the past. Just as computers have vastly changed business methods, today's knowledge of the boomerang-effects of repressed childhood emotions has revolutionized the skills of parenting.

There is an important point that bears repeating because it seems difficult to understand: It's not the painful events in our lives that cause injuries in our unconscious minds—and make us disown parts of our true-self. It's having to suppress our feelings and "invalidate" a part of our true-self that causes a "jam-up" in the *normal self-healing* of our minds. The old brain heals itself by expressing its feelings. When we were dependent children, we desperately needed someone who was "on our side"—who could let us cry our tears, mourn our griefs, express our angers, and tell them how scared we were. The unconscious mind *heals itself by expressing* its feelings.

The old brain learns from life *experiences*—not from analysis, judgments, shoulds, shouldn'ts, rights, wrongs, fairs, unfairs, or wanting to change. In a way, this makes it relatively easy to heal the old brain's injuries—*if you know how*. There are many ways to reprogram your unconscious. For example, the old brain doesn't know the difference between an abusive parent and a pillow that you *consciously imagine* to be that parent. So you can beat up the pillow, scream at it, and express your *emotional truth* about the pain your parent gave you years ago. You can vent all the rage and spiteful feelings that were unsafe to express with an abusive, angry parent when you were four years old. And the old brain can reprogram itself if it thoroughly experiences it's now safe to express its hurt and pain. The log-jam of repressed feelings can be cleared away when the old brain shovels out its moldy emotions that have been too long stored.

You can keep the quality of your life from being damaged by the simpleton old brain. Using your thinking brain, you can develop an effective "inner parent" that knows how to respond to the old brain "inner child" in a way that makes it feel safe and taken care of. We will discuss these life-enhancing techniques in Chapters 12 through 14. You'll discover how you can use your thinking new brain and *actually communicate* with your feeling old brain. This helps the old brain stay busy doing what we need it to do: giving us more energy, health, fun, and love.

For thousands of years humans have endured lives of intense conflict, not knowing that a large part of their problems were caused by the incomplete evolution of our brains—and the resulting "lifetraps." Now, thanks to the therapies and self-help techniques described in this book, it is possible for us to heal the wounds of childhood and compensate for the quirks in our brains. The future promises quantum leaps in human happiness and fulfillment. As we become liberated from so much inner turmoil, we will be free to realize our full human potential.

Part II will discuss how your well-meaning, but unskillful, childhood caretakers damaged parts of the "true-self" you were born with. To avoid pain and survive childhood, you had to develop a "false-self." Fortunately, your new brain can help you learn the skills you need to return to your whole, authentic, true-self—your birthright.

PART II

YOUR PARENTS AND YOU

4

The Birth Experience

Birth may be easy and rapid—or difficult, scary, painful, and prolonged. Although the conscious mind does not remember it, our unconscious mind was on duty. It's known today that our natal experience plays a very important part in shaping our personality. It gives us some of our first impressions about the world we've entered.

When cats give birth to kittens, the newborns seem to be squeezed out one by one without a lot of drama. The mother turns around and begins licking the kittens—and bonding begins. I once read about an Indian woman in Mexico who worked in the fields all morning. Around noontime, she excused herself and sat under a tree. She gave birth to her baby, put it on her back in papoose-style, and returned to work in the fields that afternoon. Perhaps our sedentary lives and mental attitudes have taken us a long way from our original simplicity in birthing.

Let's imagine what it may be like for a young human in the mother's body. The infant inside the womb generally lives in a state of relaxed enjoyment. It is just being—not doing. It floats in a warm, uterine sea. It is gently rocked by the movement of the mother's body. Her heartbeat, ta-dum, ta-dum, ta-dum, gives the developing human an "orchestral" background that feels peaceful and secure. All its needs for oxygen, nutrition, and elimination are met through the umbilical cord.

Information needed for future language proficiency is being programmed. In the latter part of pregnancy, it can recognize its mother's and father's voices—and tell them apart. It is emotionally quite perceptive at this time. It can accurately pick up whether it is wanted or not, and whether mommy and daddy relate harmoniously. It is the center of its small universe.

Unless the mother is involved in violence, its primary needs for safety and satisfaction are met in its womb apartment.

The Great Eviction

Unknown to this peaceful tenant, the lease on its apartment expires about nine months after the sperm penetrates the egg cell. The walls of the apartment begin to move and the infant is turned upside down. Pretty soon its head is being pushed through a terribly tight opening. Never before has it felt such constricting cervical pressure. Then it gets worse as it is tightly "straight-jacketed" by the birth canal.

Since the baby is emotionally sensitive, its natural feelings of alarm can change into terror—especially if the mother is screaming in pain. If the mother is not in good physical condition, the young child may be stuck in the constricting birth canal for hours or a day or more. It can have the experience of the ultimate old brain terror—impending death. Of course, it will have no "concept" of death—only a dreadful feeling.

Let's hope this time is short. The baby laboriously inches toward the outside opening of the birth canal. And then—bump! Something hard is pressing on its head to trap it in this claustrophobic tube. It's the mother's pubic bone that protects her lower abdominal area. If the birth has progressed smoothly to this point, the young child may now feel terror and doom for the first time. As mentioned before, although the child has a simpleton brain intellectually, it is sharp emotionally. It has sensitive feelings that are being powerfully programmed by this unexpected expulsion from its comfortable uterine nest. It's discovering that life can be rough.

The mother may be urged to take deep breaths—and bear down harder. She valiantly tries to push with all her might in spite of her pain. At this point, both mother and child may be similarly terrified—each bouncing off the other. As the vaginal opening expands or is cut or torn open, the baby's head slides by the pubic bone that may have "entombed" it. And then, perhaps with a final burst of energy from a tired, pained mother, the baby's head crowns into the air—soon to be followed by its entire body.

In some operating rooms, doctors welcome the new human being into the world with glaring lights, hold it upside down by its ankles, and slap it on the bottom until it cries. Thus it receives its first beating immediately after birth—perhaps a sample dose of the "power-based" parenting to come later on. Scissors then cut its umbilical connection to its mother. Nurses wipe its body and painfully swab out its eyes. Then it's shown to the mother who may not be encouraged to hold this sticky, crying young human.

Welcome to the world!

Intense birth trauma may contribute to developing a fear-based person who does not feel at home in this world. In *Beyond the Brain*, Dr. Stan Grof tells us:

> Individuals who relive their birth in psychedelic sessions or some nondrug experiential work repeatedly report that they have discovered a deep connection between the pattern and circumstances of their delivery and the overall quality of their life. It seems as if the experience of birth determines one's basic feelings about existence, image of the world, attitudes toward other people, the ratio of optimism to pessimism, the entire strategy of life, and even such specific elements as self-confidence and the capacity to handle problems and projects.[1]

A Greeting From the Heart

It is comforting to learn that recent developments in birthing encourage the father to emotionally support his wife as she exercises her breathing and bearing-down muscles in the months before birth. Some babies are birthed in warm tubs to minimize the shock between the uterine sea and the outside world. They are immediately put on the warm, welcoming bosom of the mother who quickly puts her arms around her precious child.

Both the mother and the father will lovingly reassure the infant after its birth ordeal. "We've been looking forward to your being here. We love you. We welcome you to the world. We want to be the best parents we can. We'll always take care of you. We want you to have fun in life. We'll be there to help you. We're so glad you're here. We love you with all our heart."

The baby does not understand these words intellectually. But since it is emotionally perceptive, it will get the message through tones of voice, gentle holding and stroking, as well as environmental friendliness such as soft lighting and music. An easy birth with a warm welcoming committee can play a part in developing a tranquil, confident, and happy child.

Nurture and Nature

We are a combination of nurture and nature. Much of our behavior is learned from our personal experience in our own unique life. And some of it is "hardwired," such as instincts or genetically determined behaviors. Research shows that identical twins reared apart in very different environments end up with similar cognitive abilities and temperaments.

While a chick can peck its way out of an egg and live without ever seeing another chicken, humans are born with only a few "instincts." (An instinct is an inborn, robot-like behavior.) This makes us totally dependent on a nurturing caregiver to survive our first years—more so than any other animal. This means that all our "mental furniture" does not have to be in place at birth. Our extended period of parental care decreases our dependence on instincts. Thus, we have an enormous flexibility in our first few years to learn languages, social customs, and explore ways to minimize pain and maximize pleasure.

In the next chapter, we will go with the precious little human on the seven stages of its psychosocial journey.

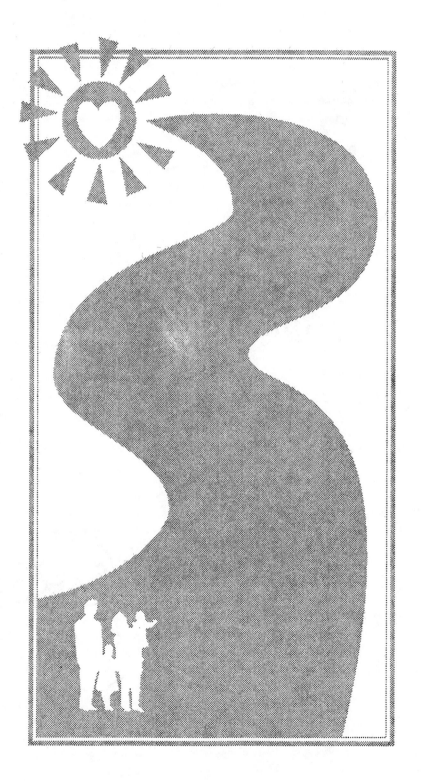

5

Our Seven Stages of Growth

By understanding the seven levels of growth, we can discover if we were deprived of any of these vital stages we need for wholeness and effectiveness in life. If our caregivers did not support us in any of these vital steps in our development, we can learn to give ourselves the parenting we missed.

The seven stages of development of a human being are awesome! What a splendid wholeness we had when we came into this world! We were whole in the sense that we had everything we needed to unfold into a fine human being. Yet there's a serious (often fatal) problem: just like a car or a boat, *we can be damaged by abuse.*

Why don't animals have this problem? It's because they usually don't have the abuse. No father dog mercilessly bites his puppy to break its will and train it into instant obedience. Mother dogs never shame their puppies for the mud on their coats. ("Your self-esteem is not important—but your coat is!") No little bird is criticized because it takes so long to make its first faltering flight. And when it first tries to fly, no observing owl tells it how poorly it did. ("You'll never learn, you klutz.") No elephant grows up self-consciously watching itself, trying to look like a good elephant when inside it has bought into parental criticism that it is a bad pachyderm.

The Best of Intentions

Not all childhood abuse involves harshly disciplining a child. Abuse can also come from unskillfully pushing a child—even with the best intentions:

Amelia's father believed that physical courage is needed to be a good person. Her father would put little Amelia on a large, spirited horse. He'd walk the horse about while bragging to others about how unafraid she was. She was ashamed to show her fear. She liked his paying attention to her. She did not want to lose it or "let him down." But the natural child in Amelia recognized, as did other adults nearby, that the situation was not really safe. A child wants a parent who looks out for its safety and best interests.

One day the horse suddenly turned, and Amelia fell. Her father was not only unable to protect her from the fall, but he harshly scolded her for falling. He became angry when she cried and shamed her for not wanting to get back on the horse. Little Amelia felt all people were courageous except her.

Her unconscious mind adapted to her father's abuse by learning to suppress her fear and disowning her common sense about dangerous situations. She gave up part of her *inborn wholeness* to get her father's approval. Her father was proud of her apparent fearlessness. She sustained a number of injuries in childhood because of her inability to recognize what was too dangerous—and thus protect herself by intelligent caution.

Her serious injuries caused her to adopt another unconscious strategy in her teens. She began to feel she could not trust herself to make good judgments about her safety. She adopted the strategy of avoiding activities with *any* danger. For example, she would be "too busy" to go to an amusement park or go hiking with her friends. Her self-esteem was deeply damaged by the shame she felt for not going with her friends to enjoy the roller coaster or camping in the mountains. She felt inferior to her friends.

Updating Parenting Skills

Today a skillful parent must know how to nurture *both* the old and new brains of their child. The worthy goals of her father were to show what a talented daughter she was and/or what a good father he was. Encouraging Amelia so she repressed her natural fears can "damage" the old brain—and set it up for mental illness later. This story of Anne illustrates both unskillful and skillful parenting:

Anne's dog had died the day before. She was sitting in a corner of her room and refused to come out and play. Her parents used their new brain to rationally console her. "Don't worry, we'll get you another dog." But Anne didn't want another dog. She wanted her Rover that she loved. "But sitting in your room isn't going to bring Rover back," her mother's new brain wisdom advised her. Anne's old brain is not logical—it feels. Her unconscious had bonded to Rover, and she was deeply hurting.

Fortunately, they had a neighbor who was a skillful parent. The neighbor realized that a modern parent must nurture both the conscious and unconscious minds. She went into Anne's room and asked Anne if she could sit down on the floor next to her. Anne apathetically said, "Yes." The neighbor feelingly said, "It's not the same without Rover, is it?" Anne looked up and felt that for the first time since Rover died, someone understood. The neighbor continued, "You just don't feel like doing anything." Tears began to form in Anne's eyes. The neighbor noticed this and put her arm around her. "You've got a lot of tears in there for Rover." Anne felt a surge of energy and hope—and more tears.

"Let them all out," the neighbor said as tears began to run down Anne's cheeks. "Let all of those tears out—you don't want to carry them around any longer." With this, Anne broke into sobbing. The neighbor held her tighter, and kept encouraging her. "Let them all out. Do it for Rover. He loves you. You love him. Let all those tears flow out."

Anne had been holding back her tears. She felt her parents would disapprove and call her a "bad girl" for crying. And here was the first person who understood how she felt. Anne was wracked with sobbing for about five minutes. Then the tears began to dry up. "Be sure you cry all those tears for Rover," the neighbor said as she hugged Anne again. And after a few more quick sobs, Anne seemed finished. Gradually she began to look around the room. She stood up, wiped her eyes with her hands, and announced, "I want to go outside and play with Joan." Joan was her best friend from down the street.

A parent who is skillful with both minds knows that emotional wounds are self-healing when fully expressed. *The parent's analytical new brain needs to temporarily take a back seat when pain hits and emotions flow.* We can have a lot of damage to our natural, whole true-self from unexpressed childhood pain. We suppress (or split off) some of our authentic true-self responses. The parts we split off are replaced by a false-self part that is like a virus in the brain. For example, to please her father, Amelia split off (sup-

The Journey of the True-Self

CREATING
Over 19 years
Developing
Responsibility
to Self and Society

INTIMACY
13 to 19 Years
Developing Heart Love
and Healthy Sexuality

CARING
7 to 13 Years
Developing Concern
for Others

COMPETING
4 to 7 Years
Developing a Sense
of Power to Achieve

IDENTITY
3 to 4 Years
Developing and Asserting
a Secure Sense of Self

EXPLORING
1 1/2 to 3 Years
Developing Curiosity and
Awareness of Self

BONDING
Birth to 1 1/2 Years
Developing Emotional
Security

From Harville Hendrix

pressed) the part of her natural true-self that triggers a legitimate fear of riding on top of a big animal. This part of her true-self was replaced by a strategic false-self programming that avoided upsetting her father by pretending not to be afraid. She paid a heavy price to please an unskillful, though loving, caregiver.

The Journey of Our True-Self

You can't go from the first grade in school to the third grade without going through the second grade. If you skip, the missing skills may keep you from getting the full benefit of the third grade. This is even truer in childhood development. If the first stage is not completed by bonding with one or more caretakers, you won't experience the safety and good feelings of loving and being loved. And you won't be ready to complete the following phases.

We have seven developmental stages we naturally go through. We were all wounded in some degree by unskillful parents, older siblings, relatives, teachers, etc., who did not understand our needs as we sallied forth on our natural stages of growth. When a parent pushes a child to complete a phase, the child may violate its natural feelings and force itself to perform for parental approval. For instance, a trait such as developing a sense of one's ability to achieve and compete will *naturally* develop in the fourth to seventh year. A well-meaning but unskillful parent may urge and push their three-year-old to win—and feel ashamed to lose. This parental eagerness can keep a character trait from naturally developing as a part of one's true-self. Instead it may be twisted into a false-self character trait.

Here is a quick glimpse of these seven stages:

1. Bonding: Birth to 18 Months. From the moment we're born, we need attention, respect, understanding, and the experience that someone is emotionally warm and there when we need them. We expect to be treated with respect (even though we don't know the word) and not be laughed at or ridiculed (or condescendingly given "baby talk") when we try to move or communicate. Have you ever heard a baby using the *adult*

49

dialect we call "baby talk?" We need lots of heartfelt love, understanding, and empathy. Our old brain is an expert in sensing feelings, and recognizing phoniness.

In this crucial first phase of unfolding our true-self, we especially need parents who are *consistently warm* and *consistently available*. When we experience loving parents, we develop a strong foundation of emotional security. We feel there's a place for us in this world. If we are not nurtured in a skillful, loving way during the crucial bonding phase, our entire life will be damaged.

John Bradshaw cautions:

> No infant has the ability to love in a mature, altruistic sense. Rather, he loves in his own age-specific fashion. A child's healthy growth depends on someone loving and accepting him unconditionally. When this need is met, the child's energy of love is released so that he can love others.
>
> When a child is not loved for his own self, his sense of I AMness is severed. Because he is so dependent, his egocentricity sets in, and his true-self never really emerges. The childish contaminations I ascribe to the wounded inner child are the consequences of this egocentric adaptation. The failure to be loved unconditionally causes the child to suffer the deepest of all deprivations.[1]

It's unfortunate that love we receive later in life can never fully make up for the lack of love in these first eighteen months—unless this injury in our unconscious mind is healed. If we don't complete the bonding phase, as adults we may fail to recognize love, be suspicious of the love that is available for us, cynically reject all love, or wrap our entire life around a mad search for more and more love. Nothing will ever be experienced as enough—no matter how many people want to love us. We may continually ask our mate, "But do you *really* love me?" It's like trying to fill a bottomless pit.

2. Exploring: 18 Months to 3 Years. From eighteen months to three years, we will try to find out what kind of world we live in. We learn there is a difference between boys and girls, cats and dogs, and Mom and Dad. With skillful parenting, our curiosity about the world and its many activities will be supported. We will be encouraged to continuously ex-

A Child Is Naturally

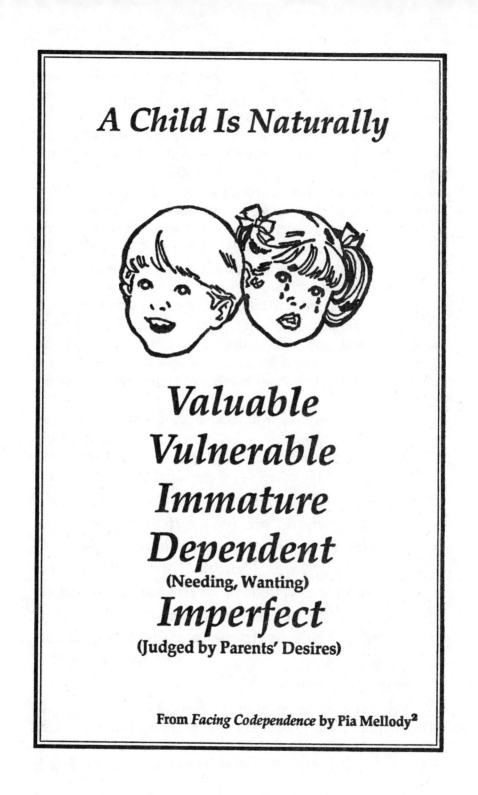

Valuable
Vulnerable
Immature
Dependent
(Needing, Wanting)
Imperfect
(Judged by Parents' Desires)

From *Facing Codependence* by Pia Mellody[2]

plore and check out our environment. We want to touch, see, hear, taste, smell, and feel everything. How else can we learn what's in the world—and how it works?

In the "terrible two's," we need to explore what happens if we say "no" to our apparently all-powerful, all-wise, all-knowing parents. A wise caretaker will give us the right to want what we want and feel what we feel. *No one has a right to have everything they want!* A love-based parent knows that the world will still turn on its axis if we say "no" when we're told to do something. They remember that behind it all, we really want to please. We're innately programmed to adapt—and become a harmonious part of it all.

If parents are fear-based, they will try to control us through fear, guilt, and shame. ("You bad boy. I've told you a thousand times you can't pull the dog's tail. The next time you do it, I'll show you how it hurts!") And our family will pay a heavy price in lost happiness because of their unskillful parenting.

Skillful parents accept our exploration phase so we can grow beyond it. Their loving patience helps us avoid getting stuck in a negative, rebellious attitude *for an entire lifetime.* We need a lot of understanding as we check out the world we live in.

> *Many parents are ignorant of the opportunities their children give them in the University of Life. Children offer a rich undergraduate curriculum in Advanced Patience, a graduate course in Love-Based Parenting, and a Ph.D. in Agape (unconditional love)! Sadly, some parents are not ready for this intense scholarship.*

We don't want to feel guilty or shamed to "grow up" fast. (For example, being pressured in toilet training before we reach the stage of development when we will naturally want to avoid being wet or soiled.) Forced development treats us as animals to be trained—rather than as human beings who are born with a *natural goodness* we can magnificently unfold if not abused.

Such premature parental pressure may give us the illusion that we're naturally bad—but we can look good if we self-consciously conform (or appear to conform) to a rule-ridden life. Many of us learn to do what's demanded. And some of us rebel and express our spirit by deliberately breaking every rule given us!

3. Identity Phase: 3 to 4 Years. Having laid a foundation of security in the bonding phase, and worldly information in the exploration phase, we are now ready from age three to four to explore our unique identity.

In the identity phase, we are ready to develop a secure sense of self if we are nurtured with love-based parenting. Here we can achieve a feeling that we are a good human being, able to assert our many selves, recognize our particular needs and desires, and continue to find out when and where they may be satisfied.

We need to feel that our parents are capable of taking care of themselves—and are not leaning on us for support. As Alice Miller explains:

> This would mean for the child: I can be sad or happy whenever anything makes me sad or happy; I don't have to look cheerful for someone else, and I don't have to suppress my distress or anxiety to fit other people's needs. I can be angry and no one will die or get a headache because of it. I can rage and smash things without losing my parents.[3]

We want the freedom to feel our feelings, want what we want, and think what we think, and express it without fear of pain or punishment. We need to be a fully human *child*—and not made to feel that we are bad because we don't act like an *adult*.

4. Competing Phase: 4 to 7 Years. From the mirrors that parents continually hold up before us, we learn who we are. If we have skillful parents, we now feel we're lovable, valuable, and secure humans with our own unique identity. During our fourth to seventh years, we will begin to "stretch our wings." In this competing phase, we can develop feelings of personal power to achieve. We learn we can begin to rely on ourselves to do what needs to be done.

We are interested in competing—and we feel winning is important. But losing will not destroy our self-esteem if we have completed the first three phases. *After all, we win some and we lose some. We're learning that's the way life is.*

5. Caring Phase: 7 to 13 Years. The preceding four stages have been stages of our self-development. If these have been successfully completed on schedule, we are now ready to embark upon the last three stages, in which we learn to relate to others in a loving, healthy, contributing, and satisfying way. Between seven and thirteen years, we will learn to sympathize and empathize with other children and adults in our world.

We're now developing a sensitivity to the feelings of other people. We can offer our toys to playmates, share our food, or even be willing to do without something for the benefit of others. If our well-meaning parents punished or shamed us prematurely into generosity, sharing, or altruism before these behaviors naturally unfold, we will do them from fear or "duty." Unfortunately for some of us, these caring behaviors *become fear-based performances instead of loving gifts from our natural true-selves.*

We are born to mature splendidly if we're given a chance. We naturally receive satisfaction as we watch ourselves grow up. This growing self-confidence may not happen if well-meaning, though unskillful, parents make us feel afraid, guilty, or ashamed—and force us to adopt a behavior as a "should" or "must." Physical or emotional penalties—a frown will do—whenever we fail to exemplify a parentally desired character trait can backfire. A skillful parent will catch us doing "right" and praise us—instead of catching us doing "wrong" and shame us. We need caregivers who can dislike something we do—*and still love us.*

6. Intimacy Phase: 13 to 19 Years. Assuming we have completed the first five stages, we are now prepared to develop a caring love for ourselves, other people, the world, and the

Children Learn What They Live

If a child lives with criticism,
  it learns to condemn.
If a child lives with hostility,
  it learns to fight.
If a child lives with pity,
  it learns to feel sorry for itself.
If a child lives with jealousy,
  it learns to hate.
If a child lives with encouragement,
  it learns to be confident.
If a child lives with praise,
  it learns to be appreciative.
If a child lives with acceptance,
  it learns to love.
If a child lives with approval,
  it learns to like itself.
If a child lives with fairness,
  it learns justice.
If a child lives with honesty,
  it learns what truth is.
If a child lives with friendliness,
  it learns that the world is a nice place
  in which to live.

Adapted from Dorothy Law Nolte

creatures and objects in it. Our natural sexual curiosity and growing energy will be supported by skillful parents so that sex is not branded "shameful," "bad," or "filthy." Instead, sex is explained as an energy that can be beautiful, when appropriately used—and create a magnetic bond with a loving partner. For teenagers, discovering sex is like learning to drive. If done skillfully, it is a life-enhancing activity. If done unskillfully, it can create fear, guilt, shame, hurt, inhibition, jealousy, murder, or AIDS.

During our teens, we learn to integrate our diverse energies into the social mores of our society. If we've had skillful parenting, we will *naturally* unfold into a warm, caring, helpful, generous person who enjoys creating deeper levels of intimacy with ourselves, our lovers, our families, and all of life.

Although opportunities for parental growth abound at all phases, the teen years offer great remedial courses for slow-learning parents. The classrooms may no longer be in the home. They may be waiting rooms of the local jail for the teenager accused of drug offenses (who projects onto them-selves—or the police—the repressed anger toward a parent who made it unsafe to say "no" in the exploration phase). Or perhaps parents may work on their advanced parenting degree sitting outside a hospital emergency room where their 25-year-old alcoholic adult/child is on the critical (!!!) list after an auto "accident." (They were taking out on society and its laws the "rebellion" their parents wouldn't accept with love as a neces-sary part of their growth 23 years earlier.)

7. **Creating or Responsibility Phase: 19 Years Through Adulthood.** If each of the first six stages has been effectively completed, we can return a precious, needed energy to the world: a loving, generous individual who knows how to be socially responsible—and who contributes in their way to society.

We can balance thoughts and feelings—"head" and "heart." We are now prepared to do our part in creating future genera-tions that will nourish the world and all of our relatives—both near and distant.

Recipe for Humans

The recipe for a wonderful human is quite simple (but skill is needed):

1. Take one human infant. Continually provide caretaker availability and emotional warmth—before birth, during, and after.

2. Skillfully avoid bruising or abusing. Don't push premature development of traits that will naturally unfold as the seven developmental stages are completed. Let the growing child feel it is okay as it is.

3. If the child feels intense fear, grief, anger, guilt, or shame, just make sure that a non-judgmental ear and empathic heart is always there for it. Encourage the child to express its fears and anger, cry its tears of grief, and tell what it wants—and be assured it is not "bad." This enables the child to integrate and self-heal its painful experiences—and not sacrifice a part of their true-self.

4. Nurture in the warmest ocean of love that you can for the next 20 years.

The above recipe will produce a healthy, secure, curious, self-confident, capable, loving, lovable human being that is concerned about others, can establish friendships, closeness, and intimacy, and who will be responsible to themselves and to society.

In the next chapter, we will learn more about the "diamond" we originally were. We'll be introduced to our whole true-self—a part of which we had to throw overboard to protect ourselves when we were dependent children.

6

Your Original True-Self

Power-based, critical parents told us, "You're a bad child. You make me so mad." This taught us to feel there was something wrong with us. How could we have learned about our natural perfection? Instead, we learned to identify ourselves with the false-self adaptations we needed to survive our childhood. To enjoy a fulfilling life, we must begin to reclaim our true-self. We can begin right now!

Let's define what we mean by "true-self" and "false-self." Your "true-self" is the real you. Ralph Waldo Emerson viewed our real self as a portion of divinity individualized as you. The qualities of divinity are love and wisdom. It's your natural, whole, complete self—body, mind, feelings, and spirit. It's the beautiful, authentic individual that when warmly and attentively nurtured will naturally unfold over the years into a relaxed woman or man who enjoys their life.

A newborn uses its true-self behavior automatically in *all* of its life situations. The true-self naturally smiles, laughs, or bonds with love when it feels emotionally close and likes what's happening. The true-self expression of emotions flows freely and naturally in response to pain or joy in moment-to-moment life situations. The true-self messes diapers and litters the floor. The true-self cries or expresses anger, fear, or grief when it hurts or its needs are not met. The true-self of a loving parent will experience the child's crying or anger as a call for help or love.

A Peek at Your True-Self

Your character was formed to a large extent by the ways in which you had to say good-bye to parts of your true-self. You learned to automatically identify with the false-self characteristics you needed to please your parents. Pages 60 and 61 con-

Your Original True-Self

If your caregivers were consistently warm and consistently available, you naturally developed these beliefs, feelings, attitudes, and self-images.

"I am welcome here in the world."

"I'm a worthy person who will be taken seriously."

"I feel safe and secure."

"I'm a part of a whole."

"People treat me fairly."

"My heart sympathizes with people who are in pain."

"It's okay to be vulnerable and show hurt feelings."

"I can trust people in authority to treat me with respect."

"People will respond when I reach out."

"I can be real and show my weakness and needs."

"I can relax and know people will stay with me."

"Love and attention are freely given to me."

"People are safe, gentle, and loving."

"I get willing support from others and can trust people."

"I feel bonded and feel people care about me."

"I can ask people to help me."

"I can get my needs met by being honest and direct."

Your Original True-Self (continued)

"I can listen to others."

"I am enough. I'm appreciated and loved just for me."

"I don't always have to act like a successful, dignified, responsible adult."

"I'm loved unconditionally."

"Enjoying myself here and now is important."

"I can say 'no' to you."

"I can get my needs met without struggling."

"I can cooperate with others and be a team player."

"I can be myself with people."

"I'm okay and lovable even if I don't do what you say."

"I feel self-esteem and self-confidence and can express and assert my own ideas."

"I can relax, play, and enjoy."

"I can tell you how I feel, what I think, and what I want."

"I can both meet my own needs and help others."

"I feel equality and self-worth."

"I can be open and fair."

"People are understanding and helpful."

"I care if people are hurting, and I can show my pain to others."

"I can seek help and don't always have to do it alone."

tain a list of some of your true-self characteristics that naturally unfold as your human birthright. You enjoy these characteristics of your true-self today—providing they were safe with your caretakers or you've reclaimed them.

From this list, you can get a glimpse of some of the most important characteristics of your true-self. To the degree that your parents weren't skillful, you will find that today you do not have the benefit of some parts of your true-self. Your life is being constantly hurt in one way or another by missing parts that you had to forsake as a child.

Splitting Our True-Self

During our first years of life, we accepted the critical mirrors our caretakers held up to us. "You'll never learn," "You're too cocky," "You're a mess," "I can't trust you," "You're hopeless," "God will punish you," etc. Our big caregivers are supposed to know about us. *We were creative and intelligent when we split off part of our naturally joyful, spontaneous, curious, loving true-self to adapt to our caregivers.*

The child's old brain has an instinct, "If I'm not loved, I will be abandoned. If I'm abandoned, I will die." In our first years, we were totally dependent on Mom and Dad. We could not afford to lose their love. We kept trying to "buy" their love by giving up another precious piece of our true-self—*the most valuable thing we owned.* And we silently asked, "Now will you love me?" But nothing can be enough for our damaged caretakers. Our parents in too many ways had not been allowed to love their true-selves. So how could they love ours?

For instance, many parents cannot stand their child crying. Yet crying is the old brain's way of *healing itself* of the fears, pains, resentments, angers, and I'll-get-even-with-you feelings when the child doesn't get what it wants. Emotional expressions such as crying or angering unloads the baggage—instead of stashing it.

Parents often spank a child for crying if it doesn't stop when the parent tells it to shut up. If it cries and heals itself, it will be scolded or punished. If it stifles its tears, it won't be punished. The child may temporarily be more comfortable for it escapes disapproval or punishment—but at a terrible price! Through pain or threat of pain it becomes afraid to express its natural true-self feelings. The false-self strategy of suppressing feelings to avoid punishment for crying begins to *feel natural or authentic*. A false-self is born!

Now the old brain does not know how to heal itself when it can't express its true-self feelings. Repressed resentments, angers, fears, rages, hates and furies are stashed away in the unconscious. They are like time bombs waiting for the quirks to explode them—usually not on the unskillful parent, but on a mate, their child, or others.

Ron Kurtz explains that the decisions we made as children about our early experiences fundamentally shape our beliefs and assumptions about ourselves and the world we live in. Our present-day emotional expression, physical posture, and "organization of our experience" were unconsciously programmed in our body-mind. Our strategic adaptation resulted in automatic, limiting false-self strategies that create problems that diminish our adult happiness.

Most of our loving, well-meaning parents were reared by power-prone caregivers. They used their "love" and approval to buy our compliance to their own physical, emotional, and intellectual needs. Thus our childhood was dominated by our parents' subtle or not so subtle, ever-present threat to control us by withdrawing support—and manipulating us to feel fear, guilt, and shame. For some of us who were continually punished, our childhood was destroyed by constant D R E A D and U N C E R T A I N T Y.

The Shadow of Your True-Self

You now know there is nothing wrong with you. You don't need fixing because *you aren't broken*. In fact, I wish to congratulate you on every false-self characteristic you had to adopt to get the love and support you needed to survive. I really mean it. You were smart when your wonderful body-mind did what it had to do to avoid pain and hopefully get love and support during your early vulnerable years. You were like the beaver whose paw was caught in a steel trap. To save its life, the beaver had to gnaw off its paw so it could escape. It's regrettable that it had to lose the paw. But it was a smart thing for the beaver to do. If it didn't survive, the intact paw would be of no use.

Like the beaver, you had to "gnaw off" a precious part of your natural, true-self. Your pain made you program a counterfeit self that in time began to feel natural. If you'd had caretakers who were consistently available and consistently warm, you wouldn't have developed the false-self characteristics that plague your life today.

The "shadow," or the missing part of our true-self, constantly seeks a way to restore our original wholeness. Unconsciously we feel guilty about the false-self we had to develop to survive physically, emotionally, intellectually, and spiritually. We can resolve to become the whole, wonderful, loving human beings *that we really are deep inside.*

The False-Self

A "false-self" character trait will be the opposite of the "true-self" trait. Suppose a caretaker repeatedly demeans or punishes the child for crying. ("If you don't come when I call you, I'll whip you till you can't sit down.") The child may try to protect itself from more hurt by suppressing its true-self expressions of anger and hurt. It can even *adapt* to this abusive life situation by programming a false-self that suppresses not only the expression *but also the feelings of hurt and anger.* This deep level of repression keeps the child from *even being aware of its true-self feelings.* Even when a caregiver is friendly, the false-self may not trust them.

Thus instead of healthily expressing its painful emotions and washing them away down the river of life, a child may be compelled to adopt strategic false-self behaviors to minimize pain. In childhood, the false-self is a needed—a smart adaptation to an unfortunate childhood situation. But our false-self habits that are so needed in childhood deeply hurt our adult life. Almost every adult lives with a partly anesthetized true-self. Our aliveness and happiness are diminished. They block us from using our adult capabilities to find more-effective responses to our adult life situations.

Childhood pain forces us to adopt false-self *screens of altered perception* to cope with the non-supportive or hostile actions of our well-meaning, but sometimes unskillful, caregivers. Thus in adulthood, our false-self creates *a world of illusion* in which we stumble from crisis to crisis.

Our Original Perfection

It must, therefore, come as a surprise to us grown-up wounded children to be told that we were originally "perfect." We genetically had a built-in ability to unfold through the various stages of childhood growth—providing our natural developmental stages were understood and supported by our caretakers. Our parents seemed like gods—all-powerful, all-knowing, and all-wise. If they were upset with us, we always blamed ourselves during our early years—there must be something wrong with us.

In Part III, we'll learn more about how our caretakers unknowingly relieved their unconscious anxiety by hitting us with *the pent-up anger it was not safe to express when they were hurt by their caretakers.* We had no way of knowing we were being abused because Grandaddy beat Daddy 25 years ago! So we usually pled guilty (especially in the first three years) to our caretakers' criticisms of being bad, sloppy, dumb, and any other denigrating judgments of our character. A toddler is trapped.

We were born excellently equipped to unfold into a happy, loving, caring, person. Perhaps you can accept your original inner "perfection" if you consider that dogs, cats, and giraffes are born with their "true-selves." Your dog was "perfect" when it was born—that is, it was "perfectly" endowed to unfold into a "perfect" *canine* life—which includes barking at strangers.

The Painful Split

So let's look again at what we mean when we use the words "true-self" and "false-self." Our true-self or "natural child" consists of the characteristics with which we were genetically endowed, and that develop in the natural unfolding of our lives with caretakers who were consistently warm and consistently available. If a specific part of our true-self was not okay with our caretakers, we repressed it and developed a false-self response that replaced it.

Sex is a crucial area that is often complicated by a parent's false-self adaptations, and our cultural conditioning. For example, a child is naturally interested in exploring how it feels when they rub their penis or clitoris. The thunderbolts of fear, guilt, and shame that some parents hurl when they see their child doing this will usually result in a false-self programming such as "I'm bad when I play with myself down there," or "My peepee is a bad thing."

One out of every three women in the U.S. have experienced some form of sexual abuse by age 18. Such abuse results in a sexual false-self that may shroud their natural true-self interest in sex—if it's not healed. When a child is *used* by adults for their sexual pleasure, the child experiences that he or she is mainly valued for sex. As the child grows up, it will have the false-self illusion that its importance to other people is based on being a terrific sexual partner. They will not feel lovable for themselves; they will only feel cared about when they fulfill someone's sexual needs.

For childhood survival, we had to perfect our performance of the strategic, false-selves required by our caregivers. John Eisman, a Hakomi therapist, says that every five-year-old deserves an Oscar. We had to learn the "right" lines provided by our caretakers. We had to convince everyone (including ourselves) as we automatically responded to life situations using our false-selves.

Some of our natural true-self responses may now feel so dangerous—even as adults—that we tremble inside and feel uneasy if we use them. (In my Caring Rapid Counseling, I've had clients who at first could not tell their truth to a pillow they called "Mom" or "Dad." With emotional appropriateness, they couldn't say to the *pillow*, "Mom, I felt hurt and unloved when you. . . .")

"Shadows" of our long-disowned true-self surface in our dreams and nightmares—shrouded in the murky mists of the distant past. Although long unavailable to the conscious mind, they are still alive in our unconscious. Reclaiming the disowned parts of your true-self is no easy task. But you can do it—and nothing else in your life can be as rewarding. Alice Miller sympathizes in *The Drama of the Gifted Child*:

> For the majority of sensitive people, the true self remains deeply and thoroughly hidden. But how can you love something you do not know, something that has never been loved? So it is that many a gifted person lives without any notion of his or her true self. Such people are enamored of an idealized, conforming, false self. They will shun their hidden and lost true self, unless depression makes them aware of its loss or psychosis confronts them harshly with that true self, whom they now have to face and to whom they are delivered up, helplessly, as to a threatening stranger.[1]

Many of us, in varying degrees, have lost our aliveness and spontaneity. We have become depressed, unhappy, and desperate. We can become alive again and free from depression and anxiety when our self-esteem is based on the *authenticity and wholeness* of our true-self feelings—and not on the *performance* of false-self adaptations that helped us survive childhood abuse. When we reclaim the anaesthesized true-self parts we had to disown, WE FEEL WHOLE. We experience that we are ENOUGH.

It is interesting to note that the enlightened state of consciousness is often described as transpersonal, timeless, and being aware of what's here and now. Higher states of consciousness are created by the *integration* of our old and new brain.

Your Life Belongs to You

It boils down to "Who's going to control our adult lives? Our parents (even though they may be dead)—or us?" If we keep going as we are, we will be the self we tailored to fit our parents' dysfunctionality. Do we want our childhood caregivers to continue directing our lives? Or, are we ready to become aware of what happened back then—and to make a decision to change, to reclaim our true-selves, and be guided by who we were born to be?

In childhood, some of us rebelled and some of us submitted. If we rebelled, we developed a false-self attitude of "I don't care what you do to me. I will keep on doing what I want to do. I don't want your love. I don't need it. The price is too big for me to pay." In spite of the uproar, the rebellious child generally has better mental health in adulthood than a submissive child.

As dependent children, we were trapped in a no-win situation. If we adopted the false-self strategies of our parents, we set ourselves up for a lifetime of unhappiness unless healed. If we rebelled, we lost their approval. There is no way we could understand at age four how *all of us would lose* no matter what choice we made—good old "Catch 22."

"We, in effect, sold our souls down the river of life," says Bob Hoffman. "Our parents were never taught to honor, respect, and love themselves. So how could they give to us what they never had? Had they been able to honor their essences, they would have honored ours, and we would have been nourished with love and nurtured with a strong sense of inner security."[2]

In the next chapter we will look closely at the false-self character strategies that today may seem completely natural to us—but are not really natural. They are responsible for almost all the problems that keep us from the relaxed enjoyment of our lives.

After reading Chapter 7, I encourage you to check yourself using the "Inventory of Childhood Survival Strategies." Your results can start you on the journey to greater joy, health, and happiness. If you carefully read and precisely follow the four steps needed to validly mark the inventory, you will be able to achieve life-giving insights that identify the childhood survival strategies you chose—and the parts of your true-self you had to disown. This inventory, which is a part of the next chapter, will lead you to your personal growth targets.

7

*True-
or
False-Self?*

By using the *Inventory of Childhood Survival Strategies*, you can begin to identify your personal growth targets for a happier and more successful life. Most people go through their lives unaware of the insights offered by this inventory. If you sift and re-sift it, you can make it a gold mine for reclaiming your authentic true-self.

"**T**here was a time for each of us," Cathryn Taylor says, "when we were not a slave to our past, a time when we were connected to our true selves and felt innocent, trusting, and free."[1] We had just begun our life. Then it began to happen. We felt afraid when our parents didn't come when we wanted them. We felt hurt and/or angry when they were critical, didn't show us love, or shamed us. We sacrificed parts of our natural true-selves to try to feel safe, loved, and nurtured by our caregivers—especially in our first years.

A Brief Review

As toddlers, to feel as safe as we could, we disowned some of our natural behaviors and replaced them with *strategic, survival* behaviors that we felt could help us handle Mom's and Dad's disapproval, anger, or shaming. These were our adopted coping strategies—our "false-self." *They became as deeply implanted as a compulsive instinct.* Some behaviors that were originally unnatural began to feel natural. Some of our original, authentic, natural actions and feelings now felt unnatural and dangerous. There was nothing else we could do. We were torn between expressing our natural feelings and needs—or risking Dad's or Mom's verbal or non-verbal punishment that made us feel shamed, afraid, hurt, terrified—or physically beaten. Some of us adopted the politically strategic path; *bow to superior power*. Others of us got stuck in the self-assertive "terrible two's"

Path of Ideal Growth

Natural Child

▼

The child experiences support and love from parents who are consistently warm and consistently available. It feels safe to be itself. The parent knows how to nurture both the conscious mind and the unconscious mind of the child.

▼

Whole Child
Child masters many life functions and skills.

The child is championed by nurturing caretakers. It is accepted as precious, valuable, vulnerable, imperfect, dependent, and immature. The child is allowed to be a child. The parents know that the child is entitled to self-confidence and self-esteem—with the right to have its feelings and thoughts heard with dignity even when the parent disagrees.

▼

Whole Person
Inner parent champions inner child.

A whole person can master new options. They have reclaimed the split-off parts of their true self. They experience life as an interesting challenge—instead of a continuous problem to be endured.

Path of Hurt/Split Child

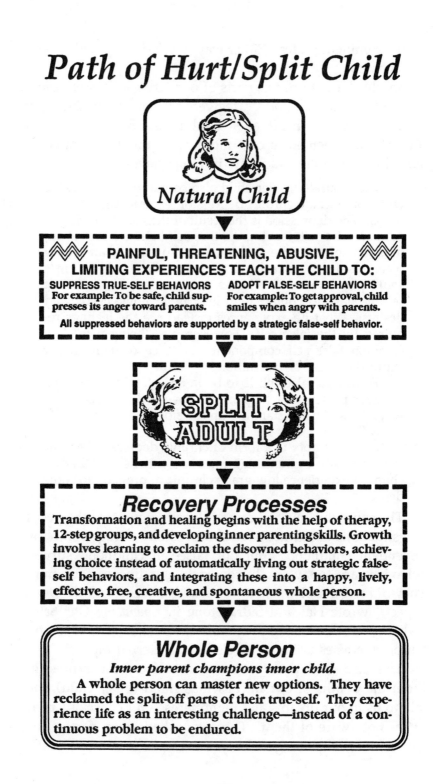

Natural Child

▼

PAINFUL, THREATENING, ABUSIVE, LIMITING EXPERIENCES TEACH THE CHILD TO:

SUPPRESS TRUE-SELF BEHAVIORS
For example: To be safe, child suppresses its anger toward parents.

ADOPT FALSE-SELF BEHAVIORS
For example: To get approval, child smiles when angry with parents.

All suppressed behaviors are supported by a strategic false-self behavior.

▼

SPLIT ADULT

▼

Recovery Processes

Transformation and healing begins with the help of therapy, 12-step groups, and developing inner parenting skills. Growth involves learning to reclaim the disowned behaviors, achieving choice instead of automatically living out strategic false-self behaviors, and integrating these into a happy, lively, effective, free, creative, and spontaneous whole person.

▼

Whole Person

Inner parent champions inner child.

A whole person can master new options. They have reclaimed the split-off parts of their true-self. They experience life as an interesting challenge—instead of a continuous problem to be endured.

for the coming decades. Either way, we ended up with a false-self behavior.

So, this blotting out of parts of our "true-self" was needed to adapt to our childhood caregivers. What was necessary in childhood became habitual in adulthood. But the "new instincts" we cemented in our unconscious mind are damaging our adult life. John Bradshaw in *Homecoming* says:

> The wounded inner child also contaminates adult life with a low-grade chronic depression experienced as emptiness. The depression is the result of the child's having to adopt a false self, leaving the true self behind. This abandonment of the true self amounts to having an empty place inside. I've referred to this as the "hole in one's soul" phenomenon. When a person loses his authentic self, he has lost contact with his true feelings, needs, and desires. What he experiences instead are the feelings required by the false self. For example, "being nice" is a common false self component. A "nice woman" never expresses anger or frustration.
>
> To have a false self is to be in an *act*. One's true self is never present. A person in recovery described it this way: "It's like I'm standing on the sidelines watching life go by."
>
> Feeling empty is a form of chronic depression, as one is perpetually in mourning for one's true self. All adult children experience low-grade chronic depression to some degree.[2]

The conscious mind of our adult-self knows that the people and situations in our life have almost totally changed since our dependent childhood. But our false-self childhood survival behaviors are today firmly rooted in our unconscious mind. They did not dissolve when we turned sixteen. "As we would expect," wrote Hal and Sidra Stone in *Embracing Our Selves*, "what we disown comes at us from the outside and, as so often happens, creates a life that feels like an eternal rape."[3]

The disowned parts in our true-self cry for expression. From the depths of our unconscious mind (inner child), they talk to us in our dreams and nightmares. Our conscious memory is not aware of them. These squashed-down parts of our true-self sap our energy. They mess up our immune system

74

and expose us to psychosomatic diseases. And they kill our aliveness and fun.

We will not feel whole until our unconscious mind is healed by *experiencing* that today we can use our adult strengths and knowledge to protect us. Our unconscious mind needs to heal itself by *experiencing* that it is safe to express our authentic, natural behaviors that we disowned to avoid childhood pain. Words or thoughts from our conscious mind will not heal the strategic programming burned in by childhood pain.

Our false-self is not easy to reprogram—unless you know how to do it. In the last several decades, leading-edge therapists have discovered *how to repair the injuries in the unconscious mind* that are destroying our adult happiness. The game is to give our unconscious mind the *here-and-now experience* that it's safe to express true-self emotions.

Another way to heal is through "inner child" work. By learning how to skillfully parent our inner child, we can transform our lives. Healing helps us return to our *original* inner peace, aliveness, and enjoyment of our life. Throughout the rest of the book, we will discuss many ways you can do this.

Children Are Little Human Beings

We are born with the ability to freely express our pain or grief through crying—or our pleasure through goo-gooing or smiling. It is a rare parent that emotionally accepts the child's *need* to express its hurt, fear, grief, or anger. By disapproving frowns or punishment, parents discourage the child's expression of their painful emotions—and encourage smiling and laughing. This communicates to the baby that expressing some of its natural feelings is not okay.

> *Our parents taught us there is something "bad" or "wrong" with us. We don't understand why we aren't okay as we are. But we must have the support of our parents. Giving up parts of our true-self can be the price we have to pay for "room and board."*

Children are not pets to be trained in ways that massage the parents' egos. Babies have feelings. They are human beings who need to be nurtured with dignity—and an empathy for both their dependence and immaturity. Pia Mellody points out that a child is naturally valuable, vulnerable, imperfect, immature, and dependent. (See page 67 in Chapter 5.) You were lucky if your parents made you feel that you were valuable, precious, and wanted—*just as you were.* Hopefully they reacted to your undesired behavior by *discouraging the behavior*—not by attacking or demeaning *you.* ("I don't like what you did," instead of, "You're a bad girl.") Traditional parenting skills attack the child—not the problem.

The child is vulnerable, imperfect, and immature when compared with adult strengths and abilities. Often busy, harried parents make children feel afraid, guilty, or ashamed of needing or wanting so much that has to be given by the adult. We were most fortunate if we were not blamed and shamed just for being dependent children.

Most of our caretakers did not understand the ever-present need of our unconscious minds to feel safe, accepted, and loved—especially during the years when our natural, true-selves were unfolding.

> *We developed a feeling that we were loved and valued because of our performance— not for who we really were. This undermined our self-esteem, self-confidence, self-appreciation, and love of ourselves.*

Don't Blame Your Parents

It is important at this point to explain that your parents did the best they were able to do—given their own abusive experiences with their parents and the false-self programming they needed to survive. Do you know why I keep repeating over and over the advice not to blame your parents? *It's because you're probably still blaming them!*

76

> *Your parents unknowingly caused your emotional problems. You can hold your parents accountable for their lack of skill in parenting. But don't blame them. When you blame your parents for what's wrong in your life, you can undermine your energy for personal growth. You have to give up your demand to have had more skillful parenting. You have to learn self-parenting.*

Your parents were *truly innocent* no matter what they did to you. They really did their best. They were only living out the way they had been programmed by their parents and society. And your grandparents were not villains either. It is essential that you understand and have compassion for their unskillfulness, and love them for the parts of their *beautiful true-self that managed to survive their own abusive childhood.*

Blaming won't change your parents—or the hurt you've endured. *It will only keep you trapped in your ego-based false-self.* As adults today, you and I are *100 percent responsible* for healing our false-self adaptations that are damaging our adult lives. Through the "inner work" described in this book, we can *return to the whole, authentic human being that we were when we came into this world.*

Skillful Parenting Means Nurturing Both Brains

Our society is faced with a fascinating challenge. It should be crystal clear by now that parents need to be sensitive to what they are setting up in the *unconscious minds* of their children. It is no longer acceptable for a parent to blissfully pass on the type of parenting they received—however good or natural it may seem to them. "Loving parents in particular," pleads Alice Miller, "should want to find out what they are unconsciously doing to their children. If they simply avoid the subject and instead point to their parental love, then they are not really concerned about their children's well-being, but rather are painstakingly trying to keep a clear conscience."[4]

> *Children who have successfully completed bonding, exploring, creating a sense of identity, competing, caring, and developing intimacy will seldom, if ever, fall into society's hellholes. A person who lives in their true-self has no need to abuse themselves with drugs, project murderous or unloving energy onto others, exploit others economically or politically, commit crimes, or to spew on themself or others any unconscious rage or hatred.*

This creates a new challenge for present and future generations of parents. Skillful parenting on both the conscious and unconscious levels requires much devotion and effort from parents. But that effort seems *minimal* compared to living with the neuroses, psychoses, suicides, murders, drugs, and criminal behavior that can bounce back on any parent who does not encourage their child to feel its feelings and express them, and to think its thoughts and express them—and support its seven phases of development.

People Are Not 100 Percent Predictable

As you know, this book tells how parents can learn to responsibly nurture both the conscious and unconscious minds of their children. By overwhelming probability, such parents will live far happier lives and have wonderful, well-adjusted, happy children who will grow into cooperative, loving adults.

Nevertheless, it is always possible that even with ideal parenting, things can go wrong. A daughter or son may develop dysfunctions because of inherited predispositions, brain injury, reaction to substances to which they are not biochemically adapted, illness, social values, individual differences, etc. All of us have limits in our ability to handle extreme pain or deprivation. Inherited metabolic abnormalities are important in anxiety, neurosis, and depression, as well as schizophrenia and perhaps depressive psychosis. There also seems to be an inherited predisposition for aggressive behaviors—as any breeder of dogs will verify.

There is much that we do not know. It is important to find out why some people brought up with harsh, authoritarian parents seem to be model citizens, spouses, and parents, while others who had abusive parents become harsh authoritarians themselves. In the latter case, they identify with the aggressor—but why? In the former case, they do the very opposite of what has been done to them—but why?

Albert Schweitzer and Carl Jung were brought up in the usual German-Swiss authoritarian fashion. This led to crises that they turned into constructive lives. Many children brought up in an "ideal" fashion may not have the intense drive to do something great for humanity. *How we choose to react to our own bad parenting and personal crisis is crucial.*

When we blame what we don't like in our lives on our parents, our relatives, the whites, the blacks, the Jews, the Arabs, the Protestants, the Catholics, the Communists, or anyone else, we may avoid assuming full responsibility for constructively responding to what we don't like about ourselves.

> *Regardless of all the words and theories, it's up to each individual to bring out the best in themselves. We need to quit blaming ourselves, our parents, or anyone or anything else. Accountable, yes; blameworthy, no.*

Compassion, humility, and forgiveness help us develop a perspective on what our old brain may feel is a certainty. Although we must go with what we think to be true in life, no one knows all about everything—or anything. We would be wise to silently add "so far as I know" to all our thoughts and conclusions.

Inventory of Childhood Survival Strategies

Based on the work of Ron Kurtz, author of *Body Centered Psychotherapy: The Hakomi Method*, I have prepared an eight-part inventory you can use to deepen your insights into parts of your true-self you left behind in your childhood. This Inventory of Childhood Survival Strategies will identify the false-self you had to construct—and clue you into your personal growth targets.

To get acquainted with this inventory, turn to the Burdened-Enduring Strategy on pages 276 and 277. First read these two pages. Then read Jean's story below. The inventory will probably give you many compassionate understandings about Jean's life.

Jean's parents grew up without any role model of how two adults could effectively communicate with each other and hunt for solutions that recognize the interests of both. Each of them came from a home where the father and mother had stopped meaningful verbal communication before they were born. And her mother was determined to control "everything."

By the time Jean was a toddler, they were engaged in abusive verbal conflict. They assigned three-year-old Jean the job of serving as referee in their arguments. They would argue, for instance, over which TV channel to watch, and ask little Jean to choose. Each, in turn, would give a long argument why their choice was the only good and logical one. Jean felt scared she would "do it wrong." She couldn't afford to say "no" to her parents. And she dreaded each session her parents used her to referee.

The natural child wants those around her to be relaxed, cheerful, and loving. The desire to please its parents is very strong. Soon little Jean learned to figure out judgments that would least upset both parents. Her motivation was to feel safe by getting as little disapproval as possible from either parent. Her parents made her feel *she was responsible for their happiness.*

She found innumerable ways to try to cheer them up and defuse their anger or crankiness. Thus her strategic response to her parents' abusive quarreling was to become a skilled codependent. (A codependent damages their life by futilely trying to "save" someone, e.g., a wife who constantly covers up the abuses and messes of her alcoholic husband.) She disowned her own need to enjoy her childhood. She took on the impossible burden of making her parents happy. And she hid her growing resentment of this job she was forced to do.

When Jean married, she and her husband were in agreement—his happiness was her responsibility. She was an automatic codependent. *She tried to fix everyone's happiness but her own.* She was unable to tell her husband what she wanted, or often, even tell herself what her needs and wants were. Since she was unable to always make her husband feel happy and cheerful, she made herself anxious and depressed by his normal moods. She also felt upset by her husband's inability to guess what her unspoken, and frequently unthought, needs and wants were. She will live a frustrated, unhappy life until she heals these codependent childhood wounds in her unconscious mind.

By considering Jean's history in the light of the Burdened-Enduring Strategy, you can develop a deep compassion for the effects of unskillful parenting that ignores the unconscious mind of the young child.

Using the Inventory

The inventory of eight childhood strategies in Appendix I can reveal to you some of the perhaps unsuspected ways your false-self keeps you stuck. *Carefully reflect on them to get a sense of each strategy.* Pay special attention to the first three columns, which describe:

1st column: Our painful experiences with our particular caretakers.

2nd column: To get our needs met and avoid pain, we adopted this false-self.

3rd column: These adaptations to our caretakers required us to disown this part of our original, true-self.

In Appendix I beginning on page 264, you will find instructions for using the Inventory of Childhood Survival Strategies. It is important to follow each instruction carefully. By checking and double-checking the instructions, you can increase the validity of your inventory results.

I strongly recommend that you complete the inventory before reading the rest of this book. Marking this book will make it more valuable to you. If it's borrowed, you can copy the pages before marking them. I am counting on your having these insights into both your true- and false-self to benefit most from the chapters that follow.

The false-self we needed to protect ourselves in childhood is like the barnacles on the bottom of a boat. We are not the barnacles that can impede our voyage. We are the boat. The barnacles must go!

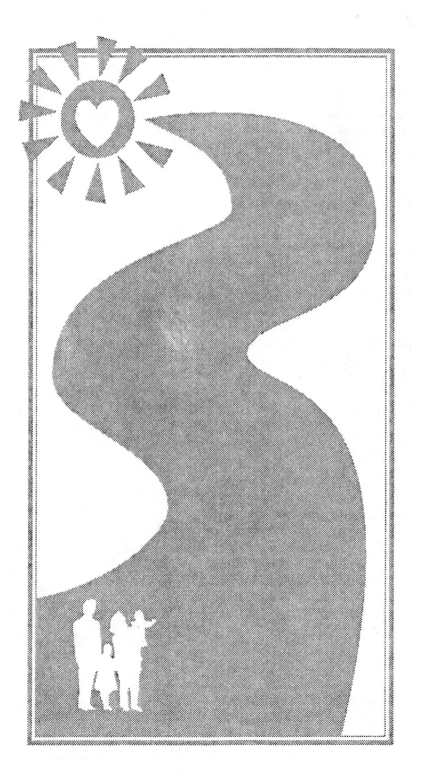

8

Killing Our Spirit

We are all wounded children trying to heal ourselves from childhood injuries we are not aware of. This chapter will expose the roots of our false-selves: the unskillful parenting we had to survive in the years before we had adult strengths and capabilities.

"T

he most dangerous place for any child is the American family," wrote Marilyn Mason in her book *Facing Shame*. Every year in the U.S., about 2,000 children are killed by their parents—and millions are psychologically crippled.

In this chapter, we will describe how our natural human aliveness can be murdered by our childhood caregivers in the first few years of life. Our parents, as we pointed out, are not to be *blamed*. But they must be held *accountable* for the degree they abused us with the "poisonous pedagogy" they learned from their parents.

When we discuss our childhood caretakers, we are usually referring to our mother and father. However, the people who are associated with the most pleasure or pain are generally the most significant in a child's development. So when we use the term "caregiver" or "caretaker," we include parents, siblings, relatives, or any others on whom the child was dependent.

John Bradshaw, who was deeply wounded in childhood, writes:

> I believe that all the ways in which the wonder child is wounded can be summed up as the loss of I AMness. Every child needs desperately to know that (a) his parents are healthy and able to take care of him, and (b) that he *matters* to his parents.
>
> Mattering means that the child's specialness is reflected in the eyes of his parents or other significant caretakers.

Mattering is also indicated by the amount of time they spend with him. Children know intuitively that people give time to what they love. Parents shame their children by not having time for them.

Any child from a dysfunctional family will receive this spiritual wound—this loss of I AMness—to some degree. An alcoholic mother and co-dependent enabling father cannot be there for their children. The alcoholic is absorbed in drinking and the co-dependent is absorbed with the alcoholic. They simply cannot be present for their children emotionally. The same is true when the parental coalition is under any chronic distress, including addictions to work or religious activities; eating disorders; addictions to control or perfectionism; or mental or physical illness. Whatever the disorder, when the parents are absorbed in their own emotional issues, they can't be there for their children.[1]

All the pains, hurts, and joys that we experienced are encoded in the old brain. In the first two or so years, they are usually beyond the *conscious recall* of the new brain in later life. If the child is abused, deep fears and pent-up anger that were unsafe to express will be programmed in its *unconscious mind*. Parents have assumed that they could train their child using punishments such as whipping, criticism that triggers fear, guilt, and shame, and demeaning the feelings, desires, and actions of the child as laughable, silly, bad, or wrong. Some parents think this harshness simply trains the young child to obey the laws of the household—and to conform to society's dictums. They don't realize that they are injuring part of the valuable wholeness of their child by *how* they teach—not necessarily by *what* they teach.

Our culture has a long tradition of treating our young children as non-entities—not fully human, not even needing human dignity. We have been unaware that even the youngest child is perceptive emotionally—although a simpleton intellectually. Caretakers have not realized that the old brain is busy programming everything that is associated with pain. Even child specialists in the past did not understand that toddler abuse plants the seed for psychological illness in adulthood.

Childhood Abuses

1. Your parent physically leaves you.

2. Your parent is so busy that you get little quality time together.

3. Your parent does not model their own emotions for you.

4. Your parent does not affirm that it is okay for you to have strong emotions.

5. Your parent does not support you in your seven stages of growth.

6. Your parent uses you to take care of their own unmet needs or desires.

7. Your parent uses you to take care of their failing marriage.

8. Your parent hides and denies their shameful secrets to the outside world, and you have to protect these hidden issues in order to keep the family balance.

9. Your parents do not give you their time, attention, and direction.

10. Your parents act shamelessly with physical violence, incest, verbal abuse, etc.

From *Bradshaw On: The Family* by John Bradshaw

Abuse creates a false-self booby trap primed to explode and project anger and rage onto future mates or others in our lives.

Fear-Based Parenting

Poisonous pedagogy is not new. It has been around for thousands of years in many cultures. (Anthropologist Margaret Mead found that Polynesia has many exceptions.) In the mid-1800's, Dr. Schreber was a well-known expert on child rearing. Some of his books went through forty printings and were translated into several languages. He counseled that as early as the fifth month of life, the parents should start aggressive training for the *child's own good*.

Dr. Schreber is very clear that a child must instantly and invariably be made to feel fear, guilt, and shame when it does anything the parent does not approve of—especially during the first three years before clear memories may begin. Thus the child will not be aware of the cruelty of the parent in stamping out its budding independence, spontaneity, curiosity, aliveness, and exploration.

As we know, a young child is totally dependent on its parents' love and support. A child usually cannot successfully oppose painful tyrannies in the first several years. Children will often blame themselves rather than their all-powerful, all-knowing, all-wise caretakers. ("If I was a good boy, Daddy would not be mad at me.")

The Roots of Mental Illness

The illusion that the parent's mental and physical cruelty on toddlers leaves no scars has destroyed the happiness of countless human lives. Both of Schreber's sons later suffered from mental illness accompanied by delusions of persecution. Alice Miller comments:

> An enormous amount can be done to a child in the first two years: he or she can be molded, dominated, taught good habits, scolded, and punished—without any repercussions for the person raising the child and without the child taking revenge. The child will overcome the serious consequences of the injustice he has suffered only if he

succeeds in defending himself, i.e., if he is allowed to express his pain and anger. If he is prevented from reacting in his own way because the parents cannot tolerate his reactions (crying, sadness, rage) and forbid them by means of looks or other pedagogical methods, then the child will learn to be silent. This silence is a sign of the effectiveness of the pedagogical principles applied, but at the same time it is a danger signal pointing to future pathological development. If there is absolutely no possibility of reacting appropriately to hurt, humiliation, and coercion, then these experiences cannot be integrated into the personality; the feelings they evoke are repressed, and the need to articulate them remains unsatisfied, without any hope of being fulfilled. It is this lack of hope of ever being able to express repressed traumata by means of relevant feelings that most often causes severe psychological problems. We already know that neuroses are a result of repression, not of events themselves. . . .

Because this process does not begin in adulthood but in the very first days of life as a result of the efforts of often well-meaning parents, in later life the individual cannot get to the roots of this repression without help. It is as though someone has had stamped on his back a mark that he will never be able to see without a mirror. One of the functions of psychotherapy is to provide the mirror.[2]

J. G. Krüger in *Some Thoughts on the Education of Children* (1752) helps us understand the pernicious philosophy that parents over the ages have felt they must follow to be a good parent:

If your son does not want to learn because it is your will, if he cries with the intent of defying you, if he does harm in order to offend you, in short, if he insists on having his own way:
Then whip him well till he cries so:
Oh no, Papa, oh no!
Such disobedience amounts to a declaration of war against you. Your son is trying to usurp your authority, and you are justified in answering force with force in order to insure his respect, without which you will be unable to train him. The blows you administer should not be merely playful ones but should convince him that you are his master. Therefore, you must not desist until he does what

89

he previously refused out of wickedness to do. If you do not pay heed to this, you will have engaged him in a battle that will cause his wicked heart to swell with triumph and him to make the firm resolve to continue disregarding your blows so that he need not submit to his parents' domination. If, however, he has seen that he is vanquished the first time and has been obliged to humble himself before you, this will rob him of his courage to rebel anew.[3]

Contemporary Abuse

Alice Miller in referring to the previous quote from Krüger comments:

> Here, everything is still stated openly; in modern books on child-rearing the authors carefully mask their emphasis on the importance of gaining control over the child. Over the years a sophisticated repertory of arguments was developed to prove the necessity of corporal punishment for the child's own good. In the eighteenth century, however, one still spoke freely of "usurping authority," of "faithful subjects," etc., and this language reveals the sad truth, which unfortunately still holds today. For parents' motives are the same today as they were then: in beating their children, they are struggling to regain the power they once lost to their own parents. For the first time, they see the vulnerability of their own earliest years, which they are unable to recall, reflected in their children. . . . Only now, when someone weaker than they is involved, do they finally fight back, often quite fiercely. There are countless rationalizations, still used today, to justify their behavior. Although parents *always* mistreat their children for psychological reasons, i.e., because of their own needs, there is a basic assumption in our society that this treatment is good for children. Last but not least, the pains that are taken to defend this line of reasoning betray its dubious nature. The arguments used contradict every psychological insight we have gained, yet they are passed on from generation to generation.
>
> There must be an explanation for this that has deep emotional roots in all of us. It is unlikely that someone could proclaim "truths" that are counter to physical laws for very long (for example, that it is healthy for children to

run around in bathing suits in winter and in fur coats in summer) without appearing ridiculous. But it is perfectly normal to speak of the necessity of striking and humiliating children and robbing them of their autonomy, at the same time using such high-sounding words as *chastising*, *upbringing*, and *guiding onto the right path*.[4]

It is difficult for parents to understand the plight of their children. Parents have a power over the young child's unconscious mind that is unique—and not likely to be duplicated in adult life. Alice Miller points out:

> The abused inmates of a concentration camp cannot of course offer any resistance, cannot defend themselves against humiliation, but they are inwardly free to hate their persecutors. The opportunity to experience their feelings, even to share them with other inmates, prevents them from having to surrender their self. This opportunity does not exist for children. They *must not* hate their father—this, the message of the Fourth Commandment, has been drummed into them from early childhood; they *cannot* hate him either, if they must fear losing his love as a result; finally, they do not even *want* to hate him, because they love him. Thus, children, unlike concentration-camp inmates, are confronted by a tormenter they love, not one they hate, and this tragic complication will have a devastating influence on their entire subsequent life.[5]

Love-Based Parenting

Many years ago, my friends Max and Virginia Frobe visited me with their son, Kai, who was then about a year old. We were discussing Living Love workshops. There was a low table with a lighted candle and a small statue about ten feet away. Virginia or Max held Kai in their laps. Every few minutes, he would squirm out of their arms and walk toward the table. Virginia would watch him without sternly saying, "Kai, stay away from that table!" As Kai slowly toddled toward the table, she would hurry over and lovingly pick him up and say something like, "You could get burned by the candle." And she would return to our conversation with Kai in her arms. Over the next two hours, this took place about 15 or 20 times!

91

In Your Personal Life

1. You can judge your own behavior, thoughts and emotions and take responsibility for their initiation and consequences upon yourself.

2. You can offer no reasons or excuses for justifying your behavior.

3. You can judge if you are responsible for judging other people's problems.

4. You can change your mind.

5. You can make mistakes and be responsible for them.

6. You can say, "I don't know."

7. You can be independent of the goodwill of others before coping with them.

8. You can be illogical in making decisions.

9. You can say, "I don't understand."

10. You can say, "I don't care."

Adapted from *When I Say No, I Feel Guilty* by Manuel Smith[6]

The style of parenting I had experienced called for stern commands designed to make me feel fear, shame, or guilt for being a "naughty boy." My shame and fear would teach me that although I didn't understand why, I was definitely not safe from attack by my parents if I "disobeyed" them.

I did not once notice that Max and Virginia were trying to control their child through fear, guilt, or shame. Although they made sure that the child did not touch the candle or the statue, all their actions were love-based. I had never before seen such patience and love radiating toward a toddler.

It takes a lot of *time, love, patience,* and *skill* to be a love-based parent. Everyone who has cared for young children knows they explore what happens when a parent says "no" during the "terrible two's." Since a child's insistent demands can test the patience of most parents, they often use their superior physical, emotional, and intellectual powers to frighten or shame the child into obedience.

When a parent controls a child through threats of punishment, they can kill the spontaneity and aliveness of the unfolding human. And both will later pay a terrible price! It occurred to me that however much patience Max and Virginia used to nurture their precious child, they would be deeply enriched as he grew up.

Styles of Parenting

Here's an example of parenting that wounds:

"Johnny, it's nine o'clock and your bedtime."

"I don't want to. I'm not going to bed."

"I don't understand you. You know that nine o'clock is the bedtime we agreed on. You promised to go to bed at nine every night when I gave you that ice cream cone last week."

"I don't feel like it. I want to stay up and look at TV."

"You should be ashamed of yourself. We've talked about this a million times. I thought I could trust you to live up to your agreement."

"I'm mad at you for making me go to bed now."

"You shouldn't feel mad at me. I'm just trying to help you. You need lots of sleep to grow up big and strong. Now look, I'm tired of going through this every night. If you don't get in there and brush your teeth and get in bed in five minutes, you're not going to the movies tomorrow."

The parent in just half a minute has demeaned the child as a person, told the child it should be ashamed to express its feelings and desires, and threatened it with punishment. The child feels unloved, afraid, overwhelmed, shamed, controlled, not heard, power tripped—and it feels it's "bad." The child probably experiences its well-meaning but unskillful parent as a danger. Notice how the parent's new brain criticized the child. Adult logic and persuasiveness are wasted. The old brain of the child only deals with safety and pleasure. And the parent struck out.

Here's how a more skillful parent might consciously nurture their child's old brain:

> "Johnny, it's nine o'clock and your bedtime."
> "I don't want to. I'm not going to bed."
> "I'm hearing you say that you don't want to go to bed now. [The parent is mirroring what the child wants.] I know there were many times when I didn't want to go to bed just like you. [The parent is validating the child as a person when it wants what it wants.] I know you're feeling upset because you have to go to bed now." [The parent has recognized the child's right to feel and want.]

At this point the parent has many options, one of which would be to lovingly take the child by the hand, or pick it up with good humor, and head for the bedroom. A *skillful parent does not always agree with the child*. However, they always respond in a way that enables their child to feel heard and understood, to feel that it's not "bad" for wanting what it wants, and that their emotions are understood and accepted by the parent. And the child may still have to go to bed since the parent has the responsibility of making this type of decision.

Unlicensed Parents

We are required to have both knowledge and skill before we can get a driver's license. This protects us and other people when we get behind the wheel of the heavy steel projectile we drive around in. But no parent needs a license to rear a child. Our society requires no knowledge about understanding and supporting our child as it unfolds into a whole, human being. No test of competency in reclaiming one's true-self or nurturing the unconscious mind is required.

Although it is appropriate to have a driver's license before we are turned loose on the road, I believe society would have an enormous drop in injuries and deaths on the road if driving were left to the common sense of individuals, *and every would-be parent had to pass a course on eliminating fear-based parenting—and demonstrate skill in lovingly nurturing both the conscious and unconscious minds of children—and themselves.*

In this chapter we have described how unskillful parenting ruins our personal happiness. It also sets us up for a life of depression, guilt, and conflict in marriage. And it damages our society—and could threaten our survival on Planet Earth.

In the next chapters, we will take a closer look at how our old brain projects a torrent of hatred onto innocent people. We will deeply examine the nightmare of unconscious projection—and how our new brain can deal with it.

PART III

THE TIME BOMB OF PROJECTION

9

Blaming
the
Innocent

The Object Quirk and the Time Quirk insidiously combine to create the craziness of psychological projection. An understanding of the mental time bomb of projection is essential so we can compensate for the life-damaging illusions it creates in our unconscious mind.

Let's look at the way we create the illusion that totally innocent children deserve our anger and aggression. Here's how it works. Our caretakers could not accept *our* true-self behaviors because their true-self wasn't accepted when *they* were children. When we were "bad," the unconscious mind of our caregiver confused or merged the present situation with the past. It is "safe" to beat a little child—sometimes even socially approved as a sign of "proper parenting." This projection acts as a handy vent for the caretaker's bottled-up anger.

The false-self of the parent always beats their child as an *unconscious* attempt to recapture the personal power and self-esteem that it lost in childhood at the hands of an abusive caregiver. While the blows are being laid on, and the child is screaming for its life, the parent's false-self ego cannot admit to itself that it is being ruthless, cruel, and unloving to the precious child they brought into the world. Alice Miller warns us:

> Until we become sensitized to the small child's suffering, this wielding of power by adults will continue to be a normal aspect of the human condition, for no one pays attention to or takes seriously what is regarded as trivial, since the victims are "only children." But in twenty years' time these children will be adults who will have to pay it all back to their own children. They may then fight vigorously against cruelty "in the world"—and yet they will

carry within themselves an experience of cruelty to which they have no access and which remains hidden behind their idealized picture of a happy childhood. . . .[1]

If an adult has been fortunate enough to get back to the sources of the specific injustice he suffered in his childhood and experience it on a conscious level, then in time he will realize on his own—preferably without the aid of any pedagogical or religious exhortations—that in most cases his parents did not torment or abuse him for their own pleasure or out of sheer strength and vitality but because they could not help it, since they were once victims themselves and thus believed in traditional methods of child-rearing.

It is very difficult for people to believe the simple fact that *every persecutor was once a victim.* Yet it should be very obvious that someone who was allowed to feel free and strong from childhood does not have the need to humiliate another person.[2]

Self-Righteous Anger

When a parent verbally or physically beats up on their child, their unconscious mind can give them a feeling they are being a good person—that is, copying *their* parents' way of parenting—even though they hated the abuse at the time. Driven by self-righteous anger, parents (who really want to be loving) are seduced by the projection mechanisms of their old brain. If our two brains were wired to eliminate such quirks, the new brain of the parent would be able to instantly stop this stupid projective mechanism of their old brain. It's crazy to punish our children for abuse perpetrated two decades earlier by our parents!

This combination of Object and Time Quirks is known by psychologists as "projection." The Tenth Edition of *Webster's Collegiate Dictionary* defines projection as "the attribution of one's own ideas and feelings to other people—especially the externalization of blame, guilt, or responsibility as a defense against anxiety." We project onto an innocent person the violence and hatred that we had to endure without venting our feelings when we were children. The energy of projected anger, rage, hate, and fury is enormous. *Yet our false-self can make it difficult for us to even understand this mental trick the jungle brain plays on us.*

As a test, read the following sentence.

> *Whenever you criticize or judge another person, you're projecting onto an innocent person a part of your injured, false-self that your unconscious mind is trying to hide from your awareness.*

Our ego, abetted by our rational mind, is not going to take this projection stuff lying down! Does a deep part of you cry out that this could not possibly be true? Is there a part of you that loudly protests that your criticisms and judgments are justified by other people's words and actions? Do you justify criticizing and judging by telling yourself, "I'm only protecting myself. I'm only trying to establish reasonable boundaries. I'm only telling the truth about how thoughtlessly, immorally, or heartlessly they are treating me. They deserve my criticism and judgmentalness. In fact, I'm performing a social service in unmasking them. How else will they learn to treat people fairly?"

Constructively and analytically sharing your opposing thoughts and ideas is okay. When you feel critical and judgmental, *you are unconsciously energized by unexpressed pain from your past.* And the other person *feels* attacked.

Kick the Cat

We laugh when we hear the "Kick the Cat" story. The boss chews out Joe. Joe goes home and speaks harshly to his wife, Jennifer. Jennifer yells at her son who has just tracked up her newly mopped kitchen floor. The son then turns around and kicks the cat. We smile condescendingly at how a verbal attack from the boss led to kicking an innocent cat through a chain of projection.

Projection makes no rational sense to the new brain. But it isn't the intelligent new brain that's doing it. It's the antediluvian old brain. Notice that only the boss was safe expressing feelings of hostility. Even the cat was cowed and afraid to attack the boy. No doubt the old brain of the boss was projecting anger that had been lurking in his unconscious since age five when his caretakers' arsenal for retaliation was too fearful to risk.

Every person in this incident was carrying pent-up, unexpressed emotions which their simpleton, unconscious mind *discharged by attacking an innocent being*. In its foggy way, the old brain tries to reclaim the power it lost to an abusive parent by attacking almost anything that seems safe. (Angry men may use their bare fist to punch a hole through an innocent plastered wall!)

Our simpleton, unconscious mind with its Time Quirk cannot distinguish between the past, present, and future. It is always experiencing the "eternal" here-and-now moment. Handicapped by the Object Quirk, your unconscious mind may not clearly distinguish between different people or objects— your mother, father, and siblings may be the same object to your unconscious as your wife, husband, or children! It cannot analyze or use logic. Since the unconscious lacks the circuitry to create concepts such as justice, fairness, letting the punishment fit the crime (or even the right "criminal"), it just flails out at a safe, handy person that has *some similarity* to the situation that injured it decades ago.

Seduced by Similarities

To survive and leave offspring in the rapacious jungles of 250 million years ago, the old brain evolved to notice one or more similarities to some element that it had noticed at the time of a painful past event. When something later has such a similarity, it can trigger the suppressed energy. For example, when a red object is moved in front of a bull, it may attack. Since red is the color of blood, perhaps the old brain of the bull is trying to kill off a bloody animal *from a past fight*. A matador can wave a red cloth held out on a stick, and the reptilian part of the bull's brain usually directs it to attack the red cloth. Since it can't think, it doesn't know that the matador with a sword is more dangerous than the red cloth he is swishing around. The bull is "projecting" its murderous anger onto an "innocent" piece of cloth. And like us, it pays a heavy price for attacking the innocent!

Imagine that you were terrorized at age four when your harried mother yelled and hit you. Decades later, your old brain may respond with fear and anger if your mate loudly shouts, "Watch out for that car!" Your mate has not hit you. The common element of both past and present is the higher volume of commanding words. But the simpleton old brain is not structured to unravel this dilemma. It shoots us up with adrenaline for fight or flight.

Suppose your mother abusively punished you, and it was not safe to express your true-self feelings of fear and anger to her. Your simpleton unconscious feels that it is appropriately retaliating against your mother's abuse when it abusively attacks your own child forty years later—even though your mother may have been dead for years!

Dealing With the Unconscious Mind

The unconscious mind is an amazing mechanism. Whether we like it or not, it works the way it works. All we can do is to learn how it works—and correct for the ways it can hurt our lives. As with a swindler, revealing the "dishonest" game tends to kill it. Although projection is behind most of our anger and demanding, most of us are blithely unaware of how it destroys our happiness.

Let's imagine that Henrietta was born into a family in which great care was taken to always appear polite, decorous, and well dressed. Clothes were conservative; voices kept low; and children were to be seen but not heard. A stiff upper lip was the proper response to any grief that might bring tears.

Young Henrietta was a vivacious little girl who was spontaneous in her laughter, her anger, and her tears. She loved to kick off her shoes and gave little value to her lace-trimmed dresses when having fun with her playmates. Years ago her parents had split off their spontaneous, alive, creative, true-self parts. To avoid punishment or loss of love from their parents, they disowned their aliveness and replaced it with a false-self facade of "dignified adult." Her parents' unconscious was programmed to immediately stifle any of their disowned true-selves that expressed human aliveness or playfulness.

Because of their own pain in childhood, her parents projected their pain on little Henrietta to restore the dignity and self-esteem they lost many years ago. They abused and punished little Henrietta for her fun-filled spirit in the same ways they had been punished in their childhood. And little Henrietta's free spirit is being crushed because of her parents' automatic projection of their childhood pain.

Restoring Lost Power

Child abuse is always based on a *caretaker's unconscious need* to restore the feeling of power lost in their childhood. The child/adult unconsciously develops a feeling of power by identifying with their verbally and/or physically violent caretakers. Children are abused for qualities *the parent hated in themselves* because it evoked so much childhood pain and disapproval from their parents. The projection mechanism of the unconscious operates so that *any disowned parts* of the parent's true-self that are exhibited by the child will make the parent perpetrate on the child the same pain that made the parent split off part of their true-self many years ago. *Projection is a universal tragedy that takes place daily in the thoughts and actions of every human being on earth.* It means blaming innocent people; it means blighting the parents' and the child's lives; and it is a major root of human unhappiness.

It is interesting to note that when Henrietta grows up and looks around for a mate, her unconscious will make her fall in love with someone who will put her in touch with her childhood pain. At first, she will be romantically attracted to a lively, free, expressive, daring male. After the honeymoon, he will probably criticize her "stuffy, rigid, unalive, no-fun, always dressed-up, always proper" way of living. ("Why don't you let your hair down and have some fun with me?") Henrietta's unconscious mind will be upset because her husband is trying to force her to do things that were not safe in childhood. And she will criticize him for being so wild, childish, and undignified. ("When will you grow up?") Henrietta and her mate will be locked into a power struggle that will most likely end up in divorce—or one of its alternatives such as psychosomatic illness, murder, suicide, or insanity—or giving up intimacy and spending little quality time together.

Although the unconscious mind's mechanism of projection may have been necessary to get our ancestors through the jungles of eons past, projection has as much place in *human* life as arsenic has in our diet. Both slowly kill us.

It makes sense to hold our parents *accountable* for our psychological problems. But it's not fair to *blame* them. They didn't know they were doing anything wrong. We can take the attitude, "I don't blame my parents for my psychological problems even though they inadvertently caused these problems. They didn't realize that what they were doing was harmful. They had problems of their own because of the way they had been treated."

Rigid Discipline Meets the Parent's Needs

Alice Miller points out in *For Your Own Good* that *all* rigid child-rearing principles meet the needs of the parent—not the child! The unconscious mind of the parent all too often is ineffectively trying to restore its long-lost dignity—and get revenge for the horrible pain it experienced. It unconsciously identifies with the power of its childhood aggressor. Among the parent's unconscious motives, she lists:

1. The unconscious need to pass on to others the humiliation one has undergone oneself.
2. The need to find an outlet for repressed affect.
3. The need to possess and have at one's disposal a vital object to manipulate.
4. Self-defense: i.e., the need to idealize one's childhood and one's parents by dogmatically applying the parents' pedagogical principles to one's own children.
5. Fear of freedom.
6. Fear of the reappearance of what one has repressed, which one re-encounters in one's child and must try

to stamp out, having killed it in oneself earlier.

7. Revenge for the pain one has suffered. . . .

Children who are lectured to, learn how to lecture; if they are admonished, they learn how to admonish; if scolded, they learn how to scold; if ridiculed, they learn how to ridicule; if humiliated, they learn how to humiliate; if their psyche is killed, they will learn how to kill—the only question is who will be killed: oneself, others, or both. [And, I must add, if they are loved unconditionally, they can learn to love with all their hearts.][3]

The Trap We're In

When children are abused and cannot express their pain to a sympathetic friend, their quirks will make them project their bottled-up anger onto others in their adulthood—or to direct it against themselves. Either one is a life-diminishing tragedy. When abused children learn to direct their rage toward themselves, their unconscious mind can create anorexia, bulimia, drug addictions, ulcers, cancers, insanity, suicide, depression, obsessive compulsions, psychosis, neurosis, sexual perversion, or innumerable psychosomatic diseases. Or they can self-destruct through driving dangerously, climbing high mountains, sky diving, and numerous other activities that may result in maiming or death. Or they may choose criminal activities, terrorism, or *socially approved violence*, such as being on a swat team, being a prison guard, or working in drug enforcement.

If an adult's aliveness has been killed by the heavy disciplined hand of a caregiver, when they have children, they will not be sufficiently cued in to the give-and-take of their own needs and their child's needs to achieve the balance needed in a close human relationship. When parents lack this sensitivity, they will use their superior power and knowledge to make the child feel fear, guilt, and shame if it does not follow the Biblical commandment, "Honor your father and your mother that your days may be prolonged, and that it may go well with you." They will take refuge in pedagogical principles and inflict pain upon their children who do not show enough respect, obedience, and submissiveness.

Parents who are strong in their true-selves will naturally find the golden mean between too much and too little guidance for their children. Parents must assume both the responsibility and the authority of their role.

> *Let's be clear. Children need parents who intelligently set limits and restraints. The healthy growth of a child requires that they respect their parents and understand that parents have feelings, needs, and grievances, too. When parents express their true-self thoughts and emotions, they will set natural limits for their child's behavior.*

Kick-the-cat projection makes us pay a huge price for the Object and Time Quirks between our two brains. Each brain has its good intention to help our life work. But we're always sitting on a keg of dynamite. Fortunately our new brain at last knows how to notice and handle these lifetraps.

In the next chapter, I will share with you how I handled a "thunderbolt" projection that my unconscious mind threw at my wife—in its illusion that she was my mother!

10

Waiting in Ambush

This chapter tells how some of my quirky "time bombs" exploded—and how I dealt with this lifetrap to minimize damage to the relationship with my wife.

I have done a lot of inner work on detecting my own projections. Nevertheless, I'm astounded by the slimy ways my false-self ego can trick me into unconsciously project-ing my childhood pain onto others. It's not only a feeling of righteousness. My false-self ego can tell me there is no other reasonable way to respond to a situation. After all, I'm only trying to defend myself. I'm just trying to communicate the "honest truth."

My wife, Lydia, hadn't noticed the apple tree on the fringes of our property. I suggested we go out to pick some cherries— and while we were out there, I'd show her the apple tree. On the way out, she picked up our mail. I saw a letter from the tax collector and I asked her to open it. I had recently protested our tax assessment at a hearing with an administrative tax of-ficial. I had not been notified of any decision from the hearing. When we opened the letter, I was surprised that the tax asses-sor had sent us a tax bill based on the assessment I had protest-ed.

Many thoughts raced through my rational mind. Why was this bill for taxes sent at this time? When would I be notified of the results of our hearing? What should I do now?

My mind was chewing on this as Lydia stood beside me holding the opened letter from the tax collector. She only vaguely knew about the hearing challenging our tax assess-ment. After I had taken a minute to silently mull over the impact of this letter, she impatiently said, "You're very inconsiderate. When we're on our way to the trees, you get sidetracked with business."

I told myself silently that when something comes up that impacts us to the tune of about $5,000, a "considerate" wife would give me a couple of minutes to assess this threat to the pocketbook. I realized later that my old brain had sneakily projected criticism onto Lydia ("inconsiderate" and "impatient") in an attempt to hide my own "inconsiderateness" and "impatience" with her!

When I was growing up, my mother would often trigger my fear, guilt, and shame by telling me that I was not "considerate" of her. These were control words that her false-self trained me to respond to. Because it was not safe to disagree with my volatile, red-haired mother in such a situation, I would not express my feelings when she hit me with this criticism.

And now, here was my wife telling me that I was not being "considerate" toward her. Although I wasn't aware of my psychological projection at the moment, my unconscious mind "exploded" with the pent-up energy of my suppressed emotions toward my mother.

Although I like to think of my general emotional state as one of balance and perspective, I felt a strong surge of anger and rage. I didn't know what was happening inside me. I quickly turned away from Lydia. I went rapidly toward the door, muttering something like, "I can't stand this any longer." Since I was rapidly getting away from her with my back toward her, she could not understand my words. But my body language spoke volumes!

Under the Apple Tree

I went out the door and headed down to the apple tree. As I sat under the tree, I was amazed by what had just happened. How could I have responded in this way to one I love? She was innocent. Her inner child was just expressing itself. It just wanted to have fun with me.

A *change of perception* gradually began to dawn on me. She had been injured by withdrawal and silence from her parents when they did not approve of her behavior. She had an unconscious injury about "abandonment." This made her critical when I shifted my attention away from her. So without any conscious calculation, I had "correctly" chosen the best way to hurt her: to go into an icy, muttering "silence"—and instantly abandon her. Even as these feelings and thoughts were welling up from my loving true-self, I still felt a rage I had not experienced for many years. I asked myself if there was a better way to respond to this situation with Lydia. I couldn't think of one. My false-self ego blocked any answer to this question. I felt trapped.

Changing My Perception

It took about three minutes for me to search out within me what this missing part of my loving true-self would have me do in this situation. It gradually occurred to me that I had responded to Lydia in the way my false-self used to protect me from my mother. She had often criticized or judged me as "inconsiderate" or "unthoughtful" to manipulate me into doing what she wanted. Although I felt resentful and angry, I didn't dare express these feelings to my mother. *My unconscious mind had just projected this unfinished business from childhood onto the woman I love!*

I do not like to think of myself as denying Lydia her right to feel what she feels—and want what she wants—and to express it. And yet here I was, projecting my childhood anger many decades later. *The old brain has no statute of limitations.*

About four minutes had now gone by. My loving self was beginning to get on top of the situation and offer me a deeper change in perception. If I had not been injured by my mother's controlling me by judgments of "inconsiderate" or "unthoughtful," I would not have responded by projecting this 50-year-old pent-up hostility toward my mother onto Lydia.

Lydia was totally innocent of my childhood pain. (Of course, her childhood sensitivity to rejection and abandonment made her critical—instead of empathetic.) She had just been letting her precious inner child ask for what it wanted when it wanted it—and to back it up with rational thoughts such as,

111

"You're very inconsiderate. When we're on our way to the trees, you get side-tracked with business."

Had it not been for my childhood injury, I could have simply heard what she said. I could have noticed that her inner child was impatiently using its right to feel what she felt and express it. Then I could have empathized with her: "You don't want anything to take me away when we're having fun. That makes sense. I feel the same way. You're feeling angry and disappointed." Or I could have said, "I'm sorry I looked at the letter at this time. It deals with a tax assessment matter, and we could lose $5,000." This would have given Lydia the information that her adult self needed to reassure her inner child that we would soon be on our way. Lydia's inner parent could have told her inner child, "It makes sense how you feel. It won't be long now before we go to pick the cherries and see the apple tree."

Working Only on MY Injured False-Self

I am aware, of course, that Lydia also has unconscious injuries from childhood pain in a family with nine brothers and sisters living in a non-affluent area of the Philippine Islands. She had repressed her cries of hurt and anger from broken promises—protests that were not safe to hurl at her parents. These unexpressed emotions were like guerrillas lying in ambush—just waiting for her husband to say or do things that release the floodgates of pent-up childhood hurt and anger.

However, I also know that blaming others will stop my own personal growth. Ignoring the part my projections play permits my false-self ego and rational mind to project more arrogantly onto innocent people. I tell myself I won't play therapist for other people unless they make an appointment in advance. I know that to complete the healing of my own injured true-self, I must not let my ego seduce me into focusing on Lydia's projections—and ignoring my own. I feel good that, in this instance, my mind did not get away with focusing me on how Lydia also was projecting her childhood pain onto me.

So the rule for me is:

> *For my own healing, I will only work on myself. It's up to you to work on yourself to reclaim your own loving true-self. If I am in conflict with you, and I blame your repressed unconscious programming, I will just keep myself stuck in my own false-self. The most helpful thing I can do for both of us is to work only on myself!*

The Treacherous False-Self

Although intellectually familiar with the psychological mechanism of projection, my false-self ego still has the ability to trip me up. It can make me do things that hurt my relationships. It triggers separating feelings in me toward those I want to love—and who want to love me. What a cosmic joke!

This incident with Lydia deepened my understanding and compassion for all of us when the ravages of our simpleton old brain continually project our pent-up angers, rages, fears, hatreds, and jealousies onto innocent people in our lives today. We spew this garbage on ourselves and other people—without knowing that we are attacking and hurting people who just happened to trigger these booby traps lurking in our old reptilian brain. Our painful unexpressed emotions don't disappear with age. Until healed they are cocked like a rat trap—always ready to come down on mates and friends, bosses or workers—or society.

Our Future Requires Conscious Parenting

Most parents today are ignorant of the world of the unconscious—and its quirks. For their own sake as well as their children's, modern parents must be *equally at home in the realms of both the conscious and the unconscious minds.* Skillful, conscious parenting is being redefined to include nurturing the old brain as well as the new brain.

Today it is "normal" to project onto innocent people one's

unconscious childhood fears, griefs, hatreds, guilts, shames—and desire for revenge and regaining lost power. How soon will the day come when parents will let their children express their tears, anger, and laughter fully *in the moment?* When that happens, one's emotions will be directed toward the person or situation causing the pain—instead of innocent surrogates many years later.

Fortunate will be the children whose parents opt for sanity and support emotional freedom—so they can become fully thinking and feeling human beings. As adults, we can do the inner work needed to feel our fears, grieve our griefs, express our angers, laugh at the absurdities, and cry and mourn the fear, guilt, shame, and rage we've carried so long in our unconscious. It will be a great step in our own personal growth when we change our perceptions to realize *we are all innocent, wounded children*—even the boss himself in the "kick-the-cat" story. A boss whose unconscious is primed to chew out his employee is wounded. His old brain is only trying to recover the self-esteem and power it lost when it was abused perhaps half a century ago. And the boss pays a price in lowered employee morale for this quirk.

We can only develop the deeper levels of understanding, compassion, and love for ourselves and all fellow beings when we understand that all of us are psychologically (not legally) innocent, no matter how horrendous our deeds have been! We are trapped because our simpleton unconscious fails to distinguish between different persons and times—and confuses aggressors with the innocent. *Because of our quirks, we live in a world with over six billion walking time bombs that can explode on any person, animal, or object—anytime!*

We deeply owe it to ourselves to develop the skills we need for stopping the ravages of this pernicious lack of communication between our conscious and unconscious minds. The old brain's automatic projection of childhood hurt onto a handy person or object today deprives us of more-helpful choices that our new brain can invent. For organisms that were programmed 250 million years ago to survive in the dog-eat-dog jungle, projection makes sense. However, today as adult humans with a neocortex, we can make better choices than projecting the bottled-up rage from our past.

We can get rid of these quirky illusions through knowledge that lets us understand what's happening, through determination to master the quirks, and through practicing with our own life situations. And we can always count on the University of Life to provide us with more lessons than we need! Let's use them to practice our skill in building a partnership between the human aliveness of our old brain and the wise, analytical abilities of our great new brain.

Since the quirks that produce illusory, false-self projections act as the *gun,* and repressed emotions function as the explosive *bullets,* the solution is simple. Get rid of the bullets. Through skillful parenting of children or adult catharsis (expressing what wasn't safe in childhood), we harmlessly detonate the bullets. **No bullets—no projections.** We can't rewire the quirks—but we can inactivate them. Like our intestinal appendix, the quirks are vestiges of our jungle past.

In the next chapter, we'll examine what's involved in healing ourselves. It's the greatest challenge of our lives. As we acquire these life-enhancing skills, we'll discover a sparkling treasure more satisfying than all the gold buried in Fort Knox— our whole true-self. It's a transformation. It is escaping from the hell of living with a false-self to the heaven of our authentic, true-self—the wonderful person we really are!

11

Our Need for Healing

A part of our human birthright is to fully live in the "Five Freedoms" that liberate our true-self. This chapter explains the freedoms you were denied in childhood—but can learn to give to yourself today.

We've examined our natural, authentic, true-self—our birthright. In every human life, painful things happen. However, if our true-self can cry out our pain, express our anger, and mourn our loss in the arms of someone who empathizes and understands, we are *self-healing*. We can psychologically integrate painful events when we safely and freely express our fear, grief, shame, and anger. For example, when someone we love dies, it may take dozens of hours of crying to heal the feeling of grief or loss in our old brain. Our new brain handles death easily. ("They had a good life, and it was their time to go.")

When we're feeling bad, we need friends whom we trust—someone who cares enough to *listen* to us. It is not even necessary for the person to tell us we're "right." They just have to be willing to hear our point of view, and to paraphrase back an understanding of what we want and name the pain we feel. We need to be reassured that our point of view makes sense—and we are not "bad" for feeling that way. A simple, empathic reply like this can help us heal an injury to our true-self: "Yes, I know you want them to pay attention to you. It makes sense that you don't feel it's fair when they ignore you. You're feeling angry, resentful, mad, and afraid." Our hurt, old brain just needs a friend who expresses understanding and compassion. It does not want *rational advice* on what to think or do at such times.

117

The Solid Parental Wall

Unskillful parents try to kill the spirit of the child in the first three years before it knows what is happening to it. To do this, there must be no cracks in the solid wall of parental authority and automatic punishment. A loving, sympathetic ear might keep it from working. The power-based parent will not usually tolerate a love-based mate who reaches out to the child with empathy. So the part of the child's true-self that cries out with pain "must not" be nurtured by any warm, loving, understanding heart. The dependent child must feel isolated—an outcast if it embarks on the second phase of exploration or the third phase of identity. (See "The Journey to Our True-Self" on page 48.)

It must feel it is in danger of losing all love and support. Every child instinctively feels that it will die if it is abandoned by its parents. (A little wolf cub separated from its mother may become a nice supper for a hawk or tiger.) A dependent two-year-old must conform to what the parent wants—or else! Children only create false-self programming under conditions that are painful and life threatening to them.

| *The false-self lifebuoy of childhood becomes the lifetrap of adulthood.*

We were smart to develop these false-self lifetraps for childhood survival of our body, mind, and spirit. Unfortunately, our unconscious mind could not erase them when we left the dominion of our early caregivers. Today we have adult strengths, capabilities, and knowledge that can do a much better job than the outdated false-self adaptations to parents who unknowingly projected their own childhood pain onto us.

Unless We Are Healed

Healing consists of taking false-self adaptations that now feel natural and making them feel unnatural again! What a twisted path we humans have to follow because our unconscious and conscious minds are not intelligently connected together! Too many quirks!

To the degree that we have been forced by our caretakers to develop false-selves, our lives will be damaged or terminated prematurely by the following four consequences:

1. Smothering Our Potential. Our alive, human spirit that is curious, creative, innovative, and fun will be impaired or missing. We lose many of our human capacities as we repress our true-self, and put on a false-self front that is rational, lacking in natural, human feelings, and needs the "safety" of submissive obedience to "authority." Our moment-to-moment train of thought is devoted to propping up a false-self *that we are afraid not to support.* In extreme cases, we join the "walking dead."

2. Psychosomatic Illness. Due to a quirk in the way our two brains operate at this time in our human evolution, power-based parenting can plant the seeds of severe mental problems both in childhood and especially later in life. Psychosomatic illness is considered by some doctors as being a root cause of perhaps 90 percent of our diseases. When the repressed injuries of childhood are creating turmoil in our unconscious minds, our bodies and minds will be continuously stressed. And stress rips us apart faster than almost anything else.

3. Destroying Our Happiness. You'll recall that throughout this book we define happiness as the relaxed enjoyment of our lives. Many of the people on earth today are living their lives in continuous stress. One stress hardly stops before two more begin. For far too many of us, relaxed enjoyment is seldom found except temporarily and partially through alcohol or drugs. Many people have such unpleasant dreams and nightmares that even their sleep cannot be said to give them a refuge of relaxed enjoyment.

4. Endangering Our Society. Dictators (whether local or international) have power because we give them our power.

On Parenting

There is no question but that your parents failed you as parents. All parents fail their children, and yours are no exception. No parent is ever adequate for the job of being a parent, and there is no way not to fail at it. No parent ever has enough love, or wisdom, or maturity, or whatever. No parent ever succeeds.

This means that part of your task—like that of every other person—is to supplement what your parents have given you, to find other sources of parenting. You need more mothering than your mother could give you, more fathering than your father had to offer, more brothering and sistering than you got from your siblings.

The problem is complicated by the demands our society makes on parents to be good parents. They are supposed to be 100% adequate, and it is a terrible disgrace if they are not. If they are successful, their children will reward them with devoted love, obedience, and success; if they are not, their children will turn out to be unloving, disobedient, and unsuccessful. This is the prevailing conviction of our society. But when parents buy this notion, they put themselves in an impossible position. They try first to be 100% adequate. When they inevitably fail at that, they try to *appear* to be 100% adequate. In either case, they cling to you, demanding that you get all your parenting from them, and thus reassure them that they have been good parents. (Such parental concern about children's "failures" can be understood in part as an attempt to force the children to succeed, and thus reassure the parents that they have been good parents.) They thus find it difficult to let you grow up; that is, to find other sources of parenting. This means that you will have to grow up in spite of them rather than wait for their permission. They will not make it easy for you, and you must do it on your own.

To grow up, it is necessary for you to forgive your parents. But you must forgive them for your sake, not theirs. Their self-forgiveness is up to them, not you, and they cannot afford to wait for you to forgive them any more than you can afford to wait for them to forgive you. When you do not forgive them it means that you are still expecting all your parenting from them. You are clinging to them in the hope that if you can make them feel guilty enough, they will finally come through with enough parenting. But this is impossible, and in order for you to be really free to find other parenting, you must forgive.

I hope you will not be embarrassed at your need for parenting, and that you will be humble enough and determined enough to find effective ways of getting it.

Henry T. Close

We let them usurp our power when we lose the power and integrity of our whole-self. When the natural self-esteem, self-worth, and self-confidence of our children are smashed by poisonous pedagogy, our society is in danger. German society in World War II paid a terrible price for its break-the-spirit-of-the-child parenting. Tyrannical parenting paves the political way for dictators. It's interesting to note that democratic nations almost never declare war on another democratic nation. When children are taught to respect and appreciate themselves, the dictators of this earth will be in trouble.

Not only are our lives placed in jeopardy by civil and international wars, we are constantly at risk from local criminals and domestic violence inside our homes. Politicians today in the United States can get elected on a "Tough on Crime" platform. The urgent plea of this book is that while we must deal with *symptoms* such as a murder or theft, it is even more important to get at the *roots* of crime. *And these roots grow in the toxic soil of power-based parenting.*

"Just a Child"

A child is not "just a child." *They are little human beings.* They have human feelings. They have endless human needs and desires just as adults do. The illusion "just a child" has ruined many lives. Children need to be respected as little humans. Conscious parents can help them develop self-esteem, self-respect, and self-confidence. Psychologists have long known that if we congratulate a child when we catch it doing things "right," it will learn much faster than if we keep a sharp, critical eye to dump fear, guilt, and shame when the child does something we don't like.

We are all precious and valuable. Unfortunately, unskillful parents sometimes react to their children as though they were a defective, inferior throwback of our species. When we plant the seeds of fear, guilt, and shame in our children, we should not be surprised when we harvest dysfunctional, depressed, should-and-shouldn't obsessed unhappy adults. When we

The Five Freedoms

1. The freedom to see and hear what is here and now, rather than comply with our caretakers distortions of what was, will be, or "should" be— and be safe to share it.

2. The freedom to think what one thinks, rather than what one "should" think—and be safe to share it.

3. The freedom to feel what one feels, rather than what one "should" feel— and be safe to share it.

4. The freedom to want and to choose what one wants, rather than what one "should" want—and be safe to share it.

5. And the freedom to imagine one's own self-actualization, rather than playing a rigid role or always playing it safe—and be safe to share it.

Adapted from Virginia Satir

plant the seeds of love, fun, appreciation, compassion, and patience in our children, we can have a bountiful harvest of a relaxed enjoyment of life—both in ourselves as parents and in our sons and daughters.

Our Declaration of Emancipation

Psychologist and family counselor Virginia Satir has formulated the five freedoms shown on the opposite page. These are the rights of all human beings, whether little or big. Unskillful parenting that denies our rights has been passed on from generation to generation. It's time for a break!

Many families violate the first freedom by making their children protect the family "shame secrets." As Bradshaw tirelessly explains, "We are as sick as our secrets." To protect the false-self of parents, children are often required to "not see" their alcoholic mother or philandering father. The children take on the shame of the parent—and feel guilty hiding or lying about these "shame secrets."

Virginia Satir's second freedom gives children the right to think as they think rather than what they "should" think—and express their thoughts without penalty. It is abusive for a parent to require their child to think that people of certain skin colors are "bad"—or that we should feel guilty and ashamed if we explore religious and political ideas not held by our parents.

Virginia Satir's third freedom gives the child the right to feel what it feels—rather than what our parents say we "should" feel—and to be safe to share it. Suppose little Johnny says, "I hate you" and the mother replies, "You don't hate me. You really love me." She is denying Johnny's freedom to feel what he feels—and express it. Painful emotions when fully expressed are like clouds that rain on us and then disappear. To deny them is to make them more important than they are. To bottle them up sets us up for depression, violence, abuse of oneself or others, suicide, illness, and stress.

The fourth freedom gives the growing child the right to want what they want. Of course no one has the right to get everything they want. You win some and you lose some.

The fifth freedom allows the young human to dream their own dreams—instead of feeling they must live out their parent's dream.

Until we understand that the little humans we've brought into the world need these "Five Freedoms," we will continue to abuse our children—and keep our lives and society in turmoil. I wish these Five Freedoms could be hung in the living room of every home in the world.

A More Abundant Life

What's past is past. We can't do anything to change our past. We can, however, do a great deal to change how our old brain *experiences* what our time-oriented new brain calls our "past." We can then perceive whatever enlarged options we now have for getting on with our lives in the best way that is available to us.

The next part of this book will help you expand your understanding of how to create a partnership between your two brains. You may learn that your own inner parent is abusing your inner child in exactly the same way your caretakers abused you! You can learn how to begin developing a satisfying, fun-filled, healing partnership between your precious inner child and your wise, nurturing inner parent.

PART IV

YOUR
INNER
PARTNERSHIP

12

*Your
Inner
Child*

When we know how to nurture and heal it, our unconscious mind gives us a lifetime of aliveness, fun, health, and energy. Our conscious mind needs to respect the functions of the unconscious mind, and also be aware of its shortcomings. We can communicate with our unconscious when our conscious inner parent learns to talk with our "inner child." Part IV tells us how to do it.

"Three things are striking about inner child work," says John Bradshaw in *Homecoming*. "The speed with which people *change* when they do this work; the depth of that change; and the power and creativity that result when the wounds from the past are healed."

In recent years, the metaphor "inner child" has been used to refer to the activities of the unconscious old brain—especially the limbic area with its palette of fear, grief, jealousy, anger, irritation, rage, hurt, resentment, boredom, etc. And, of course, the inner-child brain is also the generator of what we enjoy most: love, fun, joy, play, exhilaration, and peaceful relaxation. Your inner child is like a watch dog that instantly sniffs out possible pleasure or pain.

Let's look again at the terms we use:

	OLD BRAIN	NEW BRAIN
Product:	*Feelings*	*Thoughts*
Metaphor:	*Inner Child*	*Inner Parent/Adult*
Mind:	*Unconscious*	*Conscious*
Neurology:	*Medulla-Limbic*	*Cerebral Cortex*
Functions:	*Health, Energy,*	*Thinking, Insight,*
	Play, Loving	*Analyzing, Wisdom*

To get to know your inner child and inner parent, you must distinguish between feelings (created by the inner child) and thoughts (created by the inner parent or inner adult). For example, "I feel calm" is a feeling. But beware of "I feel senators seldom represent the people." It's not a feeling—it's a thought. It is a product of the new brain, and I can assure you that the old brain will not even know what you're talking about!

Inner-Child Activities

Barbara B. Brown in *Supermind: The Ultimate Energy* tells us:

> This failure of consciousness to know what unconsciousness knows may well be the basis for many conflicts between consciousness and unconscious activities. Freud once said that we would have no problems if there were no consciousness. But we do have conscious awareness, and the solution to conscious-unconscious conflicts would seem to be to learn how to become aware of the depth and breadth of unconscious appreciations and understandings. This is exactly what is happening now in a society that has become interested in body awareness and in exploring the interior self.[1]

The unconscious mind or inner child does many vital things in your life:

1. Energy: It increases or reduces your energy depending on your inner child's feelings of safety, pleasure, or boredom. Your inner child makes you feel bored when sensory input is too fast or too slow—or not interesting.

2. Health: Your inner child is in charge of the immune system as well as all other biochemical activities in your body. If it is heavily stressed, it can make you sick within an hour! It can also go the other way and stimulate antibodies to get you well fast. Through its operation of the immune system, it literally determines whether you live or die!

3. Fun: Your inner child creates the fun in your life. Fun and play heal us. Puppies, kittens, and young children innately know how to play. Play has no game rules. There's no winning or losing. It's just play. Two toddlers can sit in a bathtub splashing each other with water—and laugh and laugh and laugh. Adults don't understand this. ("Quit fooling around and soap yourself.")

Your Three Inner Children

Hal and Sidra Stone, in their insightful book *Embracing Our Selves*, describe three ways your inner child operates. These three modes also apply to your "outer" children—your young sons or daughters. They are:

1. The Vulnerable Child: Your inner child, as Pia Mellody said about all children, is valuable, vulnerable, imperfect, dependent, and immature. It needs to feel safe. It wants the protection, wisdom, and experience of your new brain—your "inner parent" or "inner adult." If your inner adult is not strong enough to protect your inner child when it feels unsafe, it will make you feel fear, grief, anger, frustration, resentment—or anxiety.

When your inner child is creating a tantrum inside you, your inner parent will be distracted from the balanced thinking needed to find wise solutions. For example, the emotions stirred up by your hurting inner child may lead your inner adult to angrily walk away from your lover in an argument. You may miss options that can lead to intimacy, such as responding, "I really want to know how you feel and why you're feeling that way. I'm sure we can work out a win-win so both of us can get a lot of what we want."

Like any conscious parent, your inner parent needs to make it okay for your inner child to feel what it feels. If your inner child is grieving, it is important to let it shed tears of mourning—and then encourage it to cry more. You do not help your inner child when you try to stop the flow of tears with your rational wisdom. ("Our sweetheart has gone. Don't cry any more. We'll date around to find someone else.") However wise it may be, cerebral advice makes your inner child feel you don't understand. *And you don't.* The old brain is self-healing if we don't get in the way. Tears and crying are its natural way to heal broken bonds with those we love.

2. The Playful Child: Another part of our valuable inner child is the playful child. *Life can be fun.* The relaxing effects of play and laughter help our cerebral cortex to click along processing sensory input, retrieving memories, and otherwise doing its thing. The playful child helps us lower our blood pressure and reduce heart attacks and strokes. It does a great job of tuning our biochemistry to slow down the rate at which we age.

Many of us gradually ossify into "the living dead." We don't smile; we don't belly laugh; we don't play. Our aliveness, sparkle, and joy of living may be suppressed as we grow older. We take everything seriously. We rationally deal with the people and situations in our lives. We walk stiffly, talk stuffily, and have a narrow range of choices in picking solutions to situations that confront us in life. ("What would the neighbors say?")

We *think (!)* we are having fun when we engage in "recreation." The word implies we are re-creating ourselves. We play Monopoly, bridge, and tennis and put quarters in the slot machines in Las Vegas. This is recreation—but it's not the same as play. Recreational activities may have a beneficial effect in relaxing us somewhat from the heavy "should's" and "should not's" that drive our lives. ("I should save money.") But they still keep us enmeshed in cerebral win-loss jeopardy. Recreation has strategic principles and rules that rationally compel us to watch our step—and do things "right." We may even have rules, strategies, and win-loss criteria when we engage in sex with our partner! Our false-self ego always wants to win. It keeps us self-conscious, rational, critical, and judgmental and can scare our inner child (fear, anger, shame, resentment) when we are losing.

So we need to learn the difference between play and recreation. This doesn't mean that we shouldn't try to enjoy as much recreation as we can. It just means that we should be aware of the difference between letting our inner child *play*—and engaging our inner adult in the rule-bound, win-lose climaxes of *recreation*.

So many of us have lost our playfulness. And we'd better get it back if we want to live a long, happy life. Our immune system works better when we laugh—*belly laugh*—not just smile, smirk, or chuckle. Many adults haven't belly laughed for years. And they may have high blood pressure, high cholesterol, and arthritis to mention only a few of the possibilities. We don't have to wait until something is funny in order to laugh. You can probably peel a few years off your functional age by daily belly laughing for just 20 seconds every hour!

Try standing up *right now* and belly laugh. Make your belly stick way out as you take in as much air as you can. Hold it for four seconds. Then push in with your powerful abdominal muscles to *deeply laugh as loud as you can*. Using several breaths, can you belly laugh for just 20 seconds? If you can, you may immediately feel lighter—and more relaxed. And you weren't laughing at anything!

Belly laughing gives the old brain the message that all is well. Your belly-laughing ability will strengthen with practice. It will temporarily speed up your heartbeat and give every cell in your body an added shot of oxygen and glucose. It will stimulate the flow of blood in your capillaries and massage your innards! This 20-second biochemical tune-up works every time—and it's free!

Belly laughing often during the day can tip the scales between resistance to certain diseases—and becoming a host to these diseases. If continued long enough, it can have the side effect of raising your spirits and becoming addictive. But be sure to warn your family about these hourly outbursts of belly laughter—or they'll think you've lost it.

Ornstein and Sobel in *Healthy Pleasures* tell us:

> Pleasure rewards us twice: first in immediate enjoyment and second in improved health. Although there are exceptions in the modern world, pleasure—enjoying food, sex, friends, work, and family—is the universal innate guide to health. People recognize what is healthful by the joys of life, by their pleasurable feelings—a delicious nap, a sated stomach, or the satisfaction of sexuality. These sensations signal our brain that we are on the right track and should continue.[2]

3. The Magical Child: Another face of the precious inner child within us is the magical child. This is the child whose imagination can change a dog into a horse, a house into a castle, and a parent into a king or queen—or a dragon or ogre. This child part of us can playfully dance in the world of imagination. It creates "fairy tales" that symbolically deal with what it likes or doesn't like. Children can enjoy their fantasies throughout the day. Adults may reserve fantasies to dream time at night—unless they have an insistent, magical inner child like Walter Mitty.

Psychologists tell us that the most important sex organ we have is our minds. Since the old brain blurs the distinction between fantasy and reality, fantasies even during sex can create an excitement that may be missing in our routine sex patterns.

Sexologists suggest that sexual partners work together to express their fantasies—and live them out in sex play.

New Spirit

We need a new spirit in our inner-parent–inner-child relationship. Our inner adult has often berated our vulnerable child ("Settle down so I can work"), our playful child ("That's not dignified"), and our magical child ("Don't let your mind run away from you"). Unfortunately for many of us, time plants more wrinkles in our mind than on our skin. The vulnerable, playful, and magical children within us can be active at any age. We need them to keep us lively, youthful, and healthy. This is why Hal and Sidra Stone remind us in *Embracing Our Selves:*

> The discovery of the inner child is really the discovery of a portal of the soul. A spirituality that is not grounded in understanding, experience, and an appreciation of the inner child can move people away from their simple humanity too easily. The inner child keeps us human. It never grows up, it only becomes more sensitive and trusting as we learn how to give it the time, care, and parenting it so richly deserves.[3]

We can lose a lot of happiness if we do not support both the playful and magical children in us—and nurture the hurt child—whose playroom is our old brain.

In the following chapter, you will learn how to contact your valuable inner child and communicate with it throughout the day. Even at age 100, you can revitalize your relationship with the life-enhancing inner child you always have in your unconscious mind. You can give your life a new vitality and energy that will make you feel years younger.

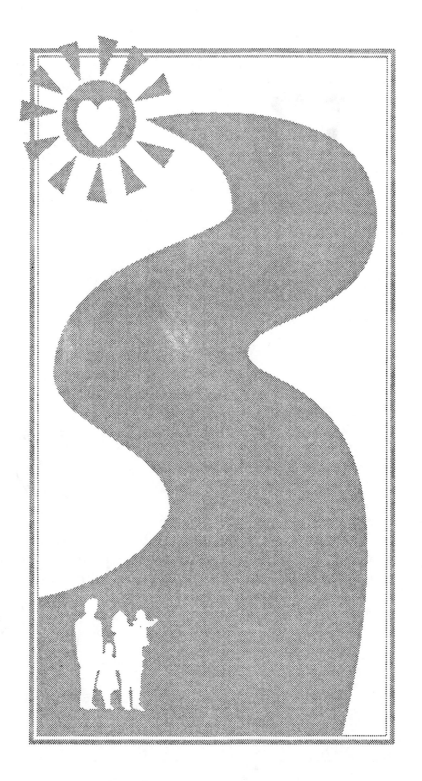

13

Your Inner Parent

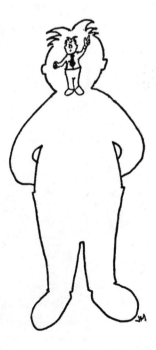

Your inner parent is the care giver. Your inner child needs and wants the loving guidance of your inner parent so it can have fun, give you energy, and take care of your immune system—and gradually heal childhood wounds. Your inner child only needs to be itself—and to be loved, nurtured, and respectfully guided by your inner parent.

If your inner adult does not skillfully parent your inner child, you may have a temper-tantruming three-year-old running your adult life!

The inner parent is like the captain of the ship. The captain makes decisions and takes responsibility. But unless the captain is fully supported by the crew (inner child), the engines may not work, the radar operator may be doing a crossword puzzle, or the navigator may fall asleep. The inner child can sabotage your life if its needs are ignored. However, it feels best when it supports the inner parent. It really likes to please.

Many excellent workshops are now available on "Healing Your Inner Child." I recommend them. However, you don't have to heal your inner child. *It's your inner adult that isn't doing its job of lovingly parenting your inner child*—and working out win-win solutions when they disagree. Your inner parent needs to change to enable your inner child to heal its fear and anger. These "inner child" workshops help your inner adult to get in touch with your inner child—and create a working "partnership."

Just Being Itself

Your inner child (just like your outer child) wants a parent who will protect, appreciate, and love it. It wants to play, laugh, and express its fear, grief, anger, or boredom. Your inner child is the part of you that is alive—right here—and right now. Your old brain or inner child does not want to be cerebral or "responsible."

It doesn't want to be lectured on the past—or concerned about the future. *It should not be expected to act like a little adult.* It wants to live with a warm, bubbly spontaneity. You abuse your inner child if you blame it for acting dependent, needy, or immature. ("I can't depend on you. You'll be the death of me yet.")

Just as your inner child has several modes (the vulnerable, playful, and magical child), your inner parent has many sides. There's the critical parent, punishing parent, rational parent, busy parent, uncaring parent, abandoning parent, hostile parent, abusive parent, rule-book parent, and always serious parent. There's also the loving parent, playful parent, wise parent, understanding parent, good-humored parent, nurturing parent, available parent, health-oriented parent, teaching parent, and protective parent. These can be boiled down to two: the functional and dysfunctional inner parents.

The adult brain's usual ideal is to have a dignified, thoughtful child. But for your inner child to be smothered by a rigid parental model is disastrous. We also need our childlike aliveness. A part of us dies if we lose our playfulness and don't experience the magic and beauty that's always there in our lives. *Without an alive inner child, it's like living in a small, stuffy room without windows or fresh air.*

> *Your inner child only needs to be itself. It can be self-healing if it feels it can trust a wise, inner parent to protect it. If your inner child has become withdrawn or aggressive, it may take several months of loving, skillful parenting to lower its defenses.*

Talking With Your Inner Child

If your inner child is neglected by a busy inner parent, or kicked around with "should's" and "should not's" by your rule-book inner parent, it may eventually try to hide from you and quit talking to you. Your inner child has to protect itself. The old reptilian and mammalian brains just do not understand new-brain reasoning. When parents "shoulded" all over us, our old brain felt afraid. ("You should never interrupt me.") Our old brain didn't understand why. It could only experience that somehow we were "bad" and our caretakers didn't like us.

John Pollard, in his book *Self-Parenting: The Complete Guide to Your Inner Conversations* and his later book, *The Self-Parenting Program*, tells you how to create a partnership between your inner child and inner parent. Pollard shows you how to develop a relationship with your inner child in which it trusts you—and talks to you! Your new brain (conscious mind) can actually hold real conversations with your inner child (unconscious mind)! Our unconscious mind doesn't understand abstract language. However, it communicates with emotions, body language, and simple sensory-based words.

Your neighbors may think you've gone nuts. But it's one of the sanest things you can do. Your inner dialogue can gradually resolve many of the inner conflicts and injuries left over from childhood.

When we acquire the skill, we can talk with our unconscious mind using either Pollard's Self-Parenting technique or the Voice Dialogue Method of Hal and Sidra Stone, or both. This can be surprisingly easy—even routine. Hypnotists talk with the unconscious mind. And in my Caring Rapid Counseling work, I consistently communicate with a client's unconscious mind in an altered state not involving hypnosis.

When you talk with your inner child, it may keep you from making mistakes in your life. It gives a here-and-nowness—to balance the past and future focus of your new brain. You'll benefit by *considering* its feelings about your work, or your proposed mate. Your life goes into a new dimension when you enrich your blend of thought, feeling, and action by creating a harmonious partnership between your two brains.

Unless you have consciously changed, you are today parenting your inner child as you were parented. It may feel it has been pushed around or abandoned—or not loved. You've been too busy to care about how it feels and to play with it. Your inner child probably does not trust you. By following Pollard's directions in *Self-Parenting*, you can gradually regain its trust.

When you first try to talk with your inner child, you may find it is withdrawn and will not talk with you. (This can happen with outer children, too!) But remember that your inner child is dying because it's missing your love and attention. It wants to talk with you so that it can begin to trust that its inner parent will keep it safe and happy. It wants to feel that the big biocomputer upstairs will deal with "scary" people and things that upset it. We cannot afford these inner-child fears. They diminish our health, happiness, fun, and energy.

Introducing Yourself

You can learn to contact an entirely different voice within you that is not your adult, rational voice. Its speech will be childlike. Its feelings and wishes may amaze you. The messages from this feeling part of your old brain will richly supplement and balance the ideas now running in your intellect.

Just to get a taste of communicating with your inner child, lie down where you are comfortable. Relax. Notice any tension within your body. If you find any tension, it's a message from your inner child that it's feeling stressed. Remember, speak slowly and use words a four-year old might use.

> Say, "Beautiful inner child, I love you and I want to help you. I am sorry I have not given you the time and help you need. I want to do better. I want to love you and care for you."

> Take six slow, deep breaths in and out. Notice any smells you can pick up. Breathe even deeper in and out—six more times. Do this slowly. You have lots of time. Say the words in the preceding paragraph again *very slowly* with heart feelings. Give it time to reply in words, images, or feelings—up to a half minute.

> Now say aloud to your inner child, "Precious, little (use the name you liked to be called in your childhood). Thank you for being with me and listening to me. Would you be willing to talk with me?" Relax and just listen for a reply.

> If you have neglected your inner child for years, it may not trust you or want to talk to you. You can regain its trust, love, and helpfulness—but it may take a while. Each time it

138

replies to you, tell it, "Thank you for talking to me." It needs to feel appreciated. Now ask your inner child, "What would you most enjoy doing today?"

Don't "think" of an answer. Just notice. Wait for your inner child to respond. If it's willing to talk to you at this time, it will answer you.

Speaking slowly, now ask your inner child, "What would you like to do tonight?" Wait for it to reply. Ask it anything else you want to find out.

You can then end this brief contact with, "I know I've been neglecting you. I want to talk with you every day. I want to know how you feel, what you don't like, and what you want."

If your inner child does not talk with you when you first try to contact it, be sure to end up with, "Thank you for listening to me." You can be sure the wily old brain is always listening!

Again, give it time to answer.

How They Work Together

The information on the following two pages will help you explore the dynamics between your inner parent and inner child. The same dynamics applied with your parents and you—and between you and your own children.

What's happening when your inner parent and inner child are in conflict? It's another mix-up between your old and new brains. The child is signaling that you are not consistently warm and consistently available. It's saying it's scared—or feels abandoned. It uses the animal behaviors of fighting (like a tiger), running away (like a rabbit), hiding (like a turtle), or submitting (like a dog). You can begin to notice these signs that you may have previously ignored.

As you read each item on the next two pages, I suggest that you pause. Apply it to your own life. If you want to improve your relationship with your inner child, what could you do immediately? In what ways would your life be happier if you go beyond the dysfunctional indifference or conflict between your inner parent and inner child? Are you ready to accept the

Your Nourishing Inner Parent Naturally:

1. Initiates analytic judgments and seeks understanding and wisdom
2. Offers intellectual advice
3. Makes rational decisions, chooses options, evaluates importance for both selves
4. Relies on reasoning to make decisions
5. Uses past experience when making decisions
6. Makes plans for the future
7. Draws up boundaries
8. Makes logical distinctions
9. Uses facts and figures
10. Wants to understand, love, support, and nurture the Inner Child
11. Does not "own" the Inner Child, but wants to accept, teach, and motivate it

When Your Critical Inner Parent Fights Your Inner Child

1. Your Inner Parent is critical and righteous and "always knows best"
2. Is quick to judge and lecture
3. Sternly delivers "should's" and predicts doom unless the Inner Child "straightens out"
4. Tries to dominate Inner Child and force it to "be good" through logic and will power
5. Attempts to control Inner Child's feelings, thoughts, and actions
6. Makes major decisions without consulting Inner Child.

Your Inner Child only needs to be itself. It cannot heal itself. Healing is the responsibility of the Inner Parent.

Your Valuable Inner Child Naturally:

1. Controls your feelings and emotional responses
2. Generates emotions such as love, anger, joy, grief, fear, rage, and shame
3. Uses feelings and emotions to make decisions
4. Is bouncy, bubbly, energetic, and enthusiastic
5. Seeks here-and-now pleasure: wants what it wants when it wants it
6. Is affectionate and has a deep desire to please the Inner Parent
7. Plays, has fun, and explores new environments
8. Does things with interest and excitement
9. Experiences freshness and joy in life
10. Generates high physical energy for both selves
11. Harmonizes with the Inner Parent to create a fulfilling, happy life for both to enjoy

When Your Rebellious Inner Child Fights Your Inner Parent

1. Your Inner Child nags, "I'm tired," "I don't want to work," "I don't feel good," "I want some candy"
2. Creates sickness, headaches, psychosomatic disease
3. Resists being warned, advised, or berated by Inner Parent
4. Creates boredom and negativity
5. Is either rebellious and at war, or shut down and repressed with deadened feelings
6. Takes the aliveness and fun out of life for both selves

Reprinted with permission from the source: *SELF-PARENTING: The Complete Guide to Your Inner Conversations* by John K. Pollard, III © 1987.

challenge of learning the skills needed to enjoy the cooperativeness essential to your highest happiness?

As a first step, you could copy these two pages and tape them to your bedroom, bathroom, or kitchen walls as a reminder. This behavioral chart can give you many insights into how your inner child and inner parent interact.

The chart lists 11 natural behaviors of the inner parent. Some of these behaviors may not be available to you today unless you have reclaimed the disowned, missing parts of your true-self. From your marking of the inventory in Appendix I, you know about the missing parts of your authentic true-self (the parts you circled in Column 3 of the Inventory).

In whatever ways *you were abused* during childhood, your critical parent *will abuse your inner child*. Some of the many ways your inner parent and inner child may be locked in conflict are shown on the bottom of page 140.

When children are supported through their various stages of growth by parents who were continuously warm and available, the child will naturally have the 11 behaviors shown at the top of page 141. When your inner child has been abused, it will retaliate against you. On the bottom of page 141, you will find six behaviors that your abused inner child may use to fight back when your inner parent is not meeting its needs.

Working With Your Inner Child

It's important for us to appreciate that the old brain (inner child) is not structurally able to *think*. It's like a dog's brain. A dog can roll over without understanding the words "roll over" as we conceptualize them. To a dog, the sound "roll over" is a *signal*. A dog or young child's memory *associates* the sound "roll over" with events it can see, hear, or feel.

With the enormous capacity of our cerebral cortex, adults can handle abstract words. The inner-child brain has difficulty with abstractions because they don't refer to anything reported by our senses. (Can you see, hear, touch, or photograph what the words "synthesis," "truth," or "grammar" refer to?) We must use *sensory-based* simple words to talk to our inner child. Adult language and the thought patterns of reasoning, rationalizing, and concepts of fairness and ethics pass "right over its head."

When you talk to your inner child, it's best ask your inner child what name it likes—rather than use the impersonal name of "inner child." (Say, "Little Ralph, how do you feel?" Not, "Inner child, how do you feel?") The inner child will get most of its understanding from your tone of voice, body language, and the way you are listening and expressing caring and love—rather than *from the words themselves.*

The role of the inner parent is to listen; not lecture or explain. Your inner parent should ask—not try to please or convince in adult terms. Your inner child gets little of its understanding from what your inner parent *says.* It feels loved or not loved through here-and-now experience—and from being able to talk and be heard.

You express love and caring as an inner parent by listening objectively, dispassionately, openly, and clearly. The words and expressions your new brain thinks appropriate may not actually feel loving to your inner child's old brain! Adult words and reasoning tend to make your inner child feel it's "bad."

Three Helpful Responses

Your inner child is really easy to get along with. Communication is most effective when all three of these responses are used by the inner parent:

1. Paraphrasing: The inner parent carefully listens to what the inner child wants. Then your inner parent paraphrases it back. ("Mary, I know you would like to go to a movie tonight.") This enables your inner child to feel that you care enough to hear it.

2. Validating: Assure your inner child that it's okay when it wants what it wants—even though the inner parent may say "no." ("I can understand your wanting to go to a movie tonight. I'd like that, too. But I've promised to do something else. Would tomorrow night be okay?") If you can't meet your inner child's desires, it will feel supported if you try to work out a win-win compromise by giving the

143

child several alternatives that you can do. Even when the options are chosen by the parent, choices give the child a feeling of dignity and empowerment.

3. Empathizing: The inner child especially needs the inner parent to acknowledge what it is feeling. ("You're feeling mad because I can't take you to see the movie tonight.") It's important for the inner parent to realize that they don't have to necessarily agree with the inner child. Although the child may protest, a nurtured inner child can quickly adapt when the parent firmly and lovingly says "no."

What your inner child really needs is to feel safe and loved—and be treated with respect. The inner child wants the inner parent to care enough to hear what it feels, hear what it wants, make it okay to want it, or try to work out a win-win trade-off. ("Little Henry, let's finish waxing the car. Then we'll go out and walk around the park and look for squirrels.")

When the alarm goes off in the morning, your inner child reaches out and shuts it off so it can sleep more. The inner adult knows that they "should" get to work on time—or the boss will find someone who does. A power-based inner adult may threaten the inner child, "We better get up or else." The loving, skillful inner parent might say to their inner child, "I need you to get up, shower, have breakfast, and be off to work. How about this: You help me do a good job working today—and we'll go to your favorite place to eat tonight?"

To summarize, daily conversations with your inner child are a great way to bridge the gaps between your conscious and unconscious minds. I suggest that you follow the guidelines in *Self-Parenting* by John Pollard, III.[1] Remember, much of your health, well-being, and intimacy depend on the harmony between your two brains.

In the next chapter, we'll discuss how you can gradually reclaim your true-self by developing a dynamic partnership between your inner child and inner parent. This partnership can give you a great boost toward the relaxed enjoyment of your life.

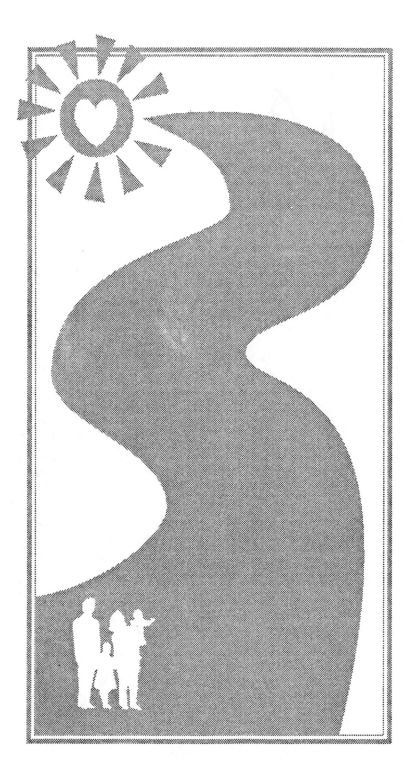

14

*Your
Inner
Partnership*

Both your inner child and inner parent need to work in partnership to give you the joy of living that you deserve. This chapter presents ways to create a partnership with your precious inner child.

"**I** believe that this neglected, wounded inner child of the past is the major source of human misery," John Bradshaw tells us. If we want to live a long time, it's important for our two brains to work in partnership. If we wish to live in relaxed enjoyment, enjoy excellent health, and rapidly get rid of the diseases we pick up, we need this partnership. If we wish to have fun, develop friendships, and create loving intimacy with a lifetime partner, we need a healthy inner child.

This means learning how to have two-way communication between our rational, new brain and our feeling, inner-child brain—*carefully supervised by our inner adult* to communicate in ways our inner child relates to. I want to emphasize again, *reasoning and analysis is not one of the ways to communicate with our inner child.* When we *reason* with it, all the inner child really hears is something like, "I'm bad for wanting what I want."

A Strong, Loving Inner Parent

Just as our caretakers were the ultimate decision makers in protecting and nurturing us in childhood, so our inner parent needs to be the ultimate decision maker for your inner child. When a parent tries to break the will of their daughter or son, train them in fear-based obedience, and consistently dominate them "for their own good," the child will feel alienated, unloved and afraid. A heavy price in happiness will be paid by all involved.

An effective inner parent understands that it is cruel to use their power to make their child feel unsafe, scared, terrified, or abandoned. Our inner parent sometimes needs to be firm—yet always gentle, compassionate, and loving while protecting the child and nurturing its growth.

Power-based parents can teach self-discipline by constantly threatening their children with the triple whips of fear, guilt, and shame. Love-based parents teach self-discipline by modeling the behavior they want their children to learn. If they want truthful children, parents cannot tell lies. If they want loving children, Mom and Dad must feel, think, and act in *ways their child will feel loved*—not in ways the parent thinks the child *should* feel loved. The child can experience the parents' discipline as helpful and kind—not selfish and angry. When parents combine love (empathy, unselfishness, kindness, acceptance) with gentle respect for law and order, their children can grow into emotionally stable and mature adults.

No inner (or outer) child needs a wishy-washy, weak parent. This kind of parenting encourages the child to run all over the parent and create a life of turmoil—both inside its head and in the outside environment. *The child who dominates a parent will not feel loved, cared for, or nurtured!* The child's greatest needs are to be protected and loved. Although the child may cry and scream about what it wants, it *intuitively feels* it needs parental protection—and sometimes a good caretaker says "no."

Our Need to Express

Parenting styles are passed on from generation to generation. My father was almost never playful with me. He maintained adult dignity and played the role of a wise judge. He made sure that as a "law breaker," I was aware of my transgressions. Through fear, guilt, and shame (for my own good, of course), I was given an opportunity to correct my errant ways.

As I got into inner-child work, I was surprised to find that I had treated my children in exactly the same way! And I've also got to admit I've treated my own inner child this way, too. With my own children, the damage is done. They have to heal themselves. No one can do it for them. All I can say is "I'm sorry." *The good news is when you learn to self-parent your inner child, it's never too late to have a second childhood!*

When I was a parent, I didn't know that energy, health, fun, spontaneity, and aliveness were dependent on the "inner child" or unconscious mind. I thought the unconscious mind was like a hellish dungeon where awful people like murderers, rapists, and arsonists guiltily stew and churn with nightmares for being bad. I didn't realize that to keep their unconscious mind clear and clean, my son and daughter needed to be able to express their hurt and pain—rather than hide their feelings to please me.

Perhaps the only psychological "sin" is fear-guilt-shame-based repression! Damming up our emotions is like plugging up a toilet. Lots of stuff overflows later when we can't *naturally* flush our painful emotions away down the river of life. Life is set up to work as long as we can express our fear, anger, grief, jealousy—and also our love, joy, fun, enthusiasm, hopes, and desires. As painful emotions arise, just expressing them to an empathetic ear flushes them down the flowing stream of life. We become mentally ill whenever this natural flow is stopped up. The focus of therapy is just to get our emotional "logjam" moving again in an area where it has been blocked.

Win-Win Solutions

Every inner child (as well as outer child) needs an inner parent who can make it okay for it to want what it wants, and feel what it feels—even if the parent does not approve. When your inner child says, "I want a big pizza with five toppings on it," it needs to be guided by an inner parent who has information on how saturated fat can deposit cholesterol plaques in coronary arteries, and how all fats will promote cross-linking of molecules that prematurely age the human body. However, your inner parent should not lecture the inner child on bio-chemistry. A good inner parent will always make sure the child *feels it is heard*. ("You want a big pizza. I like pizza, too.") And then the parent needs to make the wisest decision based on *many* factors.

When your inner parent allows your inner child to want what it wants and express it, it is supporting the child within. When your inner parent lets your inner child pick between alternatives you've chosen, you are using your power and authority to give identity and dignity to your inner child. *Its spirit is supported by giving it a choice—instead of rigidly commanding it.*

Every inner child wants an inner parent who it trusts will protect it from harm. It especially needs an inner parent who will protect it against people who are critical. ("I'm mad at you. I thought I could count on you to be on time. You're fifteen minutes late.") Your inner child needs an inner adult who will immediately step in to defend it so it does not feel fear, guilt, or shame. It needs a champion who will gently respond to the criticizer by saying something like, "Yeah, you're right. I'm fifteen minutes late. Big traffic pile-up on the freeway."

A Healing Partnership

To live with relaxed enjoyment, we need to create a living, loving relationship between our inner child and inner adult. Such a partnership will *gradually* enable us to heal the inner child injuries from our childhood. Our inner-child–inner-parent work can help us reclaim our true-self and retire the false-self which feels so real to us today. Through our inner work using the Pollard system, or any other system that works, we can increasingly become the powerful, whole, authentic human being that is our birthright.

Many people today are increasingly enjoying the benefits of fun, high energy, and an effective immune system that only the inner child partner can provide. *We don't have to live half a life.* We can expand our aliveness by talking with our inner child. As *junior and senior partners*, we can negotiate satisfying win-wins for both brains.

John Pollard in *Self-Parenting* explains eight steps to lovingly resolve disagreements with our inner child. Guiding our inner child through these eight steps can bring us rich dividends in feeling alive. It will take practice to use the eight steps effectively.

Eight Steps to Resolve Conflict Between Your Inner Parent and Inner Child

1. Your Inner Parent recognizes that you have an inner conflict.

2. Your Inner Parent makes the decision to positively self-parent your inner conflict by writing out your inner conversation.

3. You list the specific interests of each inner self.

4. Your Inner Parent and Inner Child mutually decide and agree that the solution for this inner conflict must be acceptable to both selves.

5. The inner selves search together for solutions to the inner conflict. They try to creatively find win-win solutions.

6. Your inner selves choose a mutually acceptable solution that meets both their interests.

7. Your Inner Parent and Inner Child put the solution in action.

8. Both selves evaluate the solution for workability and satisfaction.

Reprinted with permission of John K. Pollard, III, author of *Self-Parenting: The Complete Guide to Your Inner Conversations.* © 1987.

Personal growth is a lifetime adventure. Instant fixes in inner-child work are not realistic. Building a strong partnership between your inner parent and inner child can take months of inner work. And things usually begin to feel better from the first week you start. However, inner child practice will be nothing like the work and futility you will experience *if you do not create this partnership*. Your alternative is to live a more or less deadened, depressed, anxious, stressful, unhappy life.

As you create an inner partnership, you will find you are becoming a *creative cause* of your experience. Instead of playing the role of victim, you will discover a great inner power and peacefulness within you when *both of your brains are working in partnership together*. It's one of the best games in town if you want to make the most of your sojourn on Planet Earth.

Developing Your Skill

John Bradshaw's book *Homecoming: Reclaiming and Championing Your Inner Child* is an excellent resource. His brilliant "Bradshaw on Homecoming" videotapes consisting of ten one-hour programs is worth buying and sharing with your family, friends, clubs, schools, etc. It's worth watching many times to deeply absorb it. There are many fine inner child weekend workshops available today. Bradshaw offers seminars and workshops nationwide.[1]

John Pollard's *Self-Parenting: The Complete Guide to Your Inner Conversations* is enormously helpful to anyone who wants to heal the ravages of childhood—and open up to a new dimension of relaxed enjoyment.[2]

> *We've got to give up demanding a better childhood. What's past is past. That's what is.*
>
> *"The Moving Finger writes; and, having writ,*
> *Moves on; nor all they Piety nor Wit*
> *Shall lure it back to cancel half a Line,*
> *Nor all thy Tears wash out a Word of it."*
> *Omar Khayyám*

Inner-parent–inner-child work goes right to the heart of the quirks between your two brains. Every hour you spend learning to talk with your inner child—and doing it in your daily life—will be among the most valuable hours you can spend. You'll be providing yourself with a part of what's missing in your life. As you increase your skill, you can create a partnership that may unfold your life in an exciting, happy, wondrous way you never even imagined was possible!

The Next Section

In Part V, we will find that your unconscious mind determines whom you fall in love with. To shape you up, it chooses a partner who will hurt you in the way your parents did! To your amazement, you'll discover that your rational mind had little to do with falling in love—although it may erroneously take full credit for picking your partner.

You will be surprised by a fascinating exposé telling how the quirks between your two brains can ruin your marriage. Divorce could become a rarity instead of a 50 percent probability when you understand how your old and new brains change your romance into an inevitable power struggle. This conflict lets your false-self lead you to divorce, suicide, insanity, murder, psychosomatic illness, or the boredom of living in a "dead" relationship. You will learn how you and your partner can work together *to use your power struggle for healing your childhood injuries!* You can mutually create the marriage of your dreams.

Through understanding and cooperation, you and your partner can keep your quirks and your partner's quirks from ruining your relationship! You can experience the fun and aliveness that you're entitled to. *Romantic intimacy and joy can become an everyday reality for both of you.* You will discover how to go beyond the illusions of "romantic love," through the inevitable power struggle, and create a romantic, loving intimacy—enjoying the storybook ideal of "living happily ever after."

PART V

CREATING
LOVING INTIMACY

15

How You Fall in Love

It seems shocking that we "fall in love" with someone our old brain senses will injure us just like our childhood caregivers. No wonder we have a 50 percent divorce rate. How does this happen? What can we do about it? When you and your mate understand the answers to these questions, you'll know how to build a great marriage together.

Dr. Harville Hendrix has pointed out that back in the ripe old days, the husband was the "head of the household." He made final decisions for the wife and children. The husband was responsible to the Lord of the Manor, who was responsible to the King, who was responsible to God.

Therefore, the rational new brain of the father usually chose one's mate. His decision was based on his political goals, social ambitions, economic interests, and usually last, the desires of his children. This relieved sons and daughters from making a decision about whom to marry. Feelings of love from the offspring's old brain were almost irrelevant in this rational decision-making process.

With democracy, this hierarchy of power started to crumble. People began to think that the purpose of government was to serve the citizens—not vice versa. As this democratic philosophy trickled down into family folkways, sons and daughters began insisting on the right to choose their marriage partners. This removed from the father the job of deciding whom his children would marry.

So in the last few centuries, we boys and girls gradually got to pick our marriage partners. And our simpleton, though crafty, old brain took over mate selection. It makes us fall into a trance called "romantic love." This feeling is so strong that almost nothing can get in the way of two people "head-over-heels" in romantic love. As Romeo and Juliet demonstrated, if

157

they couldn't live in romantic love together, they'd rather not live at all. Powerful stuff!

Choosing Your Partner

We know that the new brain does not have good access to what's happening in the old brain. They operate in different modes. Since our two brains *seem* like they work as one, the new brain does not experience the old brain as a separate brain. If you ask someone why they fell in love, their conscious mind *thinks* it knows the answer. It will come up with stuff like, "She is intelligent," "We like to do many things together," "I am proud to introduce him to my friends," "She's physically attractive," "I feel good around him," "He's loaded with money," "We have great sex together," or "I like her sense of humor."

Whatever the rational reasons, they're pure baloney if back then you strongly felt romantic love for your partner. When your rational mind chooses your partner, you will not enjoy the electricity of romantic love. Your unconscious may even make your relationship feel boring. If you chose your partner because you felt a strong romantic passion in your heart, then it was your unconscious mind that picked your partner.

Your old brain had two basic guidelines for determining with whom you feel the ecstasy of romantic love:

1. *Painful characteristics:* Primarily, your longing for love from a hostile, rejecting parent transfers onto a *similar person* in adult life. This means that your unconscious mind makes you fall in love with a partner who will injure you in the same ways that a parent injured you when you were a child! Suppose you disown your true-self part that asks for what it wants. You'll probably end up in a romance with someone who is clear and forceful in pushing for what they want—just like your parent. Hal and Sidra Stone tell us, "The selves we disown attract people who own these selves. Then once the relationship is established, our disowned selves gradually make themselves feel alienated from such opposite 'insensitive and intolerable' parts of our partners."[1]

You'll probably be astounded to find that your unconscious has picked your mate because they will hurt you in the same way that your parents hurt you! Romantic love is nature's "anesthesia" to hook you up with the last person in the world that your thinking brain would choose—if it knew what was going on.

2. *Admired characteristics:* Secondly, your unconscious picks partners with the traits you liked in your parents. For example, if *you* felt good about your parents being well-educated and kind to animals, your unconscious mind will value a partner who has these traits.

A Basic Wisdom

However, there is a wisdom in the choice of the old brain. "The unconscious purpose of marriage," Dr. Hendrix says, "is to finish your childhood." He has formulated an insightful system that helps you relate your childhood injuries to your current disagreements. His three processes enable you to greatly improve communication, safely blow off childhood time bombs, and reach win-win solutions. His techniques (discussed in Chapter 17) can give you vastly improved odds for re-romanticizing—even if you're now firing away in a desperate court battle.

I am indebted to Dr. Harville Hendrix for much of the material in Part V, which appears in his best-selling books *Getting the Love You Want*[2] and *Keeping the Love You Find*.[3] His work is enormously helpful in learning how to spot the quirks between our two brains—and deal with them to create love, cooperation, and partnership with one's mate. (He does not use the term "quirk.")

Here's how Dr. Hendrix explains old-brain mate selection in his workshops:

> Your partner's unconscious purpose in marrying you was to get you to help him or her finish his or her childhood. And that is to get from you what your partner didn't get from his or her parent. And the worst part about this, is you can't give it to them without changing. Your partner's needs are going to call for a change in your behavior and character structure. And that's the good news because you need to change it. Given the way most of us are shaped in childhood, there is some unfinished growing to do. . . .

Now this may be a shocker: your partner is a mirror reflecting the undeveloped parts of yourself. Now what that means is that the part of you that you don't know about, your partner knows intimately. And, in fact, your partner has been informing you about that part of you for some months or years. And you have not been listening. And she or he has probably had to hit you over the head, threaten you, withdraw from you, criticize you, withhold from you, or have gone into compliance and been overly nice and generous and gracious—hoping that somehow they could get your attention.

There's a part of you that's missing, and they miss it. And there's another part of you that's distorted. And that part hurts them. And they've been trying to tell you about their pain and what they miss. And you've not been listening. Now the reason that you've not been listening is that your partner is a bad politician. They say the things that you hate to hear and they say it in ways that you can't stand. Right? Namely, they criticize you for being a stingy bastard, or a bitchy woman, or whatever else their creativity enables them to say to you. And some of us are very creative. In fact, married couples are probably the most creatively, negatively verbal people on the planet. We can say wonderfully terrible things to each other.[4]

Falling in Love

It's amazing how accurately your unconscious mind can home in on someone who will hurt you exactly like your childhood caregivers. But you already know your old brain is emotionally perceptive. If you had an alcoholic caregiver, your new brain may intelligently resolve that you won't ever date anyone who drinks even one glass of wine. So you marry someone who never imbibes. Guess who develops into an lush in the next five years!

Let's suppose ten "poker chips" add up to a torrid, passionate romantic love. Let's assume your mother was critical and made you feel put down. If your lover is critical, your old brain may credit them with three romantic love chips. If you liked the way your parents were honest, you'll be attracted to a lover who's truthful. Another chip. Now this candidate has four chips in the romantic poker game.

160

Suppose your father usually fell into a rejecting silence when you did something he didn't like. Let's assume your heart throb is also the "silent" type when they don't like what's happening. And let's say you triggered feelings of emotional abandonment when your father withdrew from you when you were young. Now your old brain has four more chips—a total of eight. If your unconscious can pick up two more romantic love chips, you'll have ten chips—and the love affair of the century! You're now deeply in love. It will seem like you've known this person before. *(You have!)* And you want to be with them forever. *(You won't unless both of you help each other's unconscious minds to stop projecting their childhood injuries onto each other.)*

Your unconscious now has you thoroughly anesthetized for the "psychosurgery" that you can use to heal your hidden childhood injuries. You have fallen in love and are committed to someone chosen by your unconscious mind who will hurt you as your parents did. You've chosen someone who has the missing part of your true-self that you split off in childhood. No wonder romantic love is notoriously unstable!

Your balloon of romantic love may explode during the honeymoon. Or you may live in this dream state for over a year. Sooner or later, your partner will rip open the old wounds inflicted by your parents. And you'll be doing the same for your mate. Then you may begin to feel most self-righteous. ("How did I ever marry you?") As the scabs on your childhood wounds are knocked off, you'll feel less safe with the partner with whom you've fallen in love. ("What did I ever see in them?")

Your battling, rational mind may decide it made a mistake. But your unconscious mind with its Object and Time Quirks is operating *as if* it wants to get the longed-for love from the parent who hurt you. Your unconscious isn't aware it has thrown you into a relationship with someone else who is *superficially* similar to your parent in some way.

Now you have an opportunity to heal your childhood injuries—*if you use the relationship for your growth.* Your marriage partner (just by being themselves) can give you the chance to heal your life-damaging childhood wounds—your false-self. But first both partners must learn *how to work together* in healing unconscious childhood injuries. And this does NOT involve either of you diagnosing or trying to play therapist for your partner. *The person you work on is you!*

Using Your Partner to Heal Yourself

Your predicament is that you really fall in love with someone you really hate—someone your simpleton unconscious mind erroneously feels injured you as a child!

To reclaim your whole-self, you must know how to use the disagreements that threaten to blow you apart. You begin to notice how they trigger the frozen fear, grief, and anger that were not safe to express with your caregivers many years ago. For example, review the incident from my life on pages 109 through 115. Notice how Lydia unintentionally ripped open a childhood wound I had not healed. And I was unknowingly triggering her childhood injuries. I tried to get from Lydia a supportive understanding that I did not get from my mother when she accused me of being "inconsiderate."

Most of us unskillfully spew these ready-to-explode childhood feelings onto our innocent partner. This is the "projection" we discussed in Part III. And our partner responds with rage—and attacks us back by projecting their unexpressed childhood angers and fears onto us. This is called the "power struggle," which we will explore in the next chapter.

You are not to blame for your unhappiness—or the failure of your marriage or marriages—and neither is your partner—and neither are your parents. *We can begin to understand how we've all been victims*—VICTIMS OF THE QUIRKS! And we can begin to take responsibility (*not blame*) for our unskillful actions that have hurt us and others.

All of us are beautiful, innocent human beings who happen to be trapped in the glitches between our two brains—and we didn't even know we had two brains—or quirks between them! Or that our quirks keep us trapped in a nightmare of error and illusion! And that our lives seem to be the pioneering "killing fields" in which evolution sorts out what's best adapted to survive.

All of this can be past history for you and your partner. You can learn how to use the painful parts of your marriage to pinpoint your own growth targets. Remember, no pain no gain. Just by honestly sharing their emotions, your partner gives you the experience needed for healing your false-self parts—and rekindling the light of love and romance that your true-self deeply wants. In the next two chapters, you'll discover how to bring back the delightful romance both of you enjoyed when you first got together. You'll find that your true-self can enable you to create a lifelong, romantic, heartfelt love. Help is on the way!

16

The Inevitable Power Struggle

Romantic love is inevitably followed by a power struggle between clashing parts of your false-self and your partner's false-self. Unless you cooperate in nurturing your partner's unconscious mind, deeper levels of love and intimacy are doomed. And finding a new partner to fall in love with just gives you more of the same! However you can learn to nurture your own and your partner's unconscious mind—and enjoy the love your heart desires.

For people who are learning to create a partnership between their two brains, the marital power struggle is not a tragedy! It's a necessity! You need it to heal your false-self—and reclaim your loving true-self.

When we find that our unconscious mind has tricked us into marrying someone who will injure us in the same ways our parents did, most of us will feel abused and self-righteous toward our partner. We enjoy feeling self-righteous because it relieves us of personal responsibility. Our rational mind tells us, "See, I told you it's not your fault. Your partner is to blame."

However, before we get too wound up, we should realize that every time we point our finger at someone else, three of our fingers are pointing back at us. Just point your finger straight at something right now—and have a laugh over what you'll notice!

Romantic love begins to drain away as our old brain throws the time-bomb pains of our childhood at our unsuspecting partner! Out of this marital power struggle can come the seeds of healing for both you and your partner. But you must first learn how to use the power struggle for your growth.

Hal and Sidra Stone in *Embracing Our Selves* describe how marriage is set up for our deeper levels of growth:

Thus, a woman who negates her sexuality and her physical being will be fascinated by a "he-man" and marry him. She will then do all she can to tame his sexuality and keep him from pursuing his outdoor life. He, in turn, may have been attracted to her timid, nonphysical way of life and intrigued by her sexual inaccessibility. Once married, he, too, is likely to object to these behaviors. Instead of learning from one another, instead of integrating these disowned selves, they live with the reflection of them in their mates, judging them and continually being angered by them.

We can be helpless victims to the multitude of relationships in our lives that reflect our disowned selves, or we can accept the challenge of these relationships and ask: "How is this person, or this situation, my teacher?" Asking this question in itself represents a major shift in consciousness. A great deal of the stress in our lives results from our tendency to attract reflections of our disowned selves in our relationships, and we continue to suffer as the same patterns are repeated in our lives.[1]

Projecting Stuff onto Our Partner

Our false-self is a master at projecting onto our partners what we are ashamed of—and want to hide about ourselves. If I accuse you of being "stingy," it's because deep down I feel that I am stingy. If I accuse you of being "unthoughtful," it's because I am ashamed to admit I'm sometimes unthoughtful. If I tell you that you don't really love me, it's because there is a part of me that has conditional love for you. Our false-self keeps us from perceiving ourselves clearly. And we certainly can't heal our false-self by projecting onto our partner the hidden stuff we don't like about ourselves!

We project our unwanted traits onto our partners. And then we criticize them for having these undesired parts of ourselves! Hendrix reminds us that *all criticism of others is a form of self-abuse!*

Now that we know about this unfortunate side effect of our two out-of-phase brains, it seems pretty stupid to beat up on another person as a surrogate for retaliating against our childhood caretakers. So notice what it reveals about you when you bash your partner!

"Your partner's needs," Hendrix tells us, "are a blueprint for your personal growth." We need a *shift in perception* to experience our partner as there to help us heal—not as an adversary. In his workshops, Hendrix has partners turn to each other and say, "Thank you for being so difficult in my life!"

Romantic Love

Romantic love is not unconditional love. Romantic love has strings attached. "I'll love you if you meet my models, but you'd better watch out because I'll throw you out of my heart if you don't." And isn't this what we felt with an unskillful parent?

The unconscious mind feels it has to somehow heal our false-self. Only then we can enjoy a lifetime of real love born of the true-self. Real love between two adults operating out of their true-selves is romantic, miraculous, and most likely sexy, lasts a lifetime, and is perhaps the most soul-satisfying experience on this earth!

So our unconscious mind makes us fall deeply in love with a partner who will open our childhood wounds so we can clean out the false-self infections. Who else can help us do the job? Who else are we willing *to be with long enough* to get deeply into these childhood wounds? Usually we're off immediately if someone starts in criticizing our false-self—which we mistakenly feel is the "real me." And then we don't have to work on our false-self—and being hidden it can continue to slash our lives without resistance!

Because our partner can give us the experiences we need to nakedly reveal our out-of-date false-self defenses against childhood fear, anger, jealousy, resentment, guilt, shame, hate, etc., they offer us a unique opportunity for do-it-yourself growth. We need a *committed* relationship that keeps us and our partner together long enough to heal.

So we see that romantic love may lead us to the marriage altar. We naively thought we would live happily thereafter.

No one told us that our unconscious mind was luring us into a committed relationship to trap us into healing our childhood wounds. We were blithely unaware that then, *and only then,* can we have the fulfillment we want with our mate. Only unconditional love, created by our true-self, can lead us to the promised land of happiness. So let's learn more about using the lover's power struggle.

Exits From Marriage

Half of our marriages terminate in divorce. Other ways to exit from marriage are suicide and psychosomatic illness. Some end up in murder. Half of the women murdered in the U.S. are by current or former lovers! Many couples gradually develop a "silent divorce." This means they provide themselves with respectable escapes or "exits" so they spend very little quality time together—and avoid openness and intimacy. An exit from intimacy could be choosing to work long hours in business so we don't have time or energy to really be with our partner. ("Do we have to talk about it now? I've had a long day.")

Oftentimes a parent will keep themselves overbusy playing with or reading to their children at night so they've used up the time available for intimacy. Hobbies and club work may be used to avoid spending quality time with each other. None of these activities in themselves are exits. *It's a matter of balance.* And both you and your partner know in your hearts when you are using an activity to avoid intimacy. If your partner criticizes you for not being there for them, you can quickly make them wrong by pointing out the fine way you are spending time with the children, serving as secretary to the local Save the Whales chapter, or working hard to provide more income for your family. Any virtue can become a vice if it's "too much" or "too little." Remember the advice of the ancient Greeks? Find the Golden Mean. Nothing in excess.

Exits do not make you a good or bad person. Neither you nor your partner is to blame. But it will be growth-producing to ask yourself, "What is there about my partner that makes me use these exits to create a 'silent divorce'?" Your answer may clue both of you into your personal growth targets.

It's really good news that at last we are learning to use the painful experiences our partner offers us to deal with the quirks between our two brains. We can use our committed relationship to heal the false-self parts we needed at age four to protect ourselves from the false-self behaviors of our caretakers. As we successfully meet the challenge of growth, we can enjoy the love and unity that arises from the union of two people who have reclaimed their whole, authentic true-selves.

In the next chapter, we will learn more about creating this seeming miracle in our lives.

17

Re-Romanticizing

How do you create more love and intimacy? How can you use your relationship to heal your false-self childhood adaptations—and create the love and intimacy you've always wanted? This chapter reveals effective ways to live in relaxed enjoyment. If both you and your partner use these techniques, you will have the tools to create the marriage of your dreams.

Your old brain makes you fall in love with someone who will "abuse" you in the ways your caregivers did. It wants your partner to change so they will give you the love you are longing for. If your unconscious senses danger (as it did with your caregiver), and develops a fear of your partner, it will begin to chip away at the romantic love you feel. Your conscious mind may not be aware of this fear in the unconscious. Your unconscious mind is trying to protect you from your caretaker's abuse of perhaps 20 years ago. Your conscious mind knows there is no threat. Your unconscious may feel TERROR. It is reacting to a projected past danger that isn't there today—another footprint of the quirks between the two brains!

A secret of romance is to help your partner's old brain feel totally safe from your unexpected attack. It's simple if you know how the reptilian and mammalian components of the old brain work. There is one key: SAFETY. This may sound easy. But as we noticed, what seems safe to your new brain may alarm the old brain.

Dr. Hendrix tells us, "Most partners are terrified of their partner at some level." This means that whenever you are critical, judgmental, or threatening, your mate's old brain will feel attacked—and the power struggle is on. The next time your partner sees you—even if you're in a good mood—the old brain will trigger, "Not safe. This one attacks. Prepare to defend yourself." Dr. Eric Berne has estimated that most human beings feel safe in their unconscious minds only about 15 minutes in their entire adult lifetime! No wonder we all suffer from the epidemic of stress, conflict, and unhappiness—and broken relationships.

"But," you might reply, "I never attack Henrietta. I always walk away when things get hot." However, the old brain, even though it's a simpleton intellectually, is always on duty emotionally. It fears abandonment. ("I'll die if I'm abandoned.") Icy, sullen, deadly silence, or refusing to talk is felt as abandonment.

Since most couples don't know how to turn the power struggle into a dynamic personal growth opportunity, they erect defenses and armor themselves to feel safe. The marriage becomes a battlefield. Playfulness is gone. Looking deeply into another's eyes, cuddling, laughing, sharing your deepest feelings and thoughts, and having great orgasms are not possible.

Their marriage becomes routine and boring—or a constant clash of egos. No opportunity for criticism is missed. Projection is rampant. The quirks have turned heaven into hell. ("Heaven" and "hell" are not being used in a theological sense. Instead, we're using Webster's definition of hell as a state of turmoil, destruction, misery, and torment. Heaven is defined as a condition of utmost happiness.)

Criticism Is Poisonous Without an Appointment

If you really want to bring the miracle of unconditional love into your marriage, it is essential to give your new brain absolute instructions *NEVER* to criticize, judge, or attack your partner—**unless you make an appointment first.** This intelligent strategy eliminates the unexpected attack that your lover's unconscious mind will program as: "This human is dangerous."

Unfortunately, criticism is a frequent behavior in most marriages. We criticize to make another person feel afraid, guilty, or ashamed. Through these painful emotions, we're trying to control them—to make them do what we want.

ROAD MAP TO COUPLE'S HEAVEN OR HELL

HEAVEN OR HELL IN YOUR RELATIONSHIP ARE ALWAYS ONLY ONE MUTUAL FEELING-THOUGHT AWAY

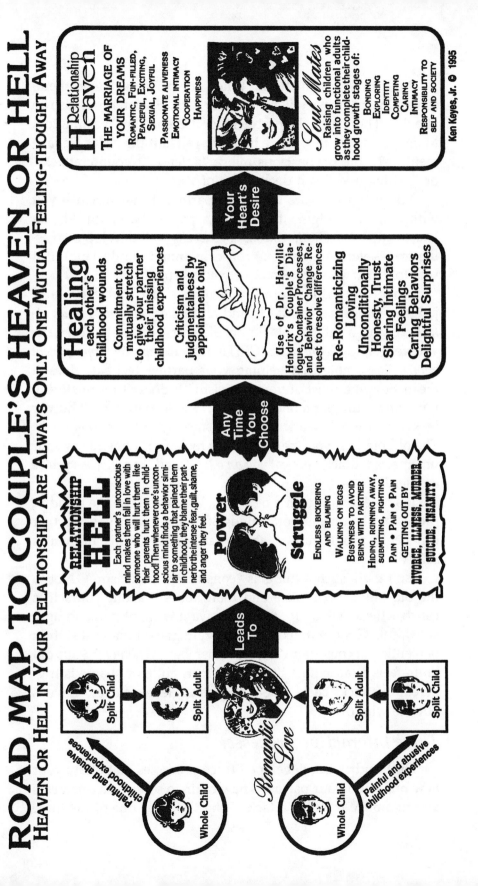

H Relationship Heaven

THE MARRIAGE OF YOUR DREAMS

ROMANTIC, FUN-FILLED, PEACEFUL, EXCITING, SEXUAL, JOYFUL

PASSIONATE ALIVENESS

EMOTIONAL INTIMACY

COOPERATION

HAPPINESS

Soul Mates

Raising children who grow into functional adults as they complete their childhood growth stages of:

BONDING
EXPLORING
IDENTITY
COMPETING
CARING
INTIMACY
RESPONSIBILITY TO SELF AND SOCIETY

Ken Keyes, Jr. © 1995

Healing
each other's childhood wounds

Commitment to mutually stretch to give your partner their missing childhood experiences

Criticism and judgmentalness by appointment only

Use of Dr. Harville Hendrix's Couple's Dialogue, Container Processes, and Behavior Change Request to resolve differences

Re-Romanticizing
Loving
Unconditionally
Honesty, Trust
Sharing Intimate Feelings
Caring Behaviors
Delightful Surprises

Your Heart's Desire (arrow)

Any Time You Choose (arrow)

RELATIONSHIP HELL

Each partner's unconscious mind makes them fall in love with someone who will hurt them like their parents hurt them in childhood! Then whenever one's unconscious mind finds a behavior similar to something that pained them in childhood, they blame their partner for the intense fear, guilt, shame, and anger they feel.

Power

Struggle

ENDLESS BICKERING AND BLAMING

WALKING ON EGGS

BUSYNESS TO AVOID BEING WITH PARTNER

HIDING, RUNNING AWAY, SUBMITTING, FIGHTING

PAIN • PAIN • PAIN

GETTING OUT BY

DIVORCE, ILLNESS, MURDER, SUICIDE, INSANITY

Leads To (arrow)

Split Child | Split Adult

Split Adult | Split Child

Romantic Love

Whole Child

Whole Child

painful and abusive childhood experiences

Painful and abusive childhood experiences

All criticism is an attack. When our partners defend themselves, their defense will be *an attack back*. So defense is also an attack. There is a Department of Defense in Washington. Many years ago, they more honestly called it the "War Department." To the unconscious mind, "defense," "counterattack," or "getting even" is a declaration of war.

You won't feel safe with your partner if they ambush you with criticism, judgments, pouting, "paying back," or "the silent treatment." *On the unconscious level* you'll develop increasing fear—even though your conscious mind would laugh if it was told that you are afraid of your partner.

Since the old brain experiences all criticism and judgmentalness as an attack, and also *all defensiveness as an attack*, if you want the old brain of your partner to feel safe, you've got to STOP ALL CRITICISM except by *appointment only*. Please note that helping your partner feel safe doesn't mean stopping most of your criticism. It doesn't mean storing it up, and dumping it once a month. Sugar coating with humor or sarcasm won't work. *It means stopping criticism completely*. The old brain of your partner is not fooled. It remembers your unexpected attack. *It's got you on a list for all the criticisms you've ever made*.

It's time to turn over a new leaf. When you use the Hendrix processes, the unconscious minds of both you and your partner can begin programming about each other, "This human is safe."

Isn't there such a thing as "constructive criticism?" Not to the old brain. Complete and total honesty about yourself is constructive. Asking for what you want without demanding it is helpful. Open-mindedness and willingness to have a shift in perception is constructive. Just remember: whenever your old brain feels attacked, its time-bomb fear, guilt, or shame is triggered. It attacks back. The power struggle takes over. Love is out the window.

Three Interactive Processes

Dr. Hendrix has developed three processes that allow your new brain and your partner's new brain to solve disagreements and minimize reptilian attack. When you use one of the three

Hendrix processes described in this chapter, you begin by asking your partner for an appointment to do one of the processes. In the Couple's Dialogue and the Container Process, you can criticize, judge, and emote to fully express how you feel. You must express your painful emotions for the well-being of your unconscious mind.

Your partner's unconscious can prepare itself so it will not feel attacked while you are letting off steam. Since your partner has been notified in advance, they can compassionately shift their perception to experience you as *wounded and needing love and understanding*—which were missing when your caretakers hurt you many years ago.

A structure for communicating is needed or your appointment for resolving a hot issue could end up in a battle royal or a resentful retreat. If either happens, your inner child will not feel safe. It's vital to fully express our emotions. If the "no criticism without appointment" agreement is to work, your old brain must have a way to blow off steam—so your two intellects can develop mutually satisfying solutions to disagreements. Dr. Hendrix offers three of the most effective communication techniques I've known:

1. **The Couple's Dialogue:** First you ask for a couple's dialogue. At the agreed time, you begin by fully expressing yourself. Your partner paraphrases what they heard you say. Then they ask, "Is that correct?" You indicate they got it right or tell them what they missed. They repeat this back to you until you're satisfied that your partner has heard you.

Then they ask, "Is there more?" If you have more, they paraphrase what they heard you say until you are satisfied they understood. This sequence continues until you've fully expressed your thoughts and feelings. Then your partner validates your statements. "I've done the same thing, too," or "It makes sense to want that." Your partner ends by naming your emotions such as fear, anger, frustration, resentment, hatred, jealousy, etc.: "You're feeling irritated and angry." Then it's your partner's turn to be heard with you paraphrasing back, validating, and empathizing (naming their emotions). You and your partner keep taking turns until a win-win emerges. It works wonderfully to reconcile both of your inner children and inner adults.

Most of the time in an argument, we only marginally listen to the other person. We are busy planning our rapier reply that will make our partner give in and say, "You're right." And it never works, huh? And neither one of you really hears and understands the other. A great thing about the Couple's Dialogue process is that you must give your *full attention* to listening to your partner, or you won't be able to paraphrase it back. And you'll discover that you often don't hear what your partner is saying!

Notice that neither you nor your partner necessarily *agrees* or *disagrees*. You're just helping each other feel they're heard. If your mate doesn't feel you've really heard them, they'll keep repeating the same thing over and over—and you'll get "fed up" fast and angrily stomp away.

2. **The Container Process:** To discharge your intensely painful emotions, you make an appointment to get together for a Container Process. This process lets you run out your pent-up pain like a non-stop express train. Instead of answering as in the Couple's Dialogue, your partner encourages you to "Get it all out." Your partner wants you to explode and spew out all the painful stuff you've kept bottled-up for so long. This is time bomb time!

Before doing the Container Process, your mate will protect their inner child by covering themselves with an imaginary shield. It works. They also shift their perception *to experience you as wounded and asking for love and help.* Your partner encourages you by repeating, "That's good. Is there more?" *But your partner doesn't defend against anything you say.*

Behind it all, both of you are cooperating to help the injured old brain heal itself by expressing what was inexpressible in childhood. You know that your mate knows, that you're just projecting your childhood stuff onto them—and they are innocent. When they view you as a wounded person asking for help and love, their inner child may not feel attacked, and their rational mind does not have to mobilize for retaliation.

Couples quickly feel much closer to each other whenever they use this process skillfully.

3. **Behavior Change Request:** A third process is called the Behavior Change Request. To do the BCR, you and your partner meet by appointment. The person who requests the appointment will ask for what they want. If their partner cannot give it to them, they offer alternative suggestions.

In this chapter, I cannot give you full instructions on these three vital processes. You will need more information on using these effective ways to heal your childhood injuries and create a heart-warming, intimate, unconditional love with your partner. You may wish to study *Getting the Love You Want* and *Keeping the Love You Find*, both by Dr. Harville Hendrix. A weekend Couples Workshop with your partner can be enormously helpful. (He also offers workshops for singles.) You may wish to see a marital therapist trained by Dr. Hendrix. I strongly urge that you get his excellent videotapes demonstrating these three processes: "Homevideo Workshop for Couples." It has four video cassettes, two audio cassettes, and an individual workbook for you and your partner. And it's reasonably priced.[2]

Love Is Blind

Here's an example from my life revealing how much I needed these processes. Within a day or two after a mutual friend introduced me to Bonita, my unconscious mind apparently sensed that she offered me a great opportunity. My mother was a dramatic, fiery redhead who hurt me by either criticizing or becoming sullen and withdrawn to coerce me into doing what she wanted. Both my mother and Bonita used the Expressive-Clinging (pages 278-279) and Sensitive-Withdrawn Strategies (pages 266-267).

My simpleton unconscious didn't know the difference between my mother and Bonita, whom I later married. My quirks gave me the most ecstatic feelings of romantic love I'd ever experienced. She was my soul mate. And I had to have her in my life. My old brain possibly felt that now I could learn to get love from a woman who would sometimes be expressively critical of me—and sometimes depressed and long-faced.

Neither Bonita nor I knew what was happening when she was critical (and it wasn't very often). I overreacted with resentment and became silent. Whenever she was depressed, I took it personally. I blamed her for my quirk-based feelings of being rejected, and I became politely withdrawn. She would get angry because I withdrew. And I would get angry because she got angry.

Since today's understanding of the quirks between the old brain and the new brain was not available then, I thought there was something wrong with our marriage. ("Are we really compatible?") The Hendrix techniques for using the power struggle to heal our childhood injuries had not yet been discovered. So we ended up in divorce a little over a year after we married. What an unnecessary tragedy!

And at the same time, this is a success story. I suffered so much pain from a "broken heart" that I resolved not to go through that again. This led me sometime later to tune into the rapidly growing technology that helps our two brains cooperate with each other. It's poignant that within ten years after our divorce, Dr. Hendrix discovered that "probably the best catalyst for personal and spiritual evolution is a partner whom you hate—if you used to love them—if you fell in love with them. That catalyst, that energy of conflict, is the most important and powerful structure for personal and spiritual evolution that is now available on the planet."[1]

Healing Each Other

When you go into a relationship with someone, you are relating to the entire history of that person. You can expect that their unconscious will quirkily attack you to retaliate for the pain their caregivers gave them back then. *And although it may feel personal, it's really an impersonal process.* Their unconscious honestly doesn't know the difference between then and now— or you and their injuring caretaker.

Let's look at another example of how quirks can ruin a marriage.

Jim's father wanted to be a good parent with high standards for his son. He worked hard at correcting him to make him "perfect." Even if Jim did things right, his father would not recognize it and compliment him. Instead he would point out how Jim could have done even better. Jim's father used the "high-jump method." When the jumper successfully clears the bar, it is always raised one inch. If he jumps over this height, the bar is again raised another inch. And the bar keeps going up until the jumper fails. With the high-jump method of parenting, the child *always* loses.

A child likes to be told they did it right. But no matter how hard Jim tried, he could never quite meet his father's escalating standards. Jim disowned the natural desire to get his father's approval. When he was four, he adopted the strategy of trying to avoid any situation in which his father would evaluate him or tell him what to do. If criticized, he would not listen and would try to get away.

When he became an adult, the survival strategy he needed with his abusive father kept him from participating in the normal give-and-take with his wife, Ellen. For example, he could not stand her telling him when they were getting ready to go to a concert, "You can relax. We've got plenty of time." Jim could not hear his partner's simple request to relax and not rush her. Inside Jim would hear, "She's telling me I'm bad because I'm worried about the time." With these injured child feelings, Jim would softly say, "I'm tired of you telling me how I should be. You don't love me." Ellen would reply, raising her voice, "I wasn't being critical. You didn't hear me. I'd feel more comfortable if you'd relax, and understand there's no need to rush." She emphasized the word "rush" by frantic up-and-down motions of her arms. Jim would then leave the room.

Jim's Sensitive-Withdrawn Strategy that helped him avoid pain with his father was ruining his marriage. He just could not hear what his partner really was saying. Jim's false-self turns an ordinary event into another example of how his mate continually attacks him, makes him wrong, tells him what to do, and tries to control him. He stays busy with his work and avoids sharing his feelings with Ellen. And Ellen is talking to a divorce lawyer.

From your experience with the Inventory of Childhood Survival Strategies in Appendix I, you have probably recognized that Jim adopted parts of the Sensitive-Withdrawn Strategy. Jim withdrew from interacting with his perfectionist, goal-setting father. And his old brain with its combined Object and Time Quirks doesn't discriminate between his father (when Joe was four) and his wife now.

In Chapter 15, we learned that the old brain makes us fall in love with someone who will injure us just like our caregivers. So Jim fell romantically in love with a woman who uses the Expressive-Clinging Strategy. Of course, she was romantically attracted to fall in love with Jim because he owned her disowned part—the quiet, reflective, withdrawn-but-carefully-watching-it-all personality.

The romantic love both of them initially felt was eroded by the power struggle that was constantly growing. Jim's inner child felt that he was continually being criticized—and not appreciated. In childhood, Ellen learned to exaggerate her feelings to get her busy parents' attention. From Ellen's point of view, she felt hurt because Jim was not expressing his feelings, maintained a wooden aloofness, and hid his feelings when they differed. She wanted a partner who was alive and responsive. And this was the part that Jim had disowned to cope with his childhood pain.

As a final attempt to save their marriage, they agreed to go to a Hendrix weekend workshop for couples. Jim and Ellen were open to learning about their childhood injuries. They discovered how their false-selves were ruining their marriage. They decided to work together to reclaim their true-selves—and re-romanticize their relationship.

Ellen was crying out for more aliveness and sharing from Jim. So Jim's growth target is to become less withdrawn and more responsive, to share emotionally, and to listen better. Ellen did not realize how quickly and deeply Jim felt about avoiding conflict and painful emotions. Her growth target was to tone down her dramatic way of expressing herself—and be more understanding when Jim withdraws. This was hard for her to do.

It is not necessary for Jim and Ellen to instantly recapture their disowned parts to save their marriage. They simply need to begin reducing the behaviors that reopen their partner's childhood wounds. Jim works on allowing himself to get in touch with his feelings and expressing them. He has learned to listen to Ellen. Ellen began easing off on her drama and is learning to speak in a lower, slower way.

The unconscious minds of both feel safer as their partner becomes more understanding and reduces their "unsafe" behavior. From one little success after another, as life pitches its daily incidents at them, they are able to gradually fulfill their partner's needs—and also meet their own growth needs!

Jim and Ellen saved their marriage by:

1. **Learning to criticize by appointment only.** This enables the unconscious mind of their partner to feel safe—and avoid staying "armored" for an unexpected attack.

2. **Using the Couple's Dialogue, the Container Process, and the Behavior Change Request.** These processes help them express their feelings and wants in a way their partner could really hear—and not feel as a personal attack. They are learning to attack their problems—not each other. They are healing their wounds in ways that do not threaten their partner—and point them toward the divorce court.

3. **Becoming aware of their adopted false-self strategies.** Jim and Ellen have learned to work on themselves by rooting out, bit by bit, the false-self strategies they had learned for childhood survival. And every success sets the stage for more success.

4. **They both began the re-romanticizing practices described in the next section.** These are tender gifts from the heart that their partner's unconscious recognizes as lovingly reaching out to create fun and joy in a relationship—and communicate love and caring.

Re-Romanticizing

To go from the power struggle to a stable, romantic relationship, you can resolve to use the three Hendrix processes whenever they're needed—with all criticism consciously given by appointment only. To relight the fire of a stable romantic love, here are loving things you can do to give powerful safety and pleasure messages to your partner's unconscious mind:

1. Find things you like, and compliment your partner.
2. Spontaneously hug and cuddle when there is nothing you want from your partner. And keep on touching and hugging frequently—*if* it is enjoyed by your partner. Notice carefully: some people limit hugs and touching.
3. Once or twice a month, with random timing, give your partner an unexpected gift. The inner child loves to get presents—but they must always be a surprise if you want more romance in the air.
4. Often ask your partner what they most want to do tonight.
5. Spontaneously join your partner in the shower, and scrub their back for them.
6. Occasionally strip their clothes off, and give them an all-over massage.
7. Play with your partner, and belly laugh.
8. Several times a day, share your loving feelings with your partner.
9. Let down your false-front dignity. Be vulnerable—and human.
10. Look for new ways you can help your partner.
11. Do the things your partner liked during courtship.
12. Notice that by contributing to your partner's happiness, you add to your happiness, too.

Relating to Your Partner's Unconscious

We're learning how to consciously work with our own and our partner's unconscious mind so we can become whole again. Our understanding new brain can learn to caringly support our partner's old brain by paraphrasing, validating, and empathizing. We know that to re-romanticize a marriage and heal the false-selves that damage our relationships, both partners need knowledge, determination, and practice. Each partner must be committed *both* to the marriage and to the processes of healing. One without the other will not help us develop what we really want—an intimate, lifetime partner with whom we can create mutual, relaxed enjoyment.

Our false-self ego would like to think that marital happiness means avoiding conflict. The truth is that intimately living together does have conflict. *But conflict is not the problem.* Our problems are created by the way we go about dealing with emotional conflict sparked by the hidden quirks in our two brains. Our projective quirks make our partner the enemy—not a friend who can offer us a golden opportunity to heal ourselves.

Our rational mind likes to think that the solution is just to tighten up a few loose screws in our partner so that they will behave in ways that allow us to feel safe—and loved. We are getting well along in our growth when we realize it's *the loose screws in ourselves* that are causing the clanging and banging in us. And it's also true that our partner has their own inner work to reclaim their whole, true-self. And that's their growth challenge.

Our world is painfully starved for examples of unconditionally loving people—and of alive, intimate, and loving marriages. The future of humanity may depend upon offsetting the quirks and healing ourselves so that our two brains are partners. Only then can we nurture children through their seven developmental phases with understanding, compassion, patience, and love. These fortunate bearers of our genes can then be a part of a new humanity.

In Part V we will explore the First Wisdom Principle. We'll learn how to use it moment-by-moment in our lives to escape from the illusion that we are a "victim" of other people and their actions. It shows us how to change our perception to go beyond anger, fear, grief, and other painful emotions.

PART VI

COMPLETING OUR HEALING

18

The First Wisdom Principle

If I think that "you make me angry," then I'm stuck in the illusion that my happiness depends on my changing you. And that's almost impossible! Only you can change you. This chapter shows how to shift your perception from being a victim of life events. You can use the First Wisdom Principle to begin changing your experience from anger or hate to acceptance and love—and thus put your happiness under your own control.

According to an old legend, a holy mountain had been discovered. Thousands were flocking to the summit to gain access to heaven. At the top were two doors. Drawing nearer, one could read the signs above them. One read "Lecture About Heaven." The other, "Heaven." And almost everyone was lining up for the lecture!

There comes a day, however, when wanting to want to do it is not enough. We're ready to do it. Among many other keys that open the door to heaven, there are two keys I call the First and Second Wisdom Principles. This chapter will examine the First Wisdom Principle that can help us enter into the promised land of relaxed enjoyment. The next chapter will give us the other key—the Second Wisdom Principle. When we practice these, we can greatly increase our insight, understanding, compassion, and love for ourselves and others.

We've all felt fear, frustration, grief, rage, anger, shame, guilt, boredom—and many other painful emotions. There have been countless times in our lives when we felt unhappy—or were even suffering. We've always thought we knew what was causing it: bad luck, other people not understanding us, other people treating us meanly, etc. The *list of who or what to blame seems endless.* And we've often thought our unhappiness was caused by things largely out of our own control. The world is "doing it to us." We are helpless victims.

Could it be this is an illusion based on a common error in perception? Could it be that our happiness does not depend on other people and events? Could it be that we don't understand what has caused us to create uncomfortable feelings and separateness? Could it be that we create our experience through widespread, but erroneous, mental habits? YES!

Taking Responsibility for Our Experience

All of us are the *creators of our own experience of life.* Enjoyable or miserable, each of us creates our own *experience.* Different people can react differently to the same situation. So it's not just the situation that determines our reaction. Through our own unique programming, we create our experience, which influences our behavior.

Regardless of the circumstances under which we live, this chapter will show how we can learn to increase our enjoyment of life. We can be the masters of our experience—even though we can't play God and control the people and the world around us—and make them fit our own models and desires. Let's look at the breakthrough insight of William James:

> The greatest revolution in our generation is the discovery that human beings, by changing the inner attitudes of their minds, can change the outer aspects of their lives.

Henry David Thoreau observed that most people endure "lives of quiet desperation." And some of us are not so quiet! Why do we so continuously trigger separating emotions of fear, frustration, anger, irritation, worry, resentment, panic, hate, impatience, anxiety, exasperation, fury, and on and on into the night? What's messing up our lives?

IT'S OUR DEMANDS! It's just our constant torrent of demands. Our demands make our minds trigger painful emotions and keep us upset when we don't get what we're demanding. "I can't stand that window rattling." "The nasty bugs are eating my flowers." "I'm pissed off because Lisa forgot our date." "John makes me angry when he asks why dinner isn't ready." "Those kids! They've messed up the living room again." "I'm getting too fat." "I'll never learn to keep my bank book straight." "Jack just isn't reasonable about wanting sex so much." "Jill spends money like it grows on trees."

The First Wisdom Principle

Let's take a close look at the empowering First Wisdom Principle:

> *My addictive demands trigger my separating emotions that create my unhappiness. Preferences never do.*

A "demand" (or an addictive demand) is a desire, expectation, or model that makes you feel upset or unhappy if it is not satisfied. A demand is "addictive" because you tell yourself you *must have it* to be happy. You might have a demand on yourself, on another person, or on a situation. For example, "I demand that I not lose my keys," or "I demand that you be on time," or "I demand that Bill agree with me." Our minds are usually preoccupied with cascades of demands—one after the other. *Our demands are quirk-based illusions.*

A "preference" is a desire that does not trigger painful emotions if it is not satisfied. For example, "I prefer that the traffic light be green when I get to it." Dealing with your quirks helps change demands into preferences.

With a preference, you *emotionally accept for now* anything you want different from the way it is. Even a lost wallet, *when accepted emotionally*, will not make you feel unhappy. You *prefer* not to lose your wallet and credit cards. But it's your internal demand that upsets you—*not the missing wallet!* When you *prefer* things to be a certain way (instead of *demanding*), you do not experience unhappiness, fear, frustration, anger, or hate.

The clue to knowing whether your brain is running an addictive demand or a preference is your *internal emotional experience.* Do you feel separating emotions, tensions in your body, or churning in your mind about something you want—or don't want? *You are running an addictive demand if you feel upset in any degree.* Take a minute to recollect the demands your mind has run in the last 24 hours. . . .

It will help to pinpoint your demands if you use this form:

PINPOINTING YOUR DEMANDS

My unconscious mind is triggering the emotion of

_____ because my programming
(emotions you feel)

is demanding _____.

(tell what you want)

In the top part of the next page, we have a list of painful emotions or feelings that give us a sure sign that our mind is running a demand instead of a preference. Choose the words that best describe your feelings and write them in the "Pinpointing Your Demands" form above.

Then fill in exactly what you are demanding. What is it you want different from way it is right now? When you've done this, you have pinpointed your demands in a way that helps you perceive what your mind is doing.

You may find it helpful to copy the "Pinpointing Your Demands" form. Keep it with you to use whenever life feels tough. When you name your emotions and pinpoint your demand, you may have a life-enhancing shift of perception. You can look at your mind creating separateness and pain. Using this mind-opening technique may help in changing a demand into a preference.

Whenever we feel worry, sadness, irritation, or any other painful emotion, we are telling ourselves there is something in our world (a life event) that is not happening the way we want. That event isn't meeting our "mental model" of how things "should" be. So, we incorrectly *blame* the life event for our unhappiness:

Erroneous Thinking

| Life Event "What Is" | → | Makes Me Feel | → | Fear, Frustration, Anger, Fury, Grief, Unhappiness, etc. |

Our Emotional Choices

When Security Demands Feel Threatened

fear	anxiety	disappointment	confusion
grief	panic	helplessness	sadness
worry	terror	apprehension	insecurity
dread	horror	hopelessness	alienation
doubt	despair	powerlessness	dejection
alarm	regret	despondency	loneliness
bitterness	shame	mournfulness	isolation
guilt	hurt	discouragement	nervousness

When Sensation or Enjoyment Demands Feel Threatened

jealousy	envy	disappointment	frustration
grief	boredom	discouragement	dismay

When Power or Control Demands Feel Threatened

frustration	anger	alienation	revulsion
annoyance	wrath	aggravation	indignation
irritation	hate	exasperation	jealousy
hostility	rage	powerlessness	impatience
resentment	fury	disdain	embarrassment

When We Shift From Demands to Preferences

satisfaction	love	compassion	benevolence
acceptance	peace	affection	appreciation
intimacy	serenity	contentment	happiness
togetherness	delight	relaxation	gladness
enjoyment	harmony	tranquility	cheerfulness
enthusiasm	courage	exultation	gratitude
buoyancy	safety	tenderness	humility
merriment	empathy	inspiration	calmness
friendliness	fun	closeness	joviality
abundance	joy	exhilaration	fulfillment
richness	elation	lightheartedness	rapture
wonder	bliss	warmheartedness	oneness

When we use the term "what is" or "life event," we are referring to "objective reality"—the way things are unfolding in our changing world. A life event (or "what is") can take place either inside us (like a tummy ache) or in the world outside our skin. Life events are reported by our senses.

How We Trap Ourselves

Sometimes, no matter what we do, how we act, or what we say, we can't get something to change. We trap ourselves by thinking that we *must* or *should* feel annoyance, resentment, anger, frustration, anxiety, jealousy, loneliness, or some separating emotion if we don't get what we want.

Our false-self ego says, "What would it *mean about you* if you didn't *demand* what you want?" We begin to think, if I don't get angry, won't people think I'm too wishy-washy? Won't people take advantage of me if I do not trigger rage in some situations? Won't I become a doormat? Will people respect me? If everything is a preference, won't I lose the ability to deal effectively with many situations? Won't life be boring? Won't I lose control—and stop trying to improve things? NO. A thousand times NO!

> *How do we make ourselves unhappy? We erroneously BELIEVE WE HAVE TO FEEL UNHAPPY if we don't get what we want. But unhappiness is not an adult necessity; it's just a strategy left over from childhood—an adult temper-tantrum. Today, with our adult capabilities, we can choose to change our demands into preferences— and peacefully enjoy our lives no matter what's happening.*

The relaxed enjoyment of your life cannot be based on getting what you want in life. Nobody gets everything they want. We win some and we lose some. It's time for us to stop making ourselves feel bad when the outside event isn't the way we want it. And we blame ourselves or others for the things we don't like.

We have usually responded by attempting to change the life event. We have put time and energy into trying to force changes on ourselves and other people. We've harmed people in trying mightily to make them change. Sometimes we've gotten what we wanted, depending on how good we were at manipulating. But let's face it: *Have we ever changed people and things enough for us to really enjoy our lives—to live peacefully thereafter?*

Let's clear up a possible misconception. There's nothing wrong with trying to change things to meet our models. We do it all the time. We have learned lots of ways to increase our skill in getting what we want. But what do we do when a life situation doesn't change? Why feel bad? Or try to make others feel bad?

> *The First Wisdom Principle shows us what to do when our lives don't give us the changes we want—which is most of the time! We shift our perception to change our demand into a preference.*

We Create Our World

Suppose Joe kept me waiting for 25 minutes when he promised to meet me at 10:00 a.m. I'm feeling impatient, frustrated, and resentful. (This was the "normal" response many people modeled for me as I grew up.) Some books I've read told me that I have to learn to "assert myself" and to "set boundaries." So I guess that means I have to get angry to prove I'm a capable, up-to-date person.

Let's ask again: *what would it mean about me if I didn't get angry?* That I don't value myself? That it's okay to treat me this way? There's no doubt about it. When Joe is late, *I have to be upset.* I don't necessarily have to blast him off the sidewalk. I can make a sarcastic remark ("Your watch stopped running?"), or I can act miffed and keep a chip on my shoulder for the next 30 minutes.

But who said I didn't have any choice? Perhaps there's no *necessary connection* between the event (Joe is late) and the emotions I trigger (impatience, frustration, resentment). Perhaps I'm a free human being who can change my perception. Joe being late doesn't *make* me feel angry: It's only my *addictive demand*—a false-self mental habit created by a quirky projection that *makes* me feel angry!

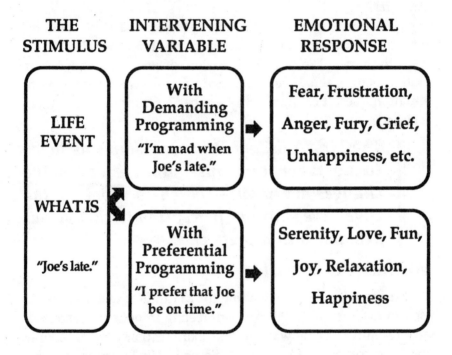

THE STIMULUS	INTERVENING VARIABLE	EMOTIONAL RESPONSE
LIFE EVENT	With Demanding Programming "I'm mad when Joe's late."	Fear, Frustration, Anger, Fury, Grief, Unhappiness, etc.
WHAT IS "Joe's late."	With Preferential Programming "I prefer that Joe be on time."	Serenity, Love, Fun, Joy, Relaxation, Happiness

I can use this life event to do inner work on *preferring* instead of *demanding* that Joe show up on time. I can enjoy watching the traffic, the people, and the birds while I'm waiting. I can realize that I don't have to create the experience of hell when I've got the keys to heaven tucked away inside me. When Joe arrives, I know he'll be relieved to hear me greet him with, "Hi! It's nice to see you. I guess something happened to delay you." (That's always a correct guess!) And another life event bites the dust of daily life without altering the relaxed enjoyment of my life—or Joe's.

A Shift in Perception

To most people freedom means "you can't tell me what to do." Those who skillfully seek a happy life know that real freedom is, "I can be happy either way. I am a versatile participant in the soap opera of life. I can play many roles. None of them is who I really am—my true-self. Shall I play a role in which you tell me what to do? Or shall I play a role in which I tell you what to do? It's all drama. I'll not get caught up in the illusions of the drama any more. I can resolve to find real freedom from my demands—and experience a relaxed enjoyment of my life.

The First Wisdom Principle offers us the realization that *we can choose to experience satisfying feelings*—instead of automatically triggering separating, painful emotions. As William James said, we can change our "inner attitudes." Rather than *blame anyone for anything*, we are learning that we can *take responsibility for what we feel*. We can choose the feelings we want to experience inside us—even if the outside event doesn't change.

All that's needed to get free of painful emotions is to CHANGE THE PROGRAMMING that triggers the emotion. This concept is empowering. It shows us that we have the potential to be the *masters of our own emotional experience*—anytime, anywhere, under any circumstances. We can't always change "what is." But with skill, we can learn to change our own programming that generates our *experience* of it!

Just as a computer is guided by its programming, we are run by ours. We are creating our projections, emotions, and actions based on the programming that went into our biocomputer over the years. Strong, painful emotions are almost always caused by childhood injuries and adaptations waiting to explode in us. It's our false-self that's booby-trapping our life. When we shift a demand into a preference, painful emotions are not triggered if we don't get what we want. With our adult abilities today, we can often reprogram our demands *unless they are too rooted in unexpressed childhood pain*. If that's where we're stuck, we can get help. (See Chapter 20.)

195

When we change a demand into a preference, we are not suppressing our emotions! We are not denying or smothering our painful feelings which are the *symptoms* or effects of our demand. Instead, we are erasing the *cause*—the demanding programs in our minds. Let's suppose Henry stays tired because he doesn't get enough sleep. He can treat the symptom (tiredness) by using lots of coffee. Or he can eliminate the *cause* by getting more sleep. If we feel angry, we can react to the *effects* or *symptoms* by expressing anger or suppressing it. Or we can change our demand into a preference—and totally eliminate the *cause* of the anger.

Changing Demands to Preferences

A preference is a desire that does not trigger any upset feelings or tensions in your mind or body—regardless of whether your desire is satisfied. With a preference you can dislike a situation. You can think you're right. You can put energy into making changes. But you do not *emotionally* demand what you want. *You simply prefer it.* And you are able to appreciate and love yourself and others even if things don't change. For example, consider the statement, "I want Bill to fill up the gas when it's low." The key to knowing if it's a preference is to notice whether you feel internally relaxed and free from any separating emotions—even when Bill forgets.

Addictive demands and preferences are both desires—*but are vastly different in how they affect your enjoyment of life.* Demands can generate a sense of exhilaration and personal power when they are satisfied—which is not too often, darn it. They create unhappiness when they aren't satisfied. A preference lets you enjoy your life—when you get your preference—*or even if you don't.* Preferences are a key to *continuously* enjoying your life.

Sometimes we hold on to demands because we have *the illusion we must have them* to be effective in life. Perhaps addictions create more powerful drives than preferences. But the cost in suffering may not be worth it. To be fully alive, let's go for what we want. *"Hold on tightly, but let go lightly."*

The addictive demands that we have programmed into our heads are the immediate, practical cause of our unhappiness when the "world" isn't the way we want it to be. In the diagram on page 194, notice that our demanding programming immediately precedes our painful internal experience. Changing our demands into preferences *gives us a way to change our internal experience.*

We often forget that:

WITH A PREFERENCE
1. *You can still want what you want.*
2. *You can still try to make changes.*
3. *You can still think you're "right."*
4. *You just don't have to make yourself upset or unhappy!*

The First Wisdom Principle enables us to become a creative cause of our experience of life—instead of a victim. If a person doesn't do what they promised, this life event *in itself* cannot make us hurt or angry. It may trigger our demanding programming that people do what they say they'll do. If we don't have this demand, a life event cannot reach into our minds and stimulate the emotional centers (limbic area) to create our experience of hurt or anger. Instead it's just noticed as another event in our personal drama.

Dr. Frank Mosca tells how our adult unhappiness (no matter what the predicament is) is always an unnecessary personal option—an unnecessary choice of our old brain that we are making in a life situation. For example, we've been taught that an insult *makes* us angry. "Not so," says Mosca. Anger is a choice we can change if we wish. In his book, *Joy Words: An Invitation to Happiness Through an Introduction to the Option Method*, he tells how to choose happiness—and avoid the robot-like triggering of unhappiness.[1]

We Are Not Our Programming

In our *essence*, we are not our programming. We are not our thoughts and feelings generated by our preferential or addictive programming. For example, no matter how beautiful or unpleasant the music on our stereo seems to us, *the music is not the stereo set.* The music is generated by the cassette or program that *we put into the stereo.* If we don't like the music, we don't criticize our stereo set. We just change the program.

If we don't like the experience we create (such as fear, frustration, anger, guilt, or shame), we don't need to criticize ourselves. We are not our false-self programs—any more than a computer is the program you install in it. As with a computer, we can change the program we're using. We are not helpless victims. We can become skillful at assessing and changing the programs we have in our head.

Just as a good stereo deserves a good cassette, we deserve every beautiful gift that life has to offer us. We can have energy, insight, love, joy, and inner peace in our lives. *It's only our demanding programming that is blocking our relaxed enjoyment.* So our next step becomes clear: let's begin to identify the demanding programs in our minds that produce the "discordant music" of separateness and painful emotions. And let's get rid of them. We can increase our skill in choosing preferential programming—or dealing with our quirks when our childhood injuries are too dominating.

The First Wisdom Principle tells us to shift our perception and mentally exchange our demanding programming for preferential programing. It also offers us another way to deal with our painful emotions: we no longer have to suppress them or project them onto others. We can work on upleveling the demands into preferences by *noticing the unhappiness and disturbance caused by our demands.* As we retrain our minds to choose preferential programming by giving new operating instructions to our biocomputer, we empower our true-self to create a more loving, peaceful, and effective life.

Gathering Power Through Insight and Love, which I coauthored (from which some of this material has been taken), gives more information for using the two wisdom principles. It also gives eight helpful methods and processes.[2]

So now you have the first key to the doorway of heaven on earth. The next chapter will give you the second key. As you learn to use these vital keys, relaxed enjoyment in your life becomes the norm—rather than the exception. Your shift in perception is gradually enabling you to reclaim the whole authentic, true-self that you were born with!

In the next chapter, we'll discover how the Second Wisdom Principle can help us develop a deep understanding, compassion, and love for ourselves and others.

19

The Second Wisdom Principle

Is there a genie that can show you how to get rid of all the "bad" people in your life? This chapter shows you how to become the genie! You can do this by learning to perceive the basic goodness in people. And we can still realistically observe the unskillful, harmful things they do or say—and protect ourselves.

Our old wildlife brain is structured to polarize quickly into *us vs. them* (us rabbits are safe; those others are dangerous). Could it be that all people are basically good? Are the "bad" things we do only *unskillful attempts* to feel good about ourselves?

Here is the Second Wisdom Principle—a key you may find helpful in unlocking the door to relaxed enjoyment:

> *Behind it all, we always have a beneficial positive intention (basically to feel good)—even though we may sometimes use unskillful ways to achieve it.*

To use this key to happiness, we must have the insight that behind every thought and action, our positive intention is *always to enjoy a desired emotional experience*. That's what we really want from any situation. If we look deeply enough, we'll discover that *behind every demand, everyone has a beneficial positive intention!* A list of beneficial positive intentions is on page 203.

In a sense, demands and positive intentions represent two sides of the same coin. Your demands help you spot what's causing the trouble. Positive intentions enable you to cut through directly to get what you really want—happiness. Understanding the beneficial positive intentions of ourselves and others helps us forgive—and get on with our life.

We Always Have Beneficial Positive Intentions

The Second Wisdom Principle carries the tremendous message that behind every thought, feeling, and voluntary action, everyone is always motivated by a beneficial positive intention.

At first this statement may seem outrageous. It's definitely not what we've been taught. One might say, "What about Hitler? Terrorists? The murderers and rapists? Surely their acts don't represent beneficial positive intentions!"

But notice, we didn't say their *acts* and *goals* represent beneficial positive intentions. *We pointed out that behind their acts, they're always motivated by beneficial positive intentions just like yours—to feel secure, effective, accepted, loved, capable, happy, etc. What they need are more skillful ways to achieve their beneficial positive intentions.* They're trapped in ways that don't work. All of this will become clearer as you read further and begin to think in terms of beneficial positive intentions in your own life—and everyone else's.

Formulating Your Beneficial Positive Intentions

Your beneficial positive intention is the *internal experience* you're trying to get through your surface goal or desire. *It is an image, thought, or feeling you want to have.* Formulating your beneficial positive intention is simple. There are only two things you need to do:

1. Make it beneficial and positive. State what you want—not what you don't want. For example, say, "My positive intention is to feel happy," instead of, "My positive intention is to not feel bad."

2. Make it specify a desired internal feeling. Just indicate the satisfying feeling you really are after if your goals or actions succeed. Choose from the list on the next page.

The form you can use for formulating your positive intentions is on the bottom of the next page.

Let's apply the two guidelines for formulating your beneficial positive intentions. For example, the guidelines for formulating your beneficial positive intention rule out "My beneficial positive intention is *not* to have a crowded house." Tell what

202

Beneficial Positive Intentions

In the Second Wisdom Principle, please remember that "Beneficial Positive Intentions" refer only to desirable emotions or feelings. Beneficial positive intentions are *internal experiences*. They are NOT actions, goals, or projects which may or may not be unskillful attempts to experience your positive intentions.

Here is a list of beneficial positive intentions:

acceptable	excited	powerful
accepted	fun-loving	prosperous
accepting	genuine	relaxed
acknowledged	happy	reliable
alive	healthy	responsible
appreciated	helpful	responsive
attractive	humorous	safe
beautiful	important	satisfied
calm	independent	secure
capable	intelligent	sexy
comfortable	joyful	strong
competent	knowledgeable	supported
complete	lovable	supportive
confident	loved	valuable
dependable	loving	valued
effective	nurtured	worthwhile
energetic	nurturing	worthy
enthusiastic	peaceful	and more!

FORMULATING BENEFICIAL POSITIVE INTENTION

My positive intention is to see myself as, to hear myself as, or feel myself as _____.

(Beneficial Positive Intentions)

you want—not what you don't want. Instead, you could formulate, "My beneficial positive intention is to feel comfortable in my home."

You would avoid stating actions or goals such as, "My beneficial positive intention is to get a new house." *This does not describe an internal experience you want.* And it could lock you into house hunting. Why do you want a new house? What *internal experience* do you think the new house will give you? If you find that your underlying, beneficial positive intention is to feel comfortable in your home, you may discover some alternatives for achieving this intention more directly than buying a new house. For example, you could add an inexpensive, prefabricated storage room in your back yard.

> *Remember that your beneficial positive intentions represent what you want your life to be about. The only thing that stops you from experiencing these 100 percent of the time is your lack of skill in achieving them.*

Good Intentions Behind Harmful Actions

In exploring your mind for its beneficial positive intentions, you may need to ask yourself, "What is my beneficial positive intention behind a negative, harmful thought?" Keep in mind that the Second Wisdom Principle says there are *always* beneficial positive intentions behind every thought or action. No exceptions! Even when you do things that you later regret or that others condemn, you still are motivated by beneficial positive intentions. The problem is that you may need *more skillful ways* to achieve your positive intention.

Suppose a friend has told a lie about you to take a business contract away from you. Let's say your thought right now is that you want to beat him up and knock his teeth in. Clearly this is a violent, separating idea. Now ask yourself, "What is my intention behind this harmful thought?" Perhaps your mind says, "I want to pay him back." This still is not a beneficial positive intention—and it certainly doesn't point to a desired internal state. So ask yourself again, "What is my intention behind *this* idea?" Exploring inside, you might answer, "It's to feel satisfied."

So now we find that feeling satisfied is your beneficial positive intention. Is beating your friend up a skillful way to achieve this beneficial positive intention of feeling satisfied? Obviously not. At this point you can ask your mind to provide you with *new ways* to help you successfully achieve your beneficial positive intention to feel satisfied.

Begin to notice the beneficial positive intentions that are always behind everything people feel, think, say, or do. For example, does a person who robs a bank have beneficial positive intentions? Yes! One of them may be to feel secure financially. Don't you have this same beneficial positive intention? Don't you want the internal emotional experience of feeling financially secure? The difference between you and the robber is that you use *more skillful ways* to achieve your beneficial positive intention to feel secure.

So we find that *the problem is not "bad" people—it's unskillful programming.* Think of the worst murderer you've heard of. Look over the list of "Beneficial Positive Intentions" and observe how many might apply to the person you're thinking about. The Second Wisdom Principle can help us develop understanding and compassion toward all human beings! *And we can still try to block the unskillful ways they are programmed to use in getting their beneficial positive intentions.*

Misusing This Principle

It is possible to misunderstand the application of the Second Wisdom Principle—and thus be unable to benefit by it. Your programming may tell you, "I just can't see the beneficial positive intention of someone who rapes and murders a woman," or "There's enough crime in this world and you shouldn't give people excuses to harm one another."

Please note that the Second Wisdom Principle does not furnish a legal defense or moral excuse for aggressive acts. We all have legal and other penalties to pay when we harm one another. In law, it is the act that is judged—not one's motive or beneficial positive intention. It would be a misuse of the Second Wisdom Principle to point out to a jury that the defendant set fire to a nursing home because he wanted the beneficial positive intention of feeling capable—just like every juror.

One of the benefits of the Second Wisdom Principle is that *you gain psychological insight into a person's antisocial or undesired behavior*. We need this understanding in a world in which people are frequently unskillful in the ways they try to get their beneficial positive intentions. When you judgmentally pigeonhole people as "bad," you limit your insight and understanding of them. This principle is designed to *help you progress* from the tunnel vision of judgmentalness and condemnation to a panoramic understanding of why people do what they do. You can use this wisdom principle to *deepen your own insight and compassion for unskillful behavior*—in both yourself and others.

The Second Wisdom Principle never "justifies" unskillful acts. People who harm others are victims of their own false-self programming—and, of course, they must live with the legal or other consequences when they act out their unskillful programming.

You can use the Second Wisdom Principle as an important vehicle to help you in your journey of inner growth. Without it, you may throw people out of your heart—and keep them out. It helps you understand what's motivating them when they do things you don't like. It helps you appreciate or love someone—*even when you dislike their unskillful actions*.

When you use this Second Wisdom Principle, it can help your friends, job associates, and family feel that your heart understands them. This may *open them to your suggestions* for more skillful actions.

We've now uncovered many of the ways our quirky brains hurt our lives. We know about the five quirks that handicap our conscious and unconscious minds. We've discussed how you can learn to talk to your old brain to improve your life, e.g., inner-child–inner-adult dialogue.

In the next chapter, we'll summarize some of the ways to integrate our two minds. Are there ways we can do it by ourselves—for ourselves? Or do we need therapists to help us? We will discuss a menu of options that are available to us.

20

*Escaping
From
Our
Lifetraps*

This chapter presents three ways (and much advice) on what you can do to heal life-damaging injuries from childhood. You may feel like a new person. But you'll only be reclaiming an adult version of the true-self with which you began your life. You'll be taking back what was rightfully yours when you began your journey on Planet Earth.

Let's review our predicament. We were put together by genes that provided us with a whole, true-self. We had what we needed to travel the road of life with fulfillment and happiness—a general feeling of relaxed enjoyment. However, when caretakers in our first few years were not available when we needed them and were not consistently warm and loving toward us, we traded parts of our true-self to buy the love and support we needed to get through childhood. We repressed the great pain of ripping out parts of our true-self.

We have the ability to heal ourselves. We could have cured our psychological wounds *if we only had someone who understood what we wanted, was aware of our pain, and assured us we were not "bad" for wanting what we wanted—and feeling what we felt.* Such an empathic person could have enabled us to integrate our pain so that it would not go bumping around like a time bomb in our unconscious for the rest of our lives.

But all too often we did not have this support. (Perhaps that's the most important role for grandmothers and grandfathers.) So we had to develop false-selves to protect ourselves from the inadvertent unskillfulness of our caregivers, who usually loved us and had good intentions.

It just doesn't seem fair that by doing what we had to do to survive childhood with our caregivers, we set up the rest of our lives for unhappiness. (But who said life was fair?) Coping with our caregivers' unskillfulness would not have been so costly if our two brains were better integrated. Since this may not happen for a million years, you and I have to compensate for our inborn quirks by developing the skills described in this book.

> *So we're stuck with a rational mind that doesn't know what's going on in the unconscious. Our unconscious mind usually feels alienated by the gobbledy-gook stuff it receives from the rational mind. It is constantly victimized by the biocomputer upstairs that erroneously thinks it knows exactly what's wrong—and how to fix it.*

Our False-Self Lifetrap

So what do we do to get out of this bottomless pit that Dr. Jeffrey E. Young calls a "lifetrap"? *Our false-self is our lifetrap.* A lifetrap acts like a pus sack in the brain. Although we may realize that our caregivers have unknowingly played their part in creating our lifetraps, you and I are *100 percent responsible* for healing them today.

Here are the three phases in learning a skill:

1. First, you need an **understanding** of what you're dealing with—and a knowledge of the techniques for getting the results you want.

2. Next you develop a **determination** to do it. You must not think that just knowing about your predicament will automatically solve it. Knowledge only enables you to take the first step. You could read a hundred books on healing, teach it in a university, work as a psychotherapist every day helping others get rid of their lifetraps, and still not free yourself from a single lifetrap that is damaging your life! *It's not your rational mind that needs help.*

3. **Then practice, practice, and more practice.** Your false-self is very sly. It is an expert at making you feel separate from yourself and other people. It will trigger your unconscious

210

mind into attacking people in the illusion that they are making you unhappy. And it will take lots of inner work to penetrate the subtle illusions your false-self uses to entrap you—over and over again.

Ways to Heal

"There isn't much we can do to alter human evolutionary history," Ornstein reminds us. "We can't rewire the nervous system."[1] However, we can gradually learn to spot the activities of our false-self. Frequently reviewing the "Inventory of Childhood Survival Strategies" has been most helpful to me (Appendix I). As we begin to understand how we were warped, we will consciously awake sooner and sooner from the trance in which our false-self has us enmeshed.

Escaping from the prison in which we have unknowingly caged ourselves is done by changing our perception. Although our false-self feels natural, it is really unnatural. We can begin to regard our "lifetraps" as part of our curriculum in the University of Life.

> *The University of Life is very handy. It's always magically located exactly wherever we are each moment! Every false-self response we unmask, and use as a part of today's lesson, is an opportunity to increase our skill in living—and get free of another lifetrap.*

A great thing is happening. Many of the people who understand our false-self lifetraps are busy discovering new ways to help us escape. The injuries to our true-self lie in our unconscious mind. It is this mind that must be healed. It cannot be healed by thoughts or words alone—however wise. It can only be healed by the old brain *experiencing now it is safe*. Then it will quickly let us use the parts of our true-selves that were blown away in childhood.

We can heal our unconscious by discovering and proclaiming *our* truth about the past. We can mourn and grieve for what happened. Alice Miller suggests:

211

Free expression of resentment against one's parents represents a great opportunity. It provides access to one's true-self, reactivates numbed feelings, opens the way for mourning and—with luck—reconciliation. In any case, it is an essential part of the process of psychic healing.[2]

So one of the first steps in healing is to tell your "truth" to your parents. Forgiveness of your parents is an essential last step in reclaiming your true-self. Complete healing in the unconscious needs your heart's compassion and forgiveness—*for your own good!*

Remember, the old brain is a here-and-now brain—there is no past and no future for it. *Its safety and pleasure programs are installed only by here-and-now experience—not by words or ideas from the new brain.*

Many people today are learning to effectively provide their unconscious mind with the experiences it needs to reclaim parts that were not safe in childhood. Let's look at three excellent ways to heal the life-damaging injuries of childhood:

1. **Twelve-Step Groups**
2. **Individual Counseling**
3. **Do-It-Yourself**

Twelve-Step Groups

Somewhere within a few minutes of where you live, there probably are regular 12-step meetings. They are free; expenses are paid by donations from participants. A list of some of these groups in a large metropolitan area appears on the next page.

When you first go to a 12-step group, you may be quiet. You're not about to reveal the shameful, humiliating, embarrassing things that you feel you must hide to maintain self-esteem. You may not have it all together inside—but at least you can look good outside.

Then you begin to experience people opening themselves, sharing the hurt they felt as children, sharing what they did as children to adapt to caretaker abuses. You hear them describe

12-Step Groups
Here is a partial list of 12-Step Groups:

Adult Children of Alcoholics
Al-Anon
Alcoholics Anonymous
CFIDS Anonymous
Chemically Dependent Anon
Cocaine Anonymous
Codependents Anonymous
Debtors Anonymous
Emotions Anonymous
Emphysema Anonymous
Gamblers Anonymous
Incest Survivors Anonymous
Learning Disabilities Anon
Marijuana Anonymous
Nar-Anon Family Group
Narcotics Anonymous
Nicotine Anonymous
Overeaters Anonymous
Prostitutes Anonymous
Partners of Survivors/Incest Anon
Racism and Bigotry Anonymous
Recovering Couples Anonymous
Self-Mutilators Anonymous
Sexaholics Anonymous
Shame Anonymous
Survivors of Incest Anonymous
Shoplifters Anonymous
Workaholics Anonymous

Al-Anon (for friends and families of alchoholics) has a national hotline (800-344-2666).

the sad state of their lives today, and how they are determined to heal. You feel they are healing. They are taking responsibility for themselves. They are hearing inspiring accounts of healing. And they are freely expressing their pain in a sympathetic group that is not judging or criticizing them—or trying to "save" them. You're accepted and respected *just as you are.*

You may begin to feel that these are caring people who are providing each other with the empathy they needed as a little child—and couldn't get. You begin to wonder if you might start healing too, just by sharing the stuff your false-self has been carefully covering up. You may discover that you've been projecting your pain onto innocent people around you—and they've fought back by projecting their childhood pain onto you. A perpetual warfare has been going on between you and the people you would like to love—and who want to love you.

You develop a deeper determination to be free. And you know that participation in these groups may be an answer for you. And perhaps even when you're healed, you'll want to continue your twelve-step work helping others.

Professional Help

Many therapists I've talked with agree that most psychotherapy takes too long, is too expensive, and is too uncertain in results. A lot of therapist training in the past (and even today) consisted of what could be called "talk" therapy. It primarily involved the new brain with occasional emotions. This meant that the rational mind of the client lengthily discussed past events ("At the supermarket last Saturday, this guy cut in line in front of me. . . ."). Or the therapist uses their experience to solve your problem ("Perhaps you and your wife can agree to. . . .").

Although it can be helpful, I feel the "talk" approach is limited. It mainly deals with symptoms, not root causes in the unconscious. I find it's more effective for the counselor to create a trust that encourages the unconscious mind of the client to take charge of healing itself. Then with techniques *offered as options* by the counselor, the unconscious will indicate the healing work it needs to do. This is done in an atmosphere of

214

loving support and respect for one's right to choose—experiences often missing in childhood.

No therapist can heal you—just as no doctor can heal your broken arm. A doctor can set up healing conditions, such as fitting the bones together and putting the arm in a cast to immobilize it. But only your old brain can orchestrate a matrix of collagen with calcium and phosphorus that heals the arm. Given skillful outside support, *your arm is self-healing*. The same thing applies to your mind.

Any therapist whose ego leads them to think that *they* heal you could be a dangerous or ineffective therapist. That's just more of the power-based parental attitude that originally injured you back then. I find that counselors who know how to cooperate with your unconscious mind can usually set up conditions *that help you escape from your lifetraps*. Only you can reclaim your authentic, whole true-self—and pull the rug out from the false-self you built to get through childhood.

Today we are in a revolution in therapy. Problem solving, "endless" free association, coping, and adjustment are out; supporting the client's unconscious mind in healing itself is in. We are developing a new kind of healer that is *tuned-in* to supporting the natural healing mechanisms of the mind—instead of trying to fix people.

> *All of us are wounded children. We don't need fixing because we aren't defective or broken. We've just been caught in some lifetraps.*

One-Week Programs

How do you find this new kind of healer? You may have to hunt—but they're out there. You might ask a counselor what techniques they use for accessing your unconscious mind—and helping it heal itself. I offer the following list with much trepidation. I don't know everything that's happening and I apologize for omissions. I can only offer a partial list of techniques that minimize "talk therapy" and maximize supporting the unconscious mind in healing itself.

The following two programs have demonstrated that in one week, they offer the likelihood of effectively healing childhood injuries in the unconscious mind. Most clients experience a dramatic transformation during this week. This *may or may not* apply to psychoses, multiple personality disorders, or other severe mental disorders.

Hoffman Quadrinity Process: Over the last 25 years, Bob Hoffman has developed one of the finest programs to rapidly and profoundly repair childhood injuries. Participants actually begin to experience their true-self as their false-self is retired. The instructors and participants intensively work together in a scenic retreat center for seven days. Childhood false-self programming is resolved by highly cathartic processes which bring understanding with no condemnation of oneself or one's parents. Instead, participants develop compassion, acceptance, forgiveness, and love for the parents they knew (or did not know) as well as for themselves and others in their lives. John Bradshaw says, "The Hoffman Process is the most effective method I know for releasing your original pain and connecting deeply and joyously with your soul. I recommend it without reservation."

The Quadrinity Process (emotional, spiritual, intellectual, physical) is structured to eliminate vicious self-sabotaging emotional patterns of feeling and behavior so that we can enjoy our true-selves, appreciate and love ourselves and others, and live in the present. By clearing away childhood blockages, participants increasingly allow the free flow of feelings, thoughts, and intuition that results in growing, developing, and contributing to others. The Quadrinity Process is available in many countries. You can get further details by writing to the Hoffman Institute, 223 San Anselmo Avenue, Suite 4, San Anselmo, CA 94960. Phone (415) 485-5220.

Caring Rapid Counseling: I've been intrigued by the new crop of healing techniques that can rapidly heal the unconscious mind where the injuries are. I adapt them to meet each client's needs—largely using EMDR, Hakomi (see below), and emotional catharsis. I call my eclectic approach "Caring Rapid

Counseling." *My goal is to drastically reduce the time and overall cost of counseling—while enormously increasing its effectiveness.* A client usually works with a CRC counselor for perhaps eight hours a day for four to six days. Most CRC clients achieve what seems to be a lifetime healing. They are required to study Pollard's *Self-Parenting* and *Your Road Map to Lifelong Happiness* before counseling begins. For a free brochure, write to CRC Registration, Caring Rapid Counseling Center, 1620 Thompson Road, Coos Bay, OR 97420. Phone (503) 267-4232. Fax (503) 269-2388.

Therapies Available in Hourly Sessions

Like other professionals, therapists vary in skill and methodology. Ask if they work directly in supporting the unconscious mind in healing itself. It may be helpful to call previous clients. Here is a list of some of the methods that target the unconscious mind:

EMDR: The name stands for Eye Movement Desensitization and Reprocessing. Originated by Dr. Francine Shapiro, this simply *elegant* technique amazingly helps the unconscious mind heal itself. Here's a bird's-eye view of how it's done. The client's eyes follow the therapist's hand as it moves from side to side about a foot from the client's face. Simultaneously, the client puts in their mind a picture of a painful event, a sentence telling what the picture *means about them*, and the painful gut emotions felt in this situation. When the emotional disturbance is greatly reduced, the client will be asked to experience the picture with a short statement of how they prefer to feel and act in such a situation. With the original issue and the preferred response in mind, the eye movements are repeated.

Somehow this seems to help the two brains communicate and integrate in a way that rapidly reprograms anger, fear, jealousy, grief, or whatever painful emotions are associated with the incident. For a list of therapists who have had advanced EMDR training, you may contact the EMDR Institute, Inc., P.O. Box 51010, Pacific Grove, CA 93950-6010. Phone (408) 372-3900.

Ericksonian Psychotherapy: Dr. Milton Erickson was a master at accessing the unconscious mind for rapid healing. Erickson occasionally helped people break through problems in a half hour or less! And he was quick to admit that he could not heal all problems.

Many therapists have been trained in his methods. Ericksonian therapists write books like *The Essence of Single-Session Success*, edited by Stephen R. Lankton and Kristina K. Erickson, the daughter of Milton Erickson. For a therapist in your area, you may wish to contact the Milton H. Erickson Foundation, Inc., 3606 North 24th Street, Phoenix, AZ 85016. Phone (602) 956-6196.

Hakomi Therapy: Ron Kurtz has developed a system for working with the unconscious mind known as "Hakomi." Kurtz spends little time working with the rational, new brain. He goes straight for the unconscious to build trust from the moment you walk through the door. After getting the trust of the unconscious, he also carefully watches the body for it constantly signals access points to the unconscious. I have used Ron Kurtz's formulation of character strategies adopted in childhood as the basis of the inventory in Appendix I. You can get a list of certified Hakomi therapists by contacting the Hakomi Institute, P. O. Box 1873, Boulder, CO 80306. Phone (303) 443-6209.

Laughter Therapy: Annette Goodheart, Ph.D., has developed a system she calls "Laughter Therapy." In Laughter Therapy, the client says a short sentence expressing what they feel bad about. ("My mother tries to control me.") Then immediately the client says "tee hee" or "ha ha." Apparently laughter tells the old brain that the situation is now safe. This can sometimes amazingly result in a rapid change of perception and feeling. Dr. Goodheart offers a one-week therapy training, which is open to therapists and non-therapists alike.

I haven't run into anyone who knows more about human emotions and laughter than Annette. She can even teach you how to use laughter therapy on yourself. If you'd like a preview, you can get a copy of her videotape "The Art of Laughter Therapy." What she teaches is worth a week of anyone's time.

She is available for individual sessions, and she gives workshops that show you how to use her techniques. You can reach Annette Goodheart at 635 North Alisos Street, Santa Barbara, CA 93103. Phone (805) 966-0025.

Imago Therapy: Harville Hendrix, Ph.D., has developed a system called "Imago Therapy," which focuses on *helping couples through the inevitable power struggle* when romantic love (nature's anesthesia) begins to wear off. *All emotional conflict between couples (not necessarily intellectual disagreements) involve projecting childhood injuries onto one's partner.* Imago Therapy tells partners how they can heal their childhood injuries and stop divorce-causing attacks on each other. ("You never think of me.") Imago Therapy shows you how to *re-romanticize* into a loving, intimate, lifelong partnership.

Imago techniques are available as a do-it-yourself approach using Dr. Hendrix's books *Getting the Love You Want* and *Keeping the Love You Find.* He also has excellent videotapes. By all means, get his marriage-repairing *Homevideo Workshop for Couples.* He also offers nationwide workshops for couples or singles. I strongly recommend that all couples take one of these outstanding workshops—whether they think they need it or not.

For information on workshops, books, tapes, study guides, or names of therapists accredited in Imago Therapy, contact The Institute for Relationship Therapy, 1255 Fifth Avenue, Suite C-2, New York, NY 10029. Phone 800-729-1121 or in New York City (212) 410-7712.

This list of breakthrough therapies is far from complete. Probably no one technique can do everything for everybody. New and more rapid ways of reprogramming the unconscious to reclaim the true-self are popping up at an increasing pace. If you know what you want, the information in this book can lead you to it.

Do-It-Yourself Healing

You'll recall that to learn any skill (whether it be painting, cooking, gardening, stock investing, or whatever), you need knowledge, determination, and practice, practice, practice. For those who are adept at applying written concepts to their moment-to-moment experience, there may be a do-it-yourself technique that will work for you.

1. **Inner Child Work:** I'm particularly impressed by self-help techniques that enable you to actually talk with your inner child as discussed in Chapters 12 through 14. John Pollard's *Self-Parenting: The Complete Guide to Your Inner Conversations* tells how to do it. It has big type, cartoons, lots of white space—and is written to introduce your inner adult to your inner child, and *vice versa*. It's fascinating to find that your conscious mind is learning to talk with your unconscious!

You may want to continue with Pollard's *The Self-Parenting Program* after you have read and reread *Self-Parenting*. Even if you are attending a 12-step group or are using professional counseling, you will find that Pollard's techniques may supplement and speed up your healing. If you look around, you'll find many inner child workshops. I suggest that my Caring Rapid Counseling clients study Pollard's *Self-Parenting* before we get together. This helps us get faster results at less cost. To tune-in to Pollard's Self-Parenting Program, or get a free information packet, or order his books, write to the Self-Parenting Program, P.O. Box 6535, Malibu, CA 90265. Phone (800) 458-0091.

2. **The Voice Dialogue Method:** Hal and Sidra Stone work together in teaching their Voice Dialogue Method of harmonizing the conscious and unconscious minds. They help you get in touch with your *Committee of Selves* that controls your thoughts and actions. They teach you to dialogue with your inner selves to direct their activities toward your highest good. The Voice Dialogue Method teaches you to talk back and forth with your amazing family of selves, which includes the inner critic, the controller, the inner child, the inner pusher, etc. Their best-known book is *Embracing Our Selves: The Voice Dialogue Method.* They also have one- and two-week training programs and are available for private consultation. For a catalog of books, tapes, and workshops, contact Hal and Sidra Stone, Delos, Inc., P.O. Box 604, Albion, CA 95410. Phone (707) 937-2424.

3. Reinventing Your Life: Jeffrey E. Young, Ph.D., Department of Psychiatry at Columbia University, wrote *Reinventing Your Life: Smart Moves for Escaping Negative Life Patterns.*[3] I am indebted to Dr. Young for the term "lifetrap." Based on Dr. Young's work, Appendix II has a six-step exercise with a sample showing how to use it. You can accelerate your insight and growth by filling out this form whenever you feel upset. There is a blank form you can copy and keep with you for on-the-spot handling of emotional "emergencies."

4. Books and Tapes: Throughout this book, I have mentioned many of the books I have personally found most helpful. For your convenience, they are listed in bold type in the footnotes in Appendix VI.

The set of six audiotapes titled *The Awakened Life* by Dr. Wayne Dyer is especially helpful.[4] By tuning-in to these books and tapes, you can acquire a background to accelerate your healing whether you choose a 12-step group, a professional counselor, or a do-it-yourself technique. And I'll repeat again: You can read every book ever written and even teach psychotherapy—*and not heal any of your own lifetraps.*

Books only give the new brain more information. Knowledge may be power, as Francis Bacon suggested. But actually dropping the false-self adaptations and reclaiming your true-self requires you to somehow create the *missing experience* (love, caring, attention, safety, telling your truth with emotional honesty, etc.) that your unconscious can use to reprogram itself. Information may provide the script, but it takes some type of action to open the curtain.

To Sum Up

Inspiration (and I hope this book inspires you) can change your perspective, values, and attitudes in such a way that pervious problems and patterns begin to lose their hold on you. Disillusionment with your present false-self adaptations is needed. Unless you are fully disillusioned, motivation may be lacking for the continuous inner work needed. And it helps to consolidate your transformation by being with people who share the same constructive perspective and way of life.

We've offered three basic ways you can go about reclaiming your authentic, true-self and retiring your false-self: 12-step groups, professional counseling in one-week comprehensive programs or in "50-minute hours," and do-it-yourself techniques. So keep your eyes and ears open. There is no one way for everybody. You may want to experience all three. Different strokes for different folks. . . .

In the next chapter, we'll examine a personal road map that can guide us to happiness.

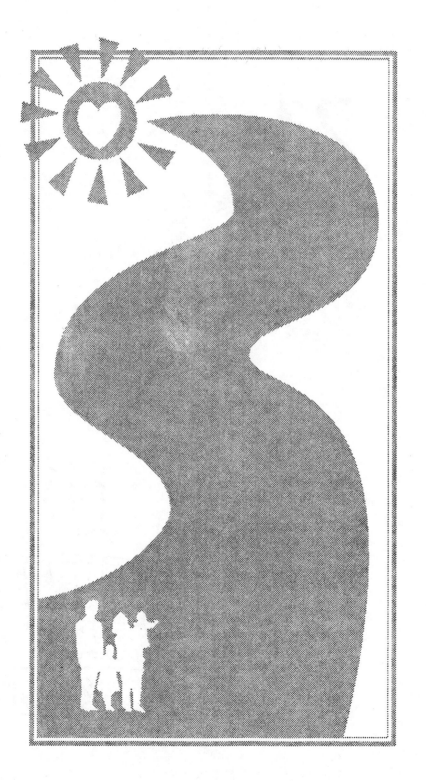

21

*Secrets
of
Happiness*

Here's a road map for finding
heaven on earth—and staying out of
hell. Good luck!

For many years, I have continually used two
Wisdom Principles as "life savers" in the storms of life. The
First Wisdom Principle enables me to avoid a "victim" consciousness—and to creatively seek the best options available to
me. To fully play the game of life, I go for what I want. By
using the First Wisdom Principle to uplevel my demands to
preferences, I can "hold on tightly" to get what I want in each
life situation—and "let go lightly" if life isn't giving it to me.
By changing my demands into preferences, I increasingly live
with relaxed enjoyment. No more beating my head against the
brick wall of "what is."

The Second Wisdom Principle helps me enrich my life by
reducing my judgments and criticisms of other people—and
myself. Considering our injuries, the pain we've experienced,
and the false-self we needed in childhood, I've learned that
we're all just doing *the best we know how*. This principle helps
me feel compassion—and to hold on to my love for people—
even when I may feel hurt by what they say and do.

Life still sends lots of "hurricanes" to test me. My wife
with whom I wanted to live the rest of my life decided she had
another agenda. A training institute I had set up to teach the
Living Love System fell apart. People I thought I could count
on let me down. My personal curriculum at the University of
Life is frequently enriched.

225

> *The two wisdom principles have taken a heavy load off of my mind. I realized that I didn't have to sweat the small stuff! Then, I realized it's all small stuff!*

Our Daily Trance

With everybody rushing around urgently doing "important" things, life can seem very serious indeed. To live in heaven while on Planet Earth, we must learn not to take our life *personally!*

Sure, what we do and say has consequences that set up the next act in the drama of our lives. But we always have *enough* to let ourselves feel relaxed enjoyment. The great power of unconditional love can enable us to enjoy whatever comes up as part of the cosmic joke that life perpetrates on us to awaken us from the trances of our false-self.

The eternal now moment is always ours to enjoy—if we make that choice. So many of us have minds that are continuously preoccupied with the past—and what can happen in the future. The past is gone forever. The future exists only in our imagination. When the *future* gets here, it will be *now*. So all we have in life is *now*. Yet the new brain often doesn't even notice what's *now* in our lives. It's too busy thinking about what's not *now*—the past and future. And we miss living in the moment of *now*. Every thought we have separates us by a millisecond from the relaxed sensory enjoyment of now—*the eternal now moment*.

Smart Drugs

Since we are subject to the ups and downs of a human body, it makes sense that we'll have more happiness if we take care of our bodies. It is known that about age 45, your body's hormones and catalysts that play a large part in maintaining the vigor of youth begin to decrease about one percent per year. By age 75, we are perhaps 30 percent under our youthful level in these vital substances. Senility is knocking at our door!

For example, by taking a daily supplement containing L-arginine, your growth hormone (made by the pituitary gland) will increase toward youthful levels. A daily capsule of DHEA (made by the adrenal glands) can enable you to *maintain* this vital substance at the level you had at age 30. Many drugs (such as hydergine or piracetum) have been proven to reduce memory loss that often comes with aging.

Unlike most drugs, life extending drugs have very few side effects. This is because you're just helping your body maintain its earlier levels of important body substances as you get older. In an experiment with rats, by increasing the supply of dopamine to the brain, a tiny amount of deprenyl added 34 percent to the average lifetime! Moreover, it restored sexual activity to rats that were no longer sexually active! ! !

For more years in your life and more life in your years, you may want to learn about this exciting new area in which the knowledge is doubling every decade. Many people (including me) are taking deprenyl and other "smart drugs" today with excellent results. For information on how to do it, see the footnote in Appendix VII.[1]

Unconditional Love

In my opinion, the two people who knew the most about happiness were Buddha, who lived 2,500 years ago, and Christ, who was born around 2,000 years ago. Buddha strongly warned against being emotionally or intellectually locked onto anything you don't have—or anything you do have that can disappear as life goes on. Buddha also stressed a second component that creates the milieu we need for the deepest happiness—the feeling of loving kindness in one's heart.

Love was Christ's speciality. He lived and taught, "Love one another." He counseled us to ". . . love your enemies, bless those who curse you, do good to those who hate you. . . ." When he had been unjustly nailed to a cross and was hanging there in pain, he is quoted as saying, "Father, forgive them; for they know not what they do." If you were crucified, and pain-

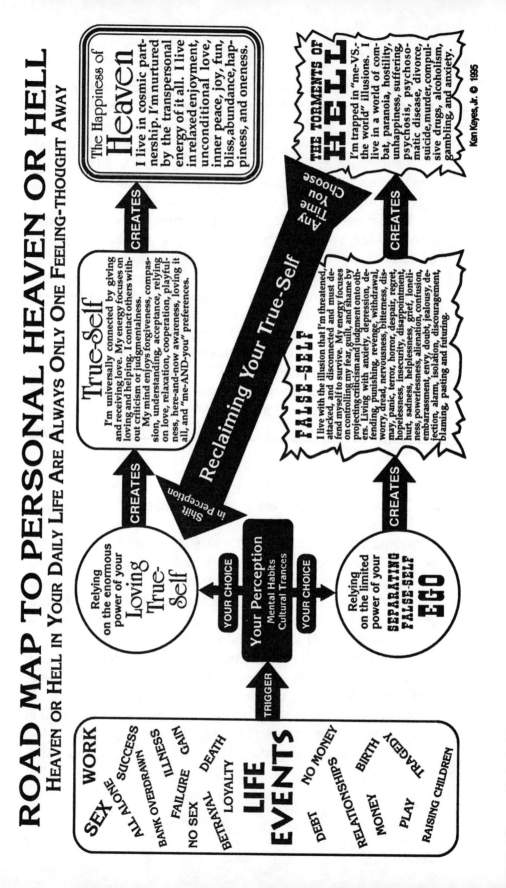

ROAD MAP TO PERSONAL HEAVEN OR HELL

HEAVEN OR HELL IN YOUR DAILY LIFE ARE ALWAYS ONLY ONE FEELING-THOUGHT AWAY

The Happiness of Heaven

I live in cosmic partnership. I'm nurtured by the transpersonal energy of it all. I live in relaxed enjoyment, unconditional love, inner peace, joy, fun, bliss, abundance, happiness, and oneness.

THE TORMENTS OF HELL

I'm trapped in "me-VS.-the world" illusions. I live in a world of combat, paranoia, hostility, unhappiness, suffering, psychosis, psychosomatic disease, divorce, suicide, murder, compulsive drugs, alcoholism, gambling and anxiety.

Ken Keyes, Jr. © 1995

True-Self

I'm universally connected by giving and receiving love. My energy focuses on loving and helping. I contact others without criticism or judgmentalness.

My mind enjoys forgiveness, compassion, understanding, acceptance, relying on love, relaxation, cooperation, playfulness, here-and-now awareness, loving it all, and "me-AND-you" preferences.

FALSE-SELF

I live with the illusion that I'm threatened, attacked, and disconnected and must defend myself to survive. My energy focuses on controlling my fear, guilt, and shame by projecting criticism and judgment onto others. Living with anxiety, depression, defending, punishing, revenge, withdrawal, worry, dread, nervousness, bitterness, dismay, panic, terror, horror, despair, regret, hopelessness, insecurity, disappointment, hurt, sadness, helplessness, grief, loneliness, powerlessness, alienation, confusion, embarrassment, envy, doubt, jealousy, dejection, alarm, isolation, discouragement, blaming, pasting and futuring.

CREATES

CREATES

Any Time You Choose

Reclaiming Your True-Self

Shift in Perception

Relying on the enormous power of your **Loving True-Self**

YOUR CHOICE

Your Perception
Mental Habits
Cultural Trances

YOUR CHOICE

Relying on the limited power of your **SEPARATING FALSE-SELF EGO**

CREATES

TRIGGER

LIFE EVENTS

SEX WORK ALL ALONE SUCCESS BANK OVERDRAWN ILLNESS GAIN FAILURE DEATH NO SEX BETRAYAL LOYALTY NO MONEY DEBT RELATIONSHIPS BIRTH MONEY TRAGEDY PLAY RAISING CHILDREN fully dying by the decree of a political judge, would your last feelings, thoughts, and words be ones of forgiveness and compassion for your executioners? If so, you've passed the unconditional love test.

In addition to love, Christ also knew how psychological attachment or demanding can destroy our peace of mind. Paul, reflecting Christ's teachings, wrote that the *love* of money is the root of evil—not money itself.[2] It's the demand, the addiction, the attachment, the craving for money that makes us do unloving things—which is exactly the point that Buddha made 500 years earlier.

Loving is a process of letting go of one's fear, suspicion, and defensive feelings—and opening our hearts to each other. *Homo sapiens* work best when we learn how to balance the head (new brain) and the heart (old brain). Our inner work toward this balance can begin our journey to the highest happiness. It's called "enlightenment." We are enlightened when our minds function consistently with here-and-now awareness, wisdom, energy, bliss and wonderment, inner peace, concentration (ability to stay with an issue long enough to deal with it), and a serene balance as the waves of life wash over us (equanimity). In case the reader is curious, I'm not enlightened. And the inner work I've done lets me enjoy most of these seven characteristics of enlightenment most of the time. If I can do it, you can too.

We have described how unskillful parenting ruins our personal happiness. It also sets us up for a life of depression, guilt, and conflict in marriage. And it inflicts a heavy price on our society. In the next chapter, we'll see how Adolf Hitler's childhood abuse was a factor in causing the deaths of 40 million people in World War II. Hitler, the arch-murderer of all time, was not born a criminal. His true-self was "murdered" by a "respectable" yet unskillful father, who continually beat and shamed him.

How soon will we understand that Planet Earth will be an increasingly dangerous place until we learn to nurture the old brain as well as the new brain of our children?

PART VII

THE FUTURE
OF HUMANITY

22

Our Dangerous Society

No one is born a murderer—or a socially conscious citizen. This chapter gives shocking information on how loving, well-meaning, but unskillful parents can be inadvertently responsible for damaging the lives of their children—and the quality of life for all of us on Earth.

We have shown how the blowtorch of fear, guilt, and shame can burn up the spirit of a child before it is three years old. Proponents of this poisonous pedagogy claim that the child's self-esteem and self-confidence must be broken, and replaced by strict obedience and subservience. This is most effectively done in the first two or three years before the child is aware of what's going on. If the parent is clever and uses a velvet tone of voice most of the time, children will bear this brutal attack on their true-self "for their own good." In their first years, they will accept the pain needed to develop a false-self. And they will usually even feel love for such a parent who will go to so much trouble to help them grow up "right!"

Breaking the Child's Will

We've seen that parenting based on autocratic, unquestioned parental power deeply damages the child's completion of the bonding, exploration, and identity phases of normal childhood development. And since the foundation of the first three phases is not complete, the competing, caring, intimacy, and creating phases will be twisted. (See "The Journey of the True-Self" chart on page 48.)

When the true-self is split, the resources of the child's unconscious mind will be focused on avoiding pain. It may choose to appear to conform to the powers that be (while resenting it)—or to rebel and stand the hell. No longer can their spirit unfold in joyful, happy, fun-filled, and eventually, socially constructive ways. Their unconscious mind will be distracted from fulfilling its primary functions of creating fun and energy and supporting the immune system.

When the child's "will" is broken, the "adult-child" may focus on avoiding "mistakes" that trigger the dreaded fear, guilt, and shame. Resistance to authority is to be avoided—or deviously done in a passive-aggressive way. Instead of engaging their creative resources to look for new solutions to problems, they mainly want to know what the "authorities" say. They may become robots who mechanically go through their safe daily routines experiencing life as a stream of dangers to be avoided—instead of a challenge to be met.

Poisonous pedagogy may drug one's aliveness and humanity—until healed. Deep within their unconscious mind, there is a continually festering wound where a part of their true-self has been ripped out. Their energy may be depleted by constantly keeping a lid on the volcano of the repressed unconscious resentment, anger, hatred, and violence that were not safe to express in childhood. The result will be pent-up anxiety, depression, illness, and occasionally violence (physical and/or verbal) when their emotional time bombs are triggered by life events.

John Bradshaw in *Homecoming* helps us understand how dysfunctional parents damage their children:

> Any child from a dysfunctional family system will feel emotional deprivation and abandonment. The natural response to emotional abandonment is a deep-seated toxic shame that engenders both primal rage and a deep-seated sense of hurt. There is no way you could grieve this in infancy. You had no ally who could be there for you and validate your pain, no one to hold you while you cried your eyes out or raged at the injustice of it all. In order to survive, your primary ego defenses kicked in and your emotional energy was left frozen and unresolved. Your unmet needs have been clamoring to be filled ever since your infancy.[1]

The World's Bloodiest Criminal

Psychoanalyst Alice Miller researched the childhood conditions of the worst arch-criminal that ever lived: Adolf Hitler. Hitler's grandmother, Maria Anna Schicklgruber, was a maid in the household of the Jewish family of Johann Trummelschlager. When Hitler's grandmother became pregnant, she wanted her employer to acknowledge that he was the father of Alois who was born on June 7, 1837. Johann, a respectable family man, denied that Alois was his son.

In the nineteenth century, the "head" of the house frequently expected sexual favors from a live-in maid. But Johann did provide financial support for young Alois until he was about 15. Thus, in addition to the anti-Semitism of Western society, from his mother, Alois grew up with an extra dose of hatred for Jews.

Alois married a docile codependent named Klara, and one of their children was Adolf Hitler. Alois was a customs official. Everyone knew he was a "good parent" as attested by his stern discipline with his children. As a "good parent," Alois knew it was necessary for Adolf to acquire the esteemed quality of unquestioned, instant obedience to parental authority.

"Pure Hell"

Alice Miller wryly observes "a parent held in high esteem by the neighbors can be pure hell for one's own child." From the time young Adolf was four, when Alois came home each evening, *he often severely beat and demeaned his son*—even if he had been a "good boy" all day. He almost beat Adolf to death when he was eleven! As a "good parent," Alois thought that when it comes to stamping out willfulness and disrespect for authority, an ounce of prevention is worth a pound of cure.

When Hitler gained power, he told one of his secretaries that in his boyhood, he had read in an adventure novel that it was a proof of courage to show no pain. He told her, "I resolved not to make a sound the next time my father whipped me. And when the time came—I still can remember my frightened mother standing outside the door—I silently counted the blows. My mother thought I had gone crazy when I beamed proudly and said, 'Father hit me thirty-two times!'"[2]

Children who are made to endure constant, severe, unexpressed pain can learn to turn off the pain. To survive such abuse they lose some of their human sensitivity. Unless healed, they cannot empathize with the pain of others.

Children are resilient. Horrible abuse by itself will not necessarily produce lifetime damage—and plant the seeds of adult violence. Children can heal themselves if there is anyone on whom they can depend to be warm, understanding, and available. They only need to feel their feelings and safely express them. They must have at least one person with whom they can vent their hurt and outrage by grieving, crying, expressing anger, *or even laughing about the painful happenings*. This is the traditional "grandmother" role. An understanding heart can make the difference between a psychopathic or sociopathic adjustment to vicious childhood abuse—or a true-self integration of terrible circumstances. Alice Miller comments,

> Hitler never had a single other human being in whom he could confide his true feelings; he was not only mistreated but also prevented from experiencing and expressing his pain; he didn't have any children who could have served as objects for. . . [projecting] his hatred, and, finally, his lack of education did not allow him to ward off his hatred by intellectualizing it. Had a single one of these factors been different, perhaps he would never have become the arch-criminal he did.[3]

The Stage Was Set

Not everyone who is the recipient of poisonous pedagogy is able to establish leadership in a gang of ruthless young men. Through the vagaries of time and place, Hitler's charisma enabled him to lead such a group and eventually gain political power in Germany in 1933.

The stage was now set for a terribly abused adult/child to guide the destiny of his nation. Hitler's anti-Semitic hatreds came in quite handy in providing a scapegoat on which everything bad could be blamed. The projections and illusions of

Hitler's false-self resulted in a holocaust that killed six million Jewish people. Since Hitler had long since turned off his empathy for himself (and hence others), such a ruthless decision was made under the righteous, rational banner of patriotism.

A schizophrenic aunt lived with young Adolf's family. He developed rage and hatred toward her because of the ruckus she constantly stirred up. Since this could not be expressed, these emotions were buried in Adolf's unconscious mind. When he came to power, Chancellor Hitler decreed that all mentally ill and retarded people must be put to death! After all, such a "healthy housecleaning" would relieve the German economy of the burden of carrying these poor people who could make no contribution to the Third Reich. Hitler's natural, human feelings of compassion and empathy had been turned off so that he could survive Alois' beatings. He could make this false-self, rational decision without being consciously aware of "heart" feelings from his true-self. To Hitler's unconscious mind, his euthanasia decision was a *personal act of revenge*, for the fear and rage he could not safely express in childhood to his trouble-causing schizophrenic aunt.[4]

Our Imperiled World

You and I, and all of our fellow human beings, will never be safe while children are abused by their parents. The world paid for the ruthless blows of Alois by making the young Hitler impervious to human feelings, human compassion, and human dignity and worth.

The World War II price tag for society's tradition of poisonous pedagogy was 40 million lives plus countless others wounded and maimed, families separated, possessions lost, and cities destroyed. In the nuclear third millennium, humankind may pay an increasingly horrible price for abusing its precious children.

Most of the people on earth today were born after World War II. Hitler seems quite remote. But what about the constant threat of injured adult/children who become dictators in Latin America, Africa, Asia, and Europe?

Abused children who grow up to rule their nation are missing vital parts of their whole-selves. *They sincerely believe they are serving their nation by the rivers of blood they create.* (For example, Saddam Hussein.) A half million human beings in Rwanda were murdered in a few months by other humans who had split off the compassionate, loving, gentle part of their true-selves.

Modern killing devices (nuclear missiles, poison gas, biological warfare) can possibly wipe out humanity. We are gradually arranging for the demise of *Homo sapiens* by ruining our environment. We urgently need to reshape our life-styles and our political and economic priorities to support peace and goodwill, and protect the ecology of the precious planet on which we live.

> *Achieving dynamic changes in our parenting skills is an international emergency today. Without vastly improved parenting skills, all other attempts to solve the problems of society will be blunted or will fail! Pruning and propping up a tree will not be helpful if the roots are rotten.*

Over half of the German terrorists in recent years have been the children of Protestant ministers. The ministers had sternly crushed the aliveness of their children so that they would *"act"* like ideal adults: considerate, unselfish, self-controlled, grateful, good, responsive, well-behaved, agreeable, undemanding, and meek. They must not appear wilful, headstrong, or defiant. When these sons and daughters in their teens discovered terrorist groups, their unconscious minds were like time bombs waiting to explode. They were repressing some of their own childhood development stages they had not been *free* to live out. Alice Miller poses the question that if terrorists kill or take innocent women and children hostage in the service of a grand and idealistic cause, are they really doing anything different from what had been done to them? They were projecting their childhood pain. When they were little children full of vitality, their parents had offered them up as human sacrifices to a grand pedagogic purpose and lofty religious values. No doubt these ministers (who taught Christ's love) felt they were performing a great and good deed by "properly" training their children. How wrong we can be![5]

We're All Wounded

The old style of parenting that most of us had to survive was ignorant of the life-damaging, false-self programming going into our unconscious mind. *All of us have a wounded child inside us.* Unless we reclaim the missing parts of our true-self, we cannot become the alive, creative, life-affirming, kind, generous, warm, and loving person that is our true-self birthright. When we murder parts of the souls of our children, they have no choice but to pass on to their children the same abusive ways they painfully experienced as a child. Without retraining, how could they parent differently? *And "they" are us!*

We live today in a dangerous society that is increasing in violence, mass destruction, and ruthlessness. We are rapidly ruining the quality of life for our descendants. Theft, white collar crime, arson, political scandals, and personal violence are increasing. We are plagued with enormous, escalating violence connected with illegal drugs. Psychopathic, serial-murderer Ted Bundy confessed to 38 murders. His conscious mind didn't know why he repeatedly killed. At this point, perhaps the reader is sensing the bloody footprints of the combined Object and Time Quirks. The old jungle brain was serially exploding time bombs to retaliate for his deep injuries. At least thirty-eight women died as innocent victims of the old brain's retaliation for little Ted's rejection by his mother and later, his first romantic partner.

Our ancient styles of parenting create a continuous turmoil between our two brains. This book has been written in the hope that it will awaken us to the Armageddon (nuclear war and environmental deterioration) we may face in the 21st century. When we begin to skillfully parent both the conscious and unconscious minds of our children, we can turn our "civilization" around. We will begin to pass on to future generations their true-self birthright of understanding, compassion, and love—instead of the increasing violence, fear, guilt, and shame that blight our lives today.

In the next chapter, we will discuss what our species must quickly do to give our children a future on Planet Earth.

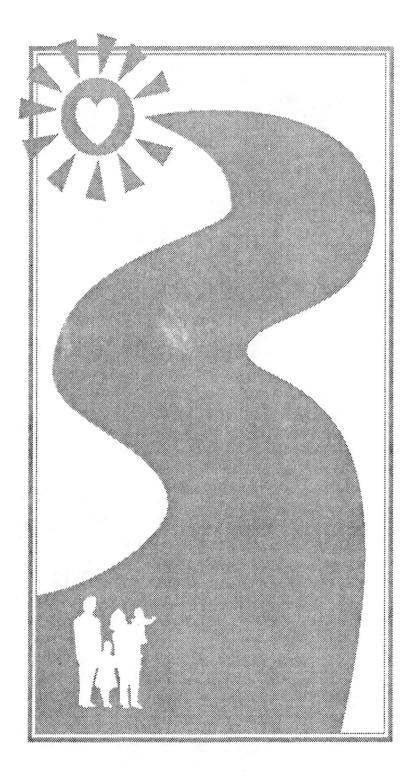

23

Our Planetary Survival

We are now capable of exterminating all human life by either nuclear war or by destroying the life-supporting environment of our planet. Our quirks have given us a world of turmoil that impacts the happiness of all of us. This chapter describes a practical solution. Many of our wisest thinkers tell us that the tried-and-proven way described in this chapter offers the *only chance* humanity has for a future on earth!

N o one has guaranteed that our species will be eternal—any more than the dinosaurs had such a guarantee. We have escalating problems such as crime, drug addiction, fatherless children, divorce, human rights violations, political deception, economic greed, and a lowering of the nourishing quality of the food we eat, the water we drink, and the air we breathe. Power-based dictators (trying to regain self-esteem and self-confidence lost in childhood) keep about 40 wars going on throughout our planet—continually trying to settle disagreements in blood. When our false-self gets some power, it often tries to control other people—and take what they have.

> *Scientists tell us that a global nuclear war can kill off all life except insects and grasses. Do we really need more death and destruction to learn the lessons that life is offering our species? Haven't we fallen enough from our true-selves?*

Our "Wild West" World

At the end of the last century, the American "Wild West" made the transition that our world must make today. In that raw society, every desperado carried his own gun and usurped the duties of lawmaker, policeman, judge, jury, and executioner—sometimes all within 20 seconds! ("You don't talk to

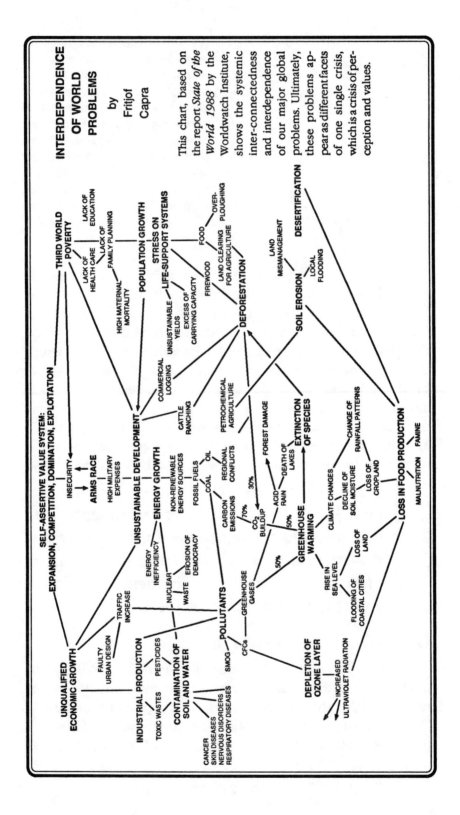

INTERDEPENDENCE OF WORLD PROBLEMS
by Fritjof Capra

This chart, based on the report *State of the World 1988* by the Worldwatch Institute, shows the systemic inter-connectedness and interdependence of our major global problems. Ultimately, these problems appear as different facets of one single crisis, which is a crisis of perception and values.

me like that. . . .") No one was safe until the guns were taken off the hips of frontiersmen and put on the hip of a sheriff who enforced laws passed by an elected legislature.

The world today has no enforced international law with a binding international court to determine who is guilty or innocent. Our world will be a dangerous, explosive place until we settle disputes *legally*—instead of *lethally*. It will remain a killing field for injured false-selves projecting their childhood pain onto innocent humans. Terrorists will continue to murder under the righteous banner of patriotism. We live today in international anarchy.

Tom Hudgens, president of the Association to Unite the Democracies, has pointed out that *no international war in the last century has been started by a democracy attacking another democratic country!* It's only the dictators or absolute rulers who keep bathing us in blood—and burden us with enormous military expenditures. Hudgens asks:

Is it enough to keep abreast of world affairs and to be an "informed citizen?" Is it enough to read about ethnic wars and contribute occasionally to the relief of refugees? Is it enough to write your representative and demand action? Is it enough to wish there were something you could do to render order out of all the chaos in the world—and then to acknowledge with regret that there isn't?

There *is* a way to resolve differences between nations and ethnic communities. It is the idea behind the success of that 200-year-old experiment in problem solving—the United States of America. Formulated by the Constitutional Convention of 1787 and further defined by two centuries of precedent, it is the idea of *federation*.

Through federation it is possible to bring together different interests, factions, regions, racial and ethnic groups—even nations—that otherwise might see armed conflict as the only mechanism to protect their interests. A federation of nation-states gives us methods short of war for peacefully resolving previously unsolvable conflicts between neighboring adversaries. Federalism is the *one idea* offering a mechanism for ensuring world peace.

What is federation? It is a structure of government in which the sovereign people of various regions or nations agree to assign certain powers to their respective states or nations. Other powers are constitutionally assigned to a

We Must Replace the *Law of Force* With the *Force of Law.*

The federal idea, which our Founding Fathers applied in their historical act of political creation in the eighteenth century, can be applied in this twentieth century in the larger context of the world of free nations—if we will but match our forefathers in courage and vision.

Nelson A. Rockefeller
U.S. Vice President

Betting on deterrence to continue to save us from nuclear annihilation is like building your house on the side of a volcano and hoping it will never erupt.

Tom A. Hudgens
Assn. to Unite the Democracies

It may be just a matter of time before the concepts of our Founding Fathers are extended to the entire human race. True, many think this is a dream, but the real dreamers may be those who expect that their children will make it, given on the one hand an arms race virtually out of control, expanding political terrorism, global pollution and nuclear proliferation, and on the other hand the rickety and inadequate global structure to contain these threats to human survival.

Eric Cox, Field Director
World Federalist Association

The only security for Americans today, or for any people, is in the creation of a system of world order that enables nations to retain sovereignty over their own cultures and institutions but that creates a workable authority for regulating the behavior of nations in their relationships with one another.

Norman Cousins, President
World Federalist Association

The United States should capitalize on the new enlightenment at work in the world by dedicating itself to taking the lead in bringing into being an effective world security arrangement, a world governed by law.

Major General Jack Kidd
United States Air Force (Ret.)

Unless some effective supranational government can be set up and brought quickly into action, the prospects of peace and human progress are dark and doubtful.

Winston Churchill
British Prime Minister

We must create world-wide law and law enforcement as we outlaw world-wide war and weapons.

John F. Kennedy
U.S. President

We Must Settle International Disputes
Legally—Not *Lethally*.

World federation is an idea that will not die. More and more people are coming to realize that peace must be more than an interlude if we are to survive; that peace is a product of law and order; that law is essential if the force of arms is not to rule the world.

William O. Douglas
Justice, U.S. Supreme Court

I believe at some future day, the nations of the earth will agree upon some sort of congress which will take cognizance of international questions of difficulty and whose decisions will be as binding as the decisions of our Supreme Court are upon us.

Ulysses S. Grant
Civil War General, U. S. Pres.

Resolve that to insure world peace and disarmament among nations, we United Methodists of the Rocky Mountain Conference urge the President and the Congress of the United States, in concert with all other willing nations, to call a World Constitutional Convention to reform the United Nations into a federal, representative world government...

United Methodist Church
Rocky Mountain Conference

The international community should support a system of laws to regularize international relations and maintain the peace in the same manner that law governs national order.

Pope John Paul II

I know war as few other men now living know it, and nothing to me is more revolting. I have long advocated its complete abolition as its very destructiveness on both friend and foe has rendered it useless as a means of settling international disputes.

General Douglas MacArthur
Address to U.S. Congress

Henceforth, every nation's foreign policy must be judged at every point by one consideration: does it lead us to a world of law and order or does it lead us back to anarchy and death?

Albert Einstein
Physicist

The world no longer has a choice between force and law. If civilization is to survive, it must choose the rule of law.

Dwight Eisenhower
Five-Star General, U. S. Pres.

larger, "federal" governing body; i.e., a group of federated nations having a directly-elected and representative central legislature, an executive branch to enforce laws they pass, and a system of courts. In so doing they create for themselves the means, under law, to resolve disputes between and among themselves. The United States of America, composed of fifty sovereign states, is an example; the proposed European Union is another. Ultimately only the creation of a strong and viable *international* federation can provide a firm foundation for world peace.

Just as no federation could survive an attempt to combine a democracy with a dictatorship, so no federation of states or regions could function without a foundation in democracy providing all their citizens a direct voice in their own governance.

The foreign policies of the world's experienced democracies should be directed, not just toward a cessation of hostilities wherever they may occur, not just toward the establishment of democratic institutions, but toward the *resolving of conflicts through the creation of a viable federation*. Laws, not guns or terror, should be the weapons of choice. Disagreements would be resolved by battalions of attorneys fighting in court—not by battalions of soldiers shooting and bombing people.

Federation is the one approach to problem solving that is working—in the United States, in Germany, in Canada, in Australia, in Switzerland, and elsewhere. And it is the one idea that can resolve the ethnic rivalries now threatening the peace of the world. Our children will not be safe until we create a democratic federation to provide world stability through the rule of law.

Appendix VI has the addresses of two organizations that are working to create a safer world by replacing the law of force by the force of law. They need our support.[1]

Benjamin B. Ferencz, a world-known international attorney, was a chief prosecutor at the Nuremburg war crimes trials. Since World War II, Dr. Ferencz has devoted his life to helping us have a future on earth. He tells us:

Substituting an effective *peace system* for the present *war system* would save a fortune by eliminating waste, mismanagement, and the present need for a continuing arms race. The United States would no longer have to be called upon to be the policeman of the world. It is up to the public to persuade the politicians. If the leaders won't lead, let the

ROAD MAP TO INTERNATIONAL HEAVEN OR HELL

HEAVEN OR HELL AMONG NATIONS ARE ALWAYS ONLY ONE SHARED FEELING-THOUGHT AWAY

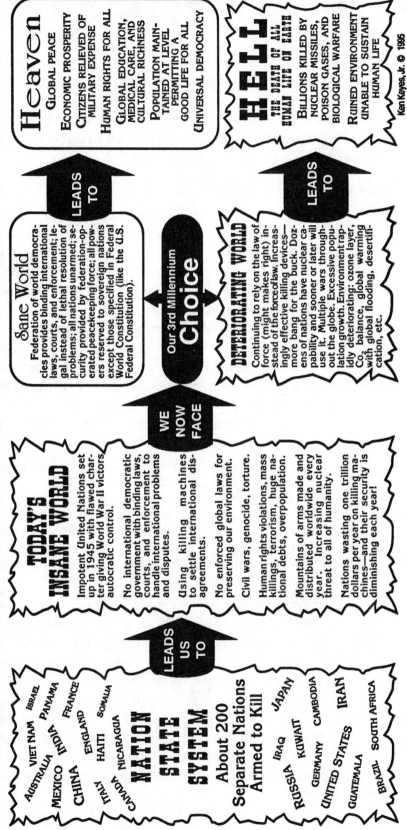

Heaven

- GLOBAL PEACE
- ECONOMIC PROSPERITY
- CITIZENS RELIEVED OF MILITARY EXPENSE
- HUMAN RIGHTS FOR ALL
- GLOBAL EDUCATION, MEDICAL CARE, AND CULTURAL RICHNESS
- POPULATION MAINTAINED AT LEVEL PERMITTING A GOOD LIFE FOR ALL
- UNIVERSAL DEMOCRACY

HELL
THE DEATH OF ALL HUMAN LIFE ON EARTH

- BILLIONS KILLED BY NUCLEAR MISSILES, POISON GASES, AND BIOLOGICAL WARFARE
- RUINED ENVIRONMENT UNABLE TO SUSTAIN HUMAN LIFE

LEADS TO

Sane World

Federation of world democracies provides binding international laws, courts, and enforcement; legal instead of lethal resolution of problems; all nations unarmed; security provided by federation-operated peacekeeping force; all powers reserved to sovereign nations except those specified in Federal World Constitution (like the U.S. Federal Constitution).

Our 3rd Millennium
Choice

LEADS TO

DETERIORATING WORLD

Continuing to rely on the law of force (might makes right) instead of the force of law. Increasingly effective killing devices—more bang for the buck. Dozens of nations have nuclear capability and sooner or later will use it. Multiple wars throughout the globe. Excessive population growth. Environment rapidly deteriorating: ozone layer, CO_2 balance, global warming with global flooding, desertification, etc.

WE NOW FACE

TODAY'S INSANE WORLD

Impotent United Nations set up in 1945 with flawed charter giving World War II victors autocratic control.

No international democratic government with binding laws, courts, and enforcement to handle international problems and disputes.

Using killing machines to settle international disagreements.

No enforced global laws for preserving our environment.

Civil wars, genocide, torture.

Human rights violations, mass killings, terrorism, huge national debts, overpopulation.

Mountains of arms made and distributed worldwide every year. Increasing nuclear threat to all of humanity.

Nations wasting one trillion dollars per year on killing machines—and their security is diminishing each year!

LEADS US TO

NATION STATE SYSTEM
About 200 Separate Nations Armed to Kill

AUSTRALIA VIET NAM ISRAEL PANAMA FRANCE
MEXICO INDIA ENGLAND SOMALIA ITALY HAITI
CANADA NICARAGUA CHINA JAPAN IRAQ KUWAIT
CAMBODIA RUSSIA GERMANY UNITED STATES IRAN
GUATEMALA BRAZIL SOUTH AFRICA

people lead and the leaders will follow. It is time for people everywhere to stop dreaming and start screaming: "We've had enough!"

In *Planethood*, coauthored by Ben Ferencz and myself, we present what we must do—and how to do it so that our grandchildren will have a future on Planet Earth.

The New Millennium

As we enter the new millennium, we need to survey the choices before us. An old Chinese proverb warns us that if we continue the way we're going, we'll end up where we're headed. Is this what we want? Is this the best that our brilliant intellects and feeling hearts can aspire to? I've written this book to show that many answers are available today to explain how we got into our predicament, what keeps us there—and how we can escape from our "species trap."

U. S. President Harry Truman was a scrappy, practical man who fought for legislation that met the needs of the people. He did not hesitate to oppose out-dated traditions. This is how he summed up what humanity must do to solve forever the insanity of war:

> When Kansas and Colorado have a quarrel over water in the Arkansas River, they don't call out the National Guard in each state and go to war over it. They bring suit in the Supreme Court of the United States and abide by the decision. There isn't a reason in the world why we cannot do that internationally. . . . It will be just as easy for nations to get along in a republic of the world as it is for you to get along in the republic of the United States.[2]

In our final chapter, we'll share a vision of a beautiful future for us—and our children. With global television and up-to-date educational technology, we can go beyond the quirks that create our lifetraps and species traps. No one knows how much time we have. I hope the reader will sense that we must wake up and eliminate world anarchy among our 200 nation-states. We must create a new world order governed by an international congress elected by the *people* of democratic nations—with global law enforcement and a world court. This is the only way we can give future generations a world free of wars and want.

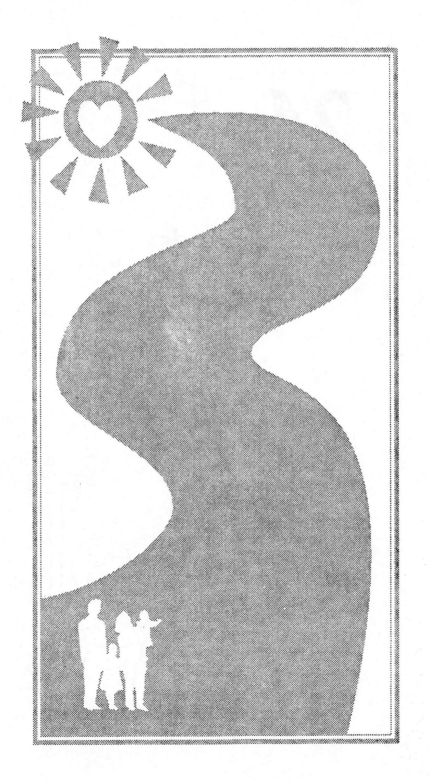

24

It's in Our Hands

We've waited too long for others to save us. Every year the future for *Homo sapiens* seems darker. Each of us must take responsibility for the future of humanity. Like Atlas, we must carry the world on our shoulders. And each of us will be capable of playing our part as we coordinate our head and our heart.

As long as we are deprived of the wholeness of our true-self, we'll be like Don Quixote attacking the arms of a windmill, deceived by the illusion that he was valiantly defending against fire-puffing dragons. The false-self constantly keeps us in a trance. What it feels is real is just an illusion. And so we beat our heads bloody fighting illusions by projecting our childhood injuries and steam-boiler rage onto innocent people. This false-self trance keeps us feeling separate from our true-selves, other people, and the world around us.

Three-to-One Against You

Suppose you're engaged in a battle in which you have two allies and yourself on one side, and one enemy to be conquered. Including yourself, that's three-to-one odds in your favor. It's a pretty good situation. However, let's suppose you don't recognize your allies—and instead mistake them for enemies. And then, to make matters even worse, suppose you don't recognize the real enemy at all.

Since you don't recognize your real enemy, it is hidden by your ignorance. So the enemy operates in the open—continually slashing and wounding you. You constantly mistake the source of your pain—and you lash back at your allies or criticize yourself instead of your real enemy. So because of tactical mistakes, you're creating odds of three-to-one against you. Your chances in such a battle are awful.

And that's our predicament. Our allies in our personal growth are (1) the people in our lives and (2) the situations we're in, and (3) ourselves. The people and situations in the ever-changing melodrama of our lives are there to teach us something. Perhaps it's patience, compassion, forgiveness, generosity, or unconditional love—or to help us recognize the cancers of our false-self that are killing us. But in our false-self trance, we constantly mistake our allies—the people around us and the situations in our lives. We play the "victim" role and fight an illusory enemy we think is outside us.

Our false-self demands are wrapped in anger, fear, irritation, jealousy, resentment—and unhappiness. We blame other people for "doing it to us." We do not compassionately understand that they are just living out their true- and false-self programming, too. In the dramas of everyday life, they are providing us with the painful "teachings" we need to work on our false-self demands—so we can reclaim our original true-self. We may not know that our true-self is our *own best friend* when we know who we really are.

The Real Enemy

The greatest tragedy of this confused fog in which we live our lives is that we don't recognize our real enemy. So we are constantly injured by an enemy we did not even know was there! Our real enemies are the quirks between our two brains that deprive us of the combined power of our feeling old brain and our thinking new brain. These quirks turn our lives over to our demanding false-self, which keeps our lives in constant turmoil—which we pass on to our children.

We forget that what our true-self really wants is not accumulations of prestige, power, pride, possessions, and pelf (money). These "Five P's" only offer the illusion of future happiness to our love-starved false-selves. The joys and contentment meretriciously dangled by the "Five P's" never seem to yield a satisfying life of relaxed enjoyment. There's nothing "bad" about them in themselves. However, when your life is wrapped around demanding them, you'll never find inner peace and relaxed enjoyment.

When we have a perceptual shift that our lives are really set up to work, and our true birthright is to enjoy the happiness of heaven on earth, a miracle begins to occur. We find that there are three-to-one odds constantly working in our favor. Our shift in perception transforms other people and the world around us into allies. As we reclaim our true-self as an ally, we feel and know that we are whole, complete, precious, valuable, worthy, and lovable—just as we are. *We don't need to prove it either to ourselves or anyone else.* We now have three-to-one odds in our favor.

Love Is Born by Experiencing Love

As we learn the lessons life offers us, we begin to experience that compassion, patience, and unconditional love are the supreme nutrients of our body and mind—the vitamins of our spirit. A child who does not *experience* unconditional love from the cradle on will be handicapped in its growth. *Most parents don't know how to give unconditional love and heartfelt warmth when they don't approve of their child's behavior.* That's because their parents didn't know how to do it. So they couldn't give us what they didn't have.

Most of us haven't learned that we can unconditionally love someone—and also lovingly tell them that we don't like what they're doing or saying, and we want them to stop. A mother can love her child, and yet not like the way it throws up its food. We can love the person—even if we don't like what they do or say. What people do or say is largely determined by their programming. We are not our programming. And as the Second Wisdom Principle tells us, everyone is doing the best they can with the unskillful programming they now have.

Our true-self is always lovable—even when smothered by a false-self. Sometimes we may have to oppose the harmful actions of others. And that's okay. But we defile ourselves and further damage our love-starved society when we withdraw our understanding, compassion, and heartfelt love from the human beings we oppose in the *drama* of our lives.

Perhaps the greatest destroyer of our true-self is our unmet childhood need for *unconditional heart-to-heart love* from our

255

caretakers. Love is a bridge of caring from heart to heart—a process of letting go of fear—and opening our hearts to each other. Too many of us scratch out our lives in a lonely emotional desert seldom watered by the flow of human warmth and touching. Too often parents have yelled at us, "I hate you when you do that." Caretakers may barter "love" for behavior they want in their child. ("You're a bad girl and I don't love you when you do that.") This is not real love.

> **True love has no price tag—no strings attached. It's given as a gift from the heart. It's unconditional.**

Love is a heart feeling generated by the old brain. Genuine love may lead us to help others as they would like to be helped—or it may not. (A mother may unconditionally love her young child and still not buy the BB gun it wants.) One's actions depend on the circumstances. Thus love is not helpful actions—although helpful actions may flow from love. You can't decide if a person loves you by whether they do everything you want. Love is a heart feeling of emotional oneness— no boundaries or ego barriers block the bridge of love between your heart and another's heart. We feel loved when we are hugged, smiled at, and warmly told "I love you."

Love is not sex—even though sex is called "making love." Sex can happen with love or without love. As we mentioned, love is a feeling—not an act. Love, like the color purple, must be experienced. You can't describe in words what you *experience* as "purple" to someone who's never seen it.

Many parents tell themselves they are loving their children when they dutifully meet their basic needs—food, shelter, medical attention, clothing, schooling, etc. Some people have never experienced unconditional love from another human being:

> Mary's parents did not know how to give her genuine heart love—a love she was entitled to just because she was their child. They only knew how to do their duty as a mother and father. That's the way they were parented. They thought love was just taking care of their child.

Young children sensitively feel love when it comes from the heart—even when they're in the womb! Mary's true-self naturally loves. We're all born with the "seeds" of love within us. But her mother couldn't nurture this part of Mary's original wholeness. Since Mary did not experience heart-to-heart love, she grew up thinking that love is supporting one's well-being. She programmed a false-self that disowned her natural ability to feel closeness and human warmth. As an adult, she could not love or feel loved—even when someone loved her. Her strategic adaptation was to let herself feel loved only when someone did something she wanted them to do.

When she married, she often said, "If you really loved me, you would. . . ." Her husband was confused when she used "love equals support" to tell whether she was loved. No one can do what she wants all the time. Her husband had his own interests and needs. Thus her feeling of being loved is intermittent and usually diminishes as the drama of her false-self plays out in a relationship. And this keeps her in a hopeless, lifelong search for "someone who really loves me."

When we truly love from our heart, we love someone just because they are there. We don't love them because they need love or because they deserve our love—or have earned our love. Love is not love unless we freely give it away.

Illusions of the False-Self Ego

Our civilization, with its constant wars, crime, and callous attitude toward human rights, is far from the best we humans can do. A new generation of parents who nurture both their own and their children's conscious and unconscious minds is essential to make our society a "paradise on earth."

On the next page, we have a list of 12 behaviors that your false-self thinks will help your life work better. Our caregivers often modeled them. Popular TV shows are built on our unconscious recognition of *our own childhood pain* from these 12

12 POPULAR ILLUSIONS OF
THE FALSE-SELF

1. Forgiveness is weakness.

2. You change others by criticizing them.

3. Your quick anger is the best way to set personal boundaries that will prevent others from taking advantage of you.

4. Your defensiveness is beneficial for it shows people that you are right.

5. You protect yourself by attacking people and/or withdrawing love in order to control them through fear, guilt, and shame.

6. Blaming yourself is important to maintain your high ideals—and show humility.

7. Blaming and shaming others is necessary to make them do things right.

8. Revenge or "paying back" helps you to establish justice.

9. It shows weakness to ever let yourself be vulnerable.

10. Righteous indignation and judging others proves what a good character you have.

11. You help a person correct their errors by interrupting them when they don't agree with you.

12. Manipulating and deceiving others can help you become successful.

false-self behaviors. Our loud laughter at high-rated TV serials is a response of our old brain to *our own pain*—not to the pain of the characters in the TV show!

Your rational mind may protest and make this list wrong. Perhaps your false-self will try to dismiss it by calling it "idealistic." ("You can't live your life that way—people would take advantage of you.") However, if you ask your true-self, it will heartily say, "Yes." Resolving to avoid these 12 separating behaviors elevates your life to a new dimension. It can be an enormous step toward reclaiming your true-self—and living in relaxed enjoyment with loving relationships.

A Vision of Our Future

And so, as sons and daughters of the great universal energy of love and unity, we can learn the head and heart skills needed to live in relaxed enjoyment. We can appreciate the beautiful future that lies within our grasp. We can understand that what we needed to protect us in childhood has made us combative, self-centered, and unhappy. And we can reclaim our true-self.

> *We can notice the experiences we create as the daily parade of people and events passes by us. We are discovering that our feelings and thoughts are altered by the "filters" of our minds. We are learning how we create our moment-to-moment experience of ourselves, others, and the world around us. We can use what life gives us to increase our skill in shifting our perceptions to create understanding, compassion, acceptance, and love. From the hard blows life gives us, we can learn to reclaim our true-selves. WE CAN LOVE IT ALL.*

We know that paradise on earth is only one shared feeling-thought away from us at all times! And the challenge of our generation is to rapidly educate our fellow humans so that heart-to-heart love, cooperation, joy, play, and happiness can be our ever-present reality.

But there's no free lunch. There's a price to be paid. We've got to learn how to tune back in to our whole, loving true-self. This can begin at any time when we enroll in the strenuous curriculum offered by the University of Life—and learn from the lessons that our lives give us.

We cannot nurture our children well until we begin to heal ourselves. Children copy what we actually do—not what we tell them they ought to do. Educators have often warned us that the future of humanity literally depends on "the hand that rocks the cradle." Until we become skillful parents who nurture *both* the conscious and unconscious minds of our valuable children, we will continue to create more hell on earth.

It's All Us

It is humbling to realize that all of us descended from a single cell organism in an ancient slimy pool. If we were to check our genealogical tree back 250 million years, we would find that our ancestors were reptiles running around on all fours with an outlandish sail-back and a long tail. Their names are Mr. and Mrs. Scale E. *Dimetrodon*.

We've come a long way, and we still have a way to go. From a cosmic perspective, all of the people, animals, and plants on earth are co-creating the great adventure of life together on this planet. We're all part of the same tree of life.

In important things, all of us humans are more alike than different. We all have a human heart. We have human feelings. And we're all doing the very best we can, given our genetic equipment, our instincts, and the learnings we picked up as we have lived our lives. And we all have beneficial positive intentions and motivations that center around feeling we are safe, loved, lovable, capable, and okay.

Let's dedicate ourselves in the new millennium to increasingly treasure the diamond of our whole, authentic, true-self. Our loving true-self contains the seeds for unfolding our divine spirit of love. This sparkling birthright is there waiting for us.

> *Right now is the first day in the rest of our life. Let's focus on the inner work that will give us a wonderful life from now on.*

We all have a basic goodness. We always have beneficial positive intentions. We now know that we can throw away our *victim* consciousness and recognize our power as *creators* of our experience!

We're all sons and daughters of the tree of life. All of us, in our innermost hearts, want a happy, fulfilling life. The good news is that we only have to reclaim it!

Appendix I

Inventory of
Childhood Survival Strategies

Because your critical inner parent is probably so good at criticizing you, I again congratulate you for the false-self strategies you have been using. Because of unskillful parenting, it was smart for you to split off parts of your true-self in the ways you did. You had no choice to survive physically, emotionally, intellectually, and/or spiritually.

Please, believe you were a good human being who did what you could do when you created your false-self parts. At age three, with limited abilities, you did the best you could to minimize pain and maximize satisfaction in *the particular world* of your caretakers. *Unfortunately, what was necessary in childhood became a locked-in habit in adulthood.* This inventory can help you identify your false-self adaptations.

These false-self habits (which feel more natural than your disowned true-self behaviors), are hurting your happiness today. Although you are not responsible for what happened back then, you are *fully responsible today* for discovering your false-self adaptations, resolving to heal these childhood injuries, and then doing what you need to heal back into the whole, authentic human being you really are! By using this inventory, you can begin to target the growth you need to reclaim your true-self.

Your day-to-day experience with your childhood caretakers played a powerful part in your choice of character strategies. And there are other factors that may have influenced your choice. A small-boned, long-limbed, thin child may not be able to get the Tough-Generous Strategy operating as easily as a big-chested, big-boned, big-muscled child. A slow-moving, heavy-set child may choose a Burdened-Enduring Strategy. A child who is plagued with constant illness during these formative years may pick a strategy (perhaps Dependent-Endearing) that is not attractive to a child with robust health and a strong identity who may go for the Self-Relying Strategy. By thoughtfully marking this inventory you will greatly increase your insights into the thoughts and actions of yourself and people around you. By understanding and labeling your adopted strategies, you will take a giant step in personal growth.

Sometimes a parent dies or leaves—and is replaced by a new mate. Sometimes older siblings or other family members will abuse a dependent child. In order to get the love, nurturing, support, and safety we needed, most of us developed several childhood strategies. And this makes us whack off more pieces of our true-self to cope with unskillful caretaking.

To get the full benefit of this inventory, you will need to exactly follow the instructions on the next two pages. Check back frequently and reread an instruction after you have completed it to be sure you have done it precisely.

Please do not innovate or shortcut. This inventory has been designed to give you life-enhancing insights into each of the eight childhood survival strategies when you carefully follow the procedures. Allow plenty of time—perhaps several hours. As you guide yourself by the instructions, you will be using your mind to examine your mind. The experience of thoughtfully marking the inventory can empower you to make life choices that enrich your life.

Instructions for Using the Inventory of Childhood Survival Strategies[1]

1 *Defining the Split of Your Whole True-self:*

    A. READ all six items listed under "Original True-Self Feelings" (Column 3) on page 267 describing the Sensitive-Withdrawn strategy.

    B. WRITE in Column 4 a number from 0 to 100% that indicates how much of each true-self part described in Column 3 applies to you *today*. Use this scale:

        0% = None of this true-self feeling is available to me today.

        25% = Seldom available.

        50% = Often available.

        75% = Usually available.

        100% = This part of my true-self is fully available to me today.

        This identifies the degree in which parts of your original, whole true-self survived in your childhood—or you have healed so they are available to you today.

    C. REPEAT A and B above with the other seven character strategies through page 281.

2 *Identifying Childhood Abuses:*

    A. READ every word on each *entire* page from top to bottom on pages 266 through 281. Include sections labeled "Cause," "False-Self Beliefs," etc. Study these eight double pages slowly and absorbingly *to get the feel of each strategy*. Notice which of the eight strategies are used by people you know well—your father, mother, sisters or brothers, relatives, mate, children, friends, teachers, boss, workers, etc. This will help you deepen your understanding of the strategies. It's best to thoroughly study the eight strategies before going on to "B."

    B. MARK with a colored pen or highlighter all the words, phrases, or sentences *outside of the five columns* that apply to you on the double pages of each of the eight strategies.

    C. Mark the words or sentences in Columns 1 and 2 that applied to you in childhood, but do not mark in Columns 3, 4, or 5.

3 *Identifying What You Need to Be Whole:*

    A. MARK an "X" on the same line in Column 5 if you marked any item in Column 2. Do this with each of the eight childhood survival strategies.

    B. CIRCLE the "Original True-Self Feelings" part in Column 3 on the same line whenever you marked from 0% to 50% in Column 4.

NOTE: The items you have circled in Column 3 are your growth targets. Unless you have healed them, they are parts of your whole, true-self that you are missing today. You vitally need to fully reclaim these repressed parts of your true-self to become the whole, authentic person that is your birthright.

4 *Identifying False-Self Character Strategies:*
A. Thumb through the double-page descriptions of the eight Character Strategies. Notice which strategy (such as Persuasive: Charming-Endearing) you have marked the most with a colored pen or highlighter when doing Step 2, Part B. Enter the name of this strategy in the first line below under "False-Self Strategies I Use."
B. Rank as "No. 2" the name of the strategy you marked the second most. Then similarly identify your third strategy, and write the name below.
C. For every false-self strategy you ranked below, you are missing a part or parts of your authentic true-self. In the "True-Self Parts to Reclaim" column below, on the same line that you listed a false-self strategy, write in all of the original, true-self feelings you circled in the six lines in Column 3.

False-Self Strategies I Use   *True-Self Parts to Reclaim*

1. _____   _____

2. _____   _____

3. _____   _____

Your Growth Targets
When you have completed these four steps on each of the eight character strategies, you will have identified which strategies you used to avoid pain and/or get your needs met in childhood. It was smart for you to use these false-self strategies to get through childhood with your caregivers. Congratulations for finding them so you could protect yourself!

Unfortunately these false-self character strategies you used automatically in childhood are life-damaging today. As an adult, you now have physical, emotional, intellectual, and spiritual strengths, plus experience, patience, perseverance, and many other abilities that were not available to you in childhood. Now it's time to let go of the compulsiveness of these false-self strategies—and reclaim the disowned parts of your true-self.

1 CONTAINING

Sensitive-Withdrawn Childhood Strategy

① Child's Abusive Experience With Caretakers	② Child's Survival Strategy (Adopted False-Self)
"I feel hostility, coldness, and abandonment."	"I'll protect myself by withdrawing, freezing, or bracing myself."
"I'm ignored or attacked."	"I'll protect myself by hiding from people and not expressing myself."
"I'm not accepted, loved, or cared about."	"I'll live in my own world of thought and fantasy."
"I'm usually afraid or in terror. It's not safe to need."	"I'll live without feeling my feelings, and I won't ask for anything."
"I don't belong here."	"I'll keep a low profile so people don't notice me."
"People are cold and hateful."	"I'll avoid personal contact, and deal with the world through my ideas."

CAUSE: Child feels rejected; child is unwelcome; mothering person either hates child before birth, or birth is traumatic and not followed by love from mother; mother is cold and hateful; child may be left alone a lot or abused; mother punishes the spontaneous energy of the child; child is extremely sensitive; environment is harsh; child is not treated gently and lovingly.

FALSE-SELF BELIEFS: There's something wrong with me; I'm no good; I'll be destroyed if I allow my life force to come through; I'm on the wrong planet; I can't trust my body; I don't belong here; I'm not welcome; they want me dead.

FEELINGS: Underlying terror; never really enters the world of feelings; fails to contact feelings; fury; hateful feelings from mothering person leads to terror of being destroyed; afraid spontaneous feelings and behaviors will blow them apart; unsafe; confused; feels isolated, alien, flat affect.

CHARACTER STRATEGY: Kurtz explains, "A person in a sensitive-withdrawn pattern uses the strategy of minimizing self-expression and emotional

This Sensitive-Withdrawn Strategy

may be used by the unconscious mind when caretakers
do not satisfy the child's natural right, and/or need to:

Exist and Bond. "I have a right to be alive, safe, and welcome."

③ Original True-Self Feelings	④ Percentage of the True-Self Feeling Adjoining in Col. 3 That I Have Today.	⑤ This Part of My True-Self (Col. 3) Was Suppressed.
"People are warm and there for me when I need them."		
"I am welcome here in the world."		
"I naturally get love, human warmth, and caring."		
"I feel safe and secure."		
"I'm a part of a whole."		
"People are safe, gentle, and loving."		

contact with self and others. The pattern reflects threats to survival and the core material will organize perceptions, feelings and actions around a theme of inescapable danger. On the surface, the basic uncertainty will be about whether or not one is welcome or belongs here. Feeling like strangers in a strange and dangerous land, these people strongly limit self-expression and contact with others. When the pattern is deeply ingrained, some of the following traits show up consistently: the person is withdrawn, shy, prefers isolation, especially under stress; likes to analyze, think, theorize, fantasize, imagine; they may seem cold, without emotions, unfriendly." They are very distant or suspicious in relationships; feel inescapable danger; can't be reached; leave one baffled, puzzled; responses are inappropriate. They are unpredictable; polarize; avoid closeness; remain distant, aloof; lack insight in relationships; overly focused on avoiding and don't want to see.

STRENGTHS: Sensitive; often psychic, intuitive, brilliant, innovative thinkers; imaginative; artists; active fantasy life; extremely perceptive; creative; spiritual; good at understanding the world symbolically.

2 CONSERVING
Dependent-Endearing Childhood Strategy

① Child's Abusive Experience With Caretakers	② Child's Survival Strategy (Adopted False-Self)
"I'm needy, alone, dependent, and abandoned."	"I'll seek help by acting weak, needy, endearing, childlike, dependent, and not understanding."
"No one is here for me."	"I can't meet my needs myself. I'll just look helpless and hopeless."
"I'm abandoned and helpless."	"I'll cling to them, hoping they'll help me."
"People don't want to help me."	"I'll get help by making them take pity on me."
"I feel lonely and abandoned — it's no use to try."	"I give up early, collapse, and want them to take care of me."
"I have to do without and be constantly seeking someone to help me."	"I'll seek their help, but I won't feel nourished even if I get it."

CAUSE: Mothering person is unavailable, for some reason, to meet child's needs; infant doesn't develop trust; child gives up when mother fails to meet needs; child feels deprived; caregiver resents taking care of the child; child is deprived of physical contact, attention, maybe food and nourishment; child cries and mother may feel angry. This pattern may be based on caregiver getting satisfaction from child's dependency and doesn't want it to grow up.

FALSE-SELF BELIEFS: There's no one there for me; everybody's going to leave me; I'm all alone; I can't get support; I feel judged and found wanting; there's something wrong with me; I never get enough; look how miserable I am, please help me.

FEELINGS: Deprivation leads to feelings of weakness; fears being abandoned, left alone; helpless; feels unfulfilled; empty; insecure. They may feel angry, guilty, or resentful toward others.

CHARACTER STRATEGY: Kurtz writes, "A person in a dependent-endearing pattern uses the strategy of seeking support by acting childlike and in need. The pattern reflects a lack of reliable nourishment and the core material will organize perceptions, feelings and actions around themes of poverty, loneliness, abandonment and

This Dependent-Endearing Strategy

may be used by the unconscious mind when caretakers do not satisfy the child's natural right, and/or need to:

Be Needy. "I have a right to need."

③ Original True-Self Feelings	④ Percentage of the True-Self Feeling Adjoining in Col. 3 That I Have Today.	⑤ This Part of My True-Self (Col. 3) Was Suppressed.
"I get willing support from others and can trust people to be helpful."		
"I'm cared for and my needs are met."		
"I feel bonded, and people care about me."		
"People will naturally help me."		
"I have reliable support."		
"I can trust that I'll get my needs met."		

loss. On the surface, the basic uncertainty will be about whether or not one will ever find reliable support. The person may feel there is some tragic flaw in them that makes them unacceptable to others and there is likely to be an inner rage about being abandoned. When this pattern is deeply ingrained, some of the following traits show up consistently: the person tends to give up easily; seeks help often but uses it poorly; has very low expectations, minimizes needs and wants and becomes depressed." They establish closeness on an infantile basis unable or unwilling to take care of themselves; they cling to others; others may at first want to take care of them, later feel drained. May block nourishment by judging help as not "right"; they don't take in what's available; they try but give up easily when not assisted.

STRENGTHS: Interested in others; tuned in to others' needs; easy to trust, talk to; relates easily; nonthreatening; good at the helping professions; affectionate; expresses feelings easily except anger.

NOTE: If the Dependent-Endearing Strategy does not work, the child often shifts to the Self-Relying Strategy to get its needs met.

269

3 SELF-RELYING

Self-Relying Childhood Strategy

① Child's Abusive Experience With Caretakers	② Child's Survival Strategy (Adopted False-Self)
"They don't take care of me. I'm needy and alone."	"I don't want to be let down any more, so I'll do it myself."
"No one is willing to help me."	"I don't need anybody or anything."
"I will be abandoned and helpless."	"I'll keep an emotional distance from others so as to avoid being let down again."
"I have to struggle to get enough."	"Life is tough, but I'll make it by myself."
"I can't rely on others."	"I seek challenges to prove my self-reliance."
"No one hears my needs."	"They didn't hear me, so I won't listen to them."

CAUSE: Child feels deprived; mothering person is unable to help or resents taking care of the child; child is deprived of physical contact, attention, maybe food and nourishment; child cries and mother may feel angry; infant doesn't develop trust.

FALSE-SELF BELIEFS: I don't need anybody; I can do it myself; I don't need support.

FEELINGS: I have to do it myself; no one will help me; I don't need anybody; life's tough; I can do it; if I don't do it, it won't get done right; only the tough survive. I won't get too close emotionally.

CHARACTER STRATEGY: May be rebellious. Kurtz says, "A person in a self-reliant pattern uses the strategy of mobilizing self-support and proving self-reliance. The pattern reflects a decision to take care of oneself and not ever rely on others. The core material will organize perceptions, feelings and actions around themes of challenge and going it alone. Surface behavior

This Self-Relying Strategy
may be used by the unconscious mind when caretakers
do not satisfy the child's natural right, and/or need to:

Be Satisfied. "I have a right to have my needs met."

③ Original True-Self Feelings	④ Percentage of the True-Self Feeling Adjoining in Col. 3 That I Have Today.	⑤ This Part of My True-Self (Col. 3) Was Suppressed.
"I can seek help and don't always have to do it alone."		
"It's O.K. to ask for help."		
"People care about me and want to help me."		
"I can get my needs met without struggling."		
"I can cooperate with others and be a team player."		
"I can listen to others."		

will reflect these themes in activities of personal challenge, like mountain climbing, and in the simple fact of doing things for themselves without expecting help from anyone. . . . When the pattern is deeply ingrained, some of the following traits show up consistently: the person seeks isolation under stress, likes to work alone, is active, takes on challenges, expects no help from others. . . ." They have trouble listening to others; may ask a lot of questions, then not listen to answers; are interested in meeting their own needs; are jealous, inappreciative; are alienated, disconnected from others; have a "nose to the grindstone" resignation. They have a subtle anger experienced more as determination; block nourishment; don't use help available; they are not team players. They want to be the parent – not the child. May select dependent instead of nurturing relationships.

STRENGTHS: Capable and responsible; self-sufficient; interested in helping others.

271

4 COMMANDING
Tough-Generous Childhood Strategy

① Child's Abusive Experience With Caretakers	② Child's Survival Strategy (Adopted False-Self)
"I'm overwhelmed and controlled."	"I'll get my needs met by controlling you."
"I'm humiliated, manipulated, betrayed, and can't trust others."	"I'll deceive you by looking tough, important, and invulnerable."
"I am put down and shamed as weak, inept, and helpless."	"I'll hide my weakness, fears, and insecurities and fool you by acting tough and dangerous."
"People don't care how much they hurt me."	"I won't feel your hurt or mine."
"If I'm close to people, they'll take advantage of me."	"I'll keep you at a distance by not letting you be my equal. I won't show you my feelings."
"I'm hurt, humiliated, and not taken seriously by authority figures."	"I won't be with you unless I'm in control. Then I'll be generous as long as you follow, admire, respect, and are loyal to me."

CAUSE: Child feels powerless; caregivers are pushing the child down; mothering person puts the child down, may try to overpower the child; child feels overwhelmed, controlled, small, weak, powerless.

FALSE-SELF BELIEFS: I won't let anyone force themselves on me; you can't hurt me; I'll show them; you can be close to me as long as you look up to me; people are disposable.

FEELINGS: Except for anger, denies feelings; inferiority complex; feels unimportant; fears being overpowered and overwhelmed; feels alienated from others and longs for intimacy; underlying neediness; lack of guilt and human empathy; ruthless; does not cry.

CHARACTER STRATEGY: Domineering, controlling; hides vulnerability. According to Kurtz, the tough-generous character strategy organizes "perceptions, feelings and actions around using others or being used by them. . . . On the surface, the basic uncertainty will be about whether or not one is respected and in control. The surface behavior will feel 'slick' and elusive. . . . When the pattern is deeply ingrained. . . , [there is] a tendency to secrecy,

This Tough-Generous Strategy
may be used by the unconscious mind when caretakers do not satisfy the child's natural right, and/or need to:

Be Respected. "I have a right to my own identity."

③ Original True-Self Feelings	④ Percentage of the True-Self Feeling Adjoining in Col. 3 That I Have Today.	⑤ This Part of My True-Self (Col. 3) Was Suppressed.
"People are safe and treat me fairly."		
"I can get my needs met by being honest and openly myself."		
"I can be real and show my weakness and needs."		
"My heart sympathizes with people who are in pain."		
"It's O.K. to be vulnerable and show hurt feelings."		
"I can trust people in authority to treat me with respect."		

great difficulty in simply being real and honest with others, and with being vulnerable, showing hurt or weakness. . . . This type... in the street version is criminal and antisocial." They intimidate others by behaving bigger, stronger, more dangerous, more intelligent, richer, more informed, or more important than they are; desire to be on top, the best, the leader. They can't form equal relationships, must be "one up"; can't easily accept favors from others; others may feel a little scared, intimidated. Relationships may be frustrating because you may want more intimacy than they will give. They can be supportive and/or generous to those who admire and respect them; they see intimacy as a fall from status; may fail to wisely evaluate risks; overconfident; act too impulsively.

STRENGTHS: Good leaders; manage people well; ability to be in public view; good with words, powerful speakers; charismatic; creative; versatile; generous; charming; entertaining; cool under fire; perceptive; adventurous.

NOTE: The Commanding and Persuasive strategies both involve deception and self-deception—and are often difficult to perceive in oneself.

273

5 PERSUASIVE
Charming-Manipulative Childhood Strategy

① Child's Abusive Experience With Caretakers	② Child's Survival Strategy (Adopted False-Self)
"I'm humiliated, used, manipulated, and tricked."	"I'll use, charm, and trick you to get what I need."
"People let me down, deceive me, and shame me."	"I'll get my needs met by being indirect, manipulative, secretive, and sly."
"People manipulate and try to fool me."	"I'll fool you by acting friendly and harmless to get your confidence."
"I feel powerless, unimportant, worthless, and taken advantage of."	"I'll get what I want through phony charm and cleverness."
"People mislead me and violate their promises."	"I'll hide my true intentions and seduce you with promises."
"People mistreat and hurt me without caring about my pain and suffering."	"I won't feel my own pain and hurt or the pain and hurt I cause others."

CAUSE: Child feels powerless; forces are pushing the child down; child is deceived and tricked; child feels overwhelmed, controlled, small, weak; mothering person may have been seductive to the child in an attempt to tie him to her; contact is for mother's needs, not child's; child kept weak, not allowed to contribute.

FALSE-SELF BELIEFS: Avoids straight-forward performance. I can get what I want by cleverness, and by persuading and manipulating others. I can only succeed through some form of devious behavior or trickery.

FEELINGS: Denies feelings, especially vulnerability; feels unimportant; fears being overpowered and overwhelmed; feels alienated from others and longs for intimacy; underlying neediness; lack of guilt or remorse.

CHARACTER STRATEGY: Plays seductive, sneaky, psychological games to manipulate people's emotions. Kurtz points out that the charming-manipulative character strategy organizes "perceptions, feelings and actions around being attractive, wanted, avoiding being exposed in some way, caught, found out, humiliated. On the surface, the basic uncertainty will be about whether or not one can have one's needs

This Charming-Manipulative Strategy

may be used by the unconscious mind when caretakers
do not satisfy the child's natural right, and/or need to:

Be Authentic. "I have a right to be an honest person."

③ Original True-Self Feelings	④ Percentage of the True-Self Feeling Adjoining in Col. 3 That I Have Today.	⑤ This Part of My True-Self (Col. 3) Was Suppressed.
"I can get my needs met by being honest and direct."		
"I can be straightforward when asking for what I want."		
"I don't have to be tricky to get support."		
"I can be myself, and be open with people."		
"I can be open and fair."		
"I care if people are hurting, and I can show my hurt and pain to others."		

met in a straightforward way. The expectation is that others will use one's needs and vulnerabilities against them. When the pattern is deeply ingrained, they may try to make themselves attractive. Movements are lithe and seductive"—often with strong sexual overtones and activities. The street version may be antisocial or criminal. People like them because they're soft, loving. They often have followers; they try to control in indirect ways; don't want anyone to have power over them. This type feels insincere and phony to others. They charm others and use them to get their needs met. A relationship may feel frustrating and insecure because you may want more intimacy than

they will give. They nourish others so as to take advantage of them. They don't feel the pain of others. Both charming-manipulative and tough-generous are deceptive—the former about motives and true feelings, the latter about strength and power.

STRENGTHS: Good with words, powerful speakers; charismatic; creative; versatile; generous; charming; entertaining; cool under fire; perceptive, good actors.

NOTE: Both the Commanding and Persuasive strategies involve deception and self-deception—and are often difficult to perceive in oneself.

6 ENDURING
Burdened-Enduring Childhood Strategy

① Child's Abusive Experience With Caretakers	② Child's Survival Strategy (Adopted False-Self)
"I'm pressured and stifled. I get love and approval only when I obey."	"I'll live without asserting myself and comply with others, but I'll resent it."
"I'm a bad person who can't do things right."	"I'm no good, but I'll bear up, wait it out, and prepare for the worst."
"I'm pressured, blamed, and kept submissive."	"I'll avoid feeling suppressed by delay, indirect defiance, or hidden sabotage."
"I'm made to feel guilty if I don't put others' needs ahead of my own."	"I'll give in to you, but I'll secretly get back at you."
"I won't be loved if I say 'no'."	"I'll do what you want, but I'll slow things down and resist."
"I'm not safe if I disagree with you or confront you."	"I insist on being in a down position."

CAUSE: Domineering, demanding, over-controlling caregiver; child feels pressured; mothering person is overbearing, fathering person may be submissive; mother pushes and nags the child; caretaker makes love conditional on obedience; strong focus on eating and defecating; mother is ambitious; wants the child to succeed; child is not allowed to be free and spontaneous; mother uses guilt: "Look how you're hurting me." All attempts at resistance are thwarted; often had thwarted temper tantrums as child; mother emphasizes material needs; denies child's spiritual needs.

FALSE-SELF BELIEFS: I'm a rotten person; I do everything wrong; I'm loved only if I do what people want; I'm hopeless; I'm a martyr; it's not O.K. to have fun.

FEELINGS: Inhibited; hopeless; stuck; feels defeated; has much stored rage; feelings of resentment and loss; spite; feels great guilt.

CHARACTER STRATEGY: According to Kurtz, the burdened-enduring character

This Burdened-Enduring Strategy

may be used by the unconscious mind when caretakers do not satisfy the child's natural right, and/or need to:

Be Self-Determined. "I have a right to assert myself."

③ Original True-Self Feelings	④ Percentage of the True-Self Feeling Adjoining in Col. 3 That I Have Today.	⑤ This Part of My True-Self (Col. 3) Was Suppressed.
"I feel self-esteem and self-confidence and can express and assert my own ideas."		
"I'm O.K. and lovable even if I don't do what you say."		
"I can tell you how I feel, what I think, and what I want."		
"I can both meet my own needs and help others."		
"I can say 'no' to you."		
"I feel equality and self-worth."		

strategy "organizes perceptions, feelings and actions around guilt, inadequacy, inferiority, and avoiding mistakes and hurting others . . . . On the surface, the basic uncertainty will be about whether or not one can be effective, how well they can do things without making a mess of it, and self-worth. This inhibits and delays action. When the pattern is deeply ingrained," they may feel "stuck, impotent, incompetent, and not as attractive or effective" as others. They are passive-aggressive; won't give you what you want; may try to bring others down and make them look foolish; provoke others into anger and impatience. They desire to be close, loved, want others to make them feel better—others may feel bogged down. They keep themselves in a down position; can only be close with submissive attitude; unable to respond with own ideas; spitefully slows down or resists action and responsibility. Like a turtle, they build a strong, insensitive shell that will wear you out if you try to force them. Under stress they slow down, prepare for the worst, and delay the inevitable.

STRENGTHS: Reliable; dependable; persevering; hard workers; loyal; thorough; patient; capable of great love.

7 ATTRACTING
Expressive-Clinging Childhood Strategy

① Child's Abusive Experience With Caretakers	② Child's Survival Strategy (Adopted False-Self)
"I'm ignored, betrayed, rejected, and not understood."	"I'll dramatize events and my feelings to get attention and avoid being ignored."
"I'll be rejected and ignored if I show my needs and open my heart."	"I'll live without love and express my feelings loud and clear."
"No one listens to me."	"I'll get their attention by acting seductive or sick or flamboyant."
"I'm not heard or noticed."	"I have to struggle for attention, closeness, love, and a lasting relationship."
"People ignore me and leave me."	"I have to do a dance clinging to relationships, or they'll leave me."
"I'm left out and not cared about."	"I'll act up, make noise, or be outrageous to be noticed."

CAUSE: Neglectful or busy parents; caretakers do not treat child as person in its own right; don't pay attention to child; don't take child's feelings seriously; don't listen; child must increase volume to be heard; fathering person was loving in early years, but freezes up at child's sexuality; pushes child away; in our culture this character type is most often found among females; father may be afraid of his own sexual feelings toward child.

FALSE-SELF BELIEFS: No one understands or listens to me; my feelings are unacceptable; I won't give in to my feelings of love, so you can't hurt me; I can't get the attention I need.

FEELINGS: Disappointed; disregarded; defeated; yearns to be protected and loved; afraid of deep emotional involvement; deep sense of hurt, betrayal.

CHARACTER STRATEGY: The expressive-clinging character strategy, writes Kurtz, organizes "perceptions, feelings and actions around separation, being pushed away and not being loved, cared for, appreciated and attended to. On the surface, the basic uncertainty will be about whether or not one is interesting, attractive or wanted. When the pattern is deeply ingrained, some of the following traits show up consistently:

This Expressive-Clinging Strategy

may be used by the unconscious mind when caretakers
do not satisfy the child's natural right, and/or need to:

Be Valued. "I have a right to be heard and understood."

③ Original True-Self Feelings	④ Percentage of the True-Self Feeling Adjoining in Col. 3 That I Have Today.	⑤ This Part of My True-Self (Col. 3) Was Suppressed.
"People are understanding and give me attention."		
"People respond when I reach out."		
"People are interested in me; and take me seriously."		
"I'm a worthy person with whom others can relate."		
"I can relax and know people will stay with me."		
"Caring and helpfulness are freely given to me."		

the person is easily upset and often makes a show of it. He or she can be loud and/or very emotional..., seductive, in a flamboyant, attention-getting way, or girlish and innocent, if that will keep things going. . . . They can feel anxious or very sensitive." They are generally seductive; may be mothering or childlike; may idealize others; may try to sabotage relationships by making unreasonable demands. They look for proof that you care; can't tolerate distance; can't be objective; others may feel trapped, pressured, manipulated. They are desperate for closeness but have difficulty having sexual and love feelings in same place. They want stability in relationships but have inadequate insight; won't focus long enough to gain clarity; will whoop up loudness to get attention; create sickness, destructiveness; want to be interesting, attractive and wanted. They delay separations of all kinds and have trouble letting go of a conversation or a relationship.

STRENGTHS: Sensitive; flexible; expresses strong feelings; empathetic; can be very loving; stimulating to be with; enthusiastic; spontaneous; good actors and actresses; can be very caring and motherly especially in an ongoing relationship; psychic abilities.

8 PRODUCING
Industrious-Overfocused Childhood Strategy

① Child's Abusive Experience With Caretakers	② Child's Survival Strategy (Adopted False-Self)
"I'm inadequate, judged, pushed away, ignored, and must earn love."	"I'll live without love and get what I want by doing a good job and impressing people."
"My father won't love me if I'm not perfect. I've got to achieve — or do it right to get love."	"I'll stay busy and meet adversity by trying harder — trying to be perfect."
"I must be grown-up and adult."	"I'll work hard, compete, keep going, get results, and let nothing distract me."
"I must be serious and stay busy doing my best."	"I'll work hard and earn my self-esteem and the support of others."
"I don't feel good enough."	"I'll get love and support by being conscientious and overachieving."
"Only the future is important."	"I won't relax now, but I'll keep on building for tomorrow."

CAUSE: Main problem is usually with fathering person; father is busy, ignores or rejects the child; does not accept the child as is; child struggles for adult status; the child is not quite good enough; poor self-esteem; feels they will be betrayed if they express love freely; frustrated in attempts to get pleasure; grows up fast; given responsibility prematurely; love from father is conditional on performance; child is pushed to be a "little man" or "little lady" before ready; not allowed to be a child; expected to be perfect; learns to overachieve to get parent's favor.

FALSE-SELF BELIEFS: I have to work to be O.K.; there's always something else to do; I have to be on guard or I'll get hurt; I can't relax or let down; I have to achieve to be appreciated or loved; I'll be used if I don't watch out.

FEELINGS: Fears losing control; frustration; feels unaccepted; fears being held back; afraid of heart feelings being hurt; longs for love from father; longs for tenderness; feels opposed, challenged, pressured.

CHARACTER STRATEGY: Kurtz points out that the industrious-overfocused character strategy organizes "percep- tions, feelings and actions around perfec-

This Industrious-Overfocused Strategy
may be used by the unconscious mind when caretakers
do not satisfy the child's natural right, and/or need to:

Be Imperfect. "I have a right to relax and be loved."

③ Original True-Self Feelings	④ Percentage of the True-Self Feeling Adjoining in Col. 3 That I Have Today.	⑤ This Part of My True-Self (Col. 3) Was Suppressed.
"I'm accepted and loved just as I am."		
"I am enough. I'm appreciated and loved just for me."		
"I don't always have to act like a successful, dignified, responsible adult."		
"I can relax, play, and enjoy."		
"I'm loved unconditionally."		
"Enjoying myself here and now is important."		

tion, competition, failure, effort and striving; not being loved for oneself. On the surface, the basic uncertainty will be about whether or not one is worthy in the eyes of significant others, whether one is competent, adult and successful." He goes on to say that when this pattern is deeply ingrained, they may be "workaholic and serious, interested primarily in getting the job done right, and then doing the next job even better." They work hard; are perfectionistic; keep on going and aren't distracted. They take refuge in action; maneuver to gain closeness; energize others around them. They seek challenges; may be easily angered; have difficulty in letting down and relaxing; have trouble letting themselves be loved. They want equality in relationships; can form fairly close relationships. They avoid surrendering to soft feelings; avoid completing jobs and relationships. To others they may seem cold and business-like. They may feel a need to relax, but stay busy; feel unappreciated and under pressure to perform.

STRENGTHS: High achievers; successful; fast workers; gets things done; responsible, down to earth; self-confident; exciting to be with; good breadwinners; dependable.

Appendix II
Identifying and Escaping
From a Lifetrap

This appendix contains:

1. Sample Lifetrap Worksheets: Pages 284 and 285 show how these life trap worksheets can be used. Notice how they lead you to the childhood roots of the fear, grief, anger, guilt, shame, rage, etc. in your life today—and help you get free of them. You'll get the most helpful insights when you use the lifetrap worksheets *at the time* when a painful emotion first arises.

2. Extra Lifetrap Worksheets: On pages 286 and 287, there is a blank form you can copy. You may wish to carry this with you so you can deal immediately with painful emotions when they are triggered by life events. To speed up reclaiming your true-self, I suggest you fill out this form *EVERY TIME YOU HAVE A PAINFUL EMOTION.*

As you use this growth exercise, you may find it helpful to bear in mind:

1. **Underneath all childhood hurt and pains are unmet childhood needs for love and attention.**

2. **Underneath all painful emotions TODAY (fear, grief, shame, anger, etc.) is an attempt by the unconscious mind to alert us so we can avoid hurt and pain like we experienced in our dependent childhood. Thus, unexpressed, painful childhood emotions are automatically projected into your present life situ-**

ations, and acted out today by life-damaging aggression, withdrawal, submission, or hiding.

3. Becoming aware of the childhood origins helps you get free from painful, separating emotions that diminish your happiness today. You do not need these upsetting emotions to *automatically* grab you today. Your adult skills, physical strengths, and knowledge are more effective than these painful emotions in responding to challenging situations in your adult life.

Please feel free to copy pages 286 and 287 so you can keep a supply with you. By habitually using them at the moment you are disturbed, you can take advantage of the sometimes painful curriculum of the University of Life.

Identifying and Escaping
From a Lifetrap

STEP 1:   List your present painful gut emotions and feelings (not thoughts) about a disturbing area in your life. Use single words like fear, guilt, shame, grief, jealousy, anger, rage, hate, hurt, disdain, resentment, worry, etc. Choose emotions from page 191.

I create the lifetrap experience of _____

irritation, resentment, hate,

anger, rage

because I am demanding (write what you are demanding)

Mary listen to me and not

interrupt me while I'm

talking — and not raise her voice.

STEP 2:   Behind all adult pain, fear, guilt, and shame are conscious and/or unconscious memories of childhood pain when your needs were not met.

I felt the same painful emotions listed in STEP 1 in my childhood when *My parents*

interrupted me and wouldn't

let me finish telling my side.

They would often shout at me

when I tried to answer what

they were saying.

284

STEP 3: To survive physically and emotionally, and to protect my spirit and self-esteem when I was a child, I learned to respond to this pain by *hiding my hurt and not even trying to tell what I want, and what I'm feeling.*

STEP 4: I have the life-enhancing adult insight that it is not true that everyone in my life TODAY will (Copy situation described in Step 2) *keep me from telling my side of an issue.*

STEP 5: When I feel that way today, it is because when I was a child, my caretakers hurt me by *loudly interrupting me and not letting me tell my side.*

STEP 6: With my adult capabilities and strengths today, I can find more effective ways to respond to such situations in my life. I can escape from this lifetrap by choosing behaviors such as *not assuming that when Mary interrupts me and raises her voice that I will not be able to express my point of view. When she breaks in, I can say, "Please don't interrupt me. I want to tell you my side."*

From *Your Road Map to Lifelong Happiness* by Ken Keyes, Jr.

Identifying and Escaping
From a Lifetrap

STEP 1: List your present painful gut emotions and feelings (not thoughts) about a disturbing area in your life. Use single words like fear, guilt, shame, grief, jealousy, anger, rage, hate, hurt, disdain, resentment, worry, etc. Choose emotions from page 191.

I create the lifetrap experience of _____

_____

_____

because I am demanding (write what you are demanding)

_____

_____

_____

STEP 2: Behind all adult pain, fear, guilt, and shame are conscious and/or unconscious memories of childhood pain when your needs were not met.

I felt the same painful emotions listed in STEP 1 in my

childhood when_____

_____

_____

_____

_____

_____

STEP 3: To survive physically and emotionally, and to protect my spirit and self-esteem when I was a child, I learned to respond to this pain by _____

_____

_____

STEP 4: I have the life-enhancing adult insight that it is not true that everyone in my life TODAY will (Copy situation described in Step 2)_____

_____

_____

STEP 5: When I feel that way today, it is because when I was a child, my caretakers hurt me by_____

_____

_____

STEP 6: With my adult capabilities and strengths today, I can find more effective ways to respond to such situations in my life. I can escape from this lifetrap by choosing behaviors such as

_____

_____

_____

_____

_____

From *Your Road Map to Lifelong Happiness* by Ken Keyes, Jr.

Appendix III

Caring Rapid Counseling

Therapy is usually a costly and time-consuming process. It often involves hundreds of sessions at a cost of many thousands of dollars—over many years. Breakthrough methods that can produce rapid and effective healing of lifetraps are long overdue. Ken Keyes, Jr., a leader in the field of personal growth, has accepted the challenge of developing a counseling program that heals childhood wounds in only five days. He calls his work "Caring Rapid Counseling" (CRC).

Results with CRC have been phenomenal. It works directly with one's unconscious mind where the life-damaging injuries are locked in. The five days are focused on the *client's particular requests for change.* CRC offers the opportunity to heal these "injuries" that are destroying relationships, tearing one's self-esteem and self-confidence, and reducing fulfillment, aliveness, fun, inner peace, and happiness.

In the five-day CRC program, we work on one or several problem areas chosen by the client. Although most people find five days sufficient, sometimes more time may be required if one's problems are unusually complex and multi-layered.

CRC is available to clients who are active, non-psychotic, and without drug addiction and who can focus their energy into healing their false-self injuries so they can enjoy their lives.

For a brochure contact: CRC Registration, Caring Rapid Counseling Center, 1620 Thompson Road, Coos Bay, OR 97420. Phone (503) 267-6412. Fax (503) 269-2388.

Caring Rapid Counseling May Help in. . .

Healing These Feelings:

"I'm not good enough."

"I can't speak for myself."

"I should be perfect."

"I'm helpless, hopeless, alone."

"I feel insecure."

"I'm anxious about the future."

"I'll never do it right."

"I'll never find the right person."

"I'll get hurt if I get too close."

"I can't cope."

"I don't enjoy sex."

"I'm afraid of men/women."

"I'm a loser."

"I'm afraid my mate will leave me."

"I have to take what I can get."

"I can't live my own life."

"I can't rely on anyone."

"I have to rescue my partner."

"Relationships don't last."

"I feel guilty and undeserving."

"I'm afraid to express the true me."

"I feel shy."

"I'm ashamed of myself."

Changing These Conditions:

Codependence

Chronic anger, frustration, resentment

Fear of going forward

Body rejection

Chronic sorrow, pity, grief

Repressed anger toward parents

Fear of living fully

Need to be a "victim"

Plagued by unwanted images

Tendency to be lonely and alone

Trauma from sexual abuse

Guilt, self-hate, shame

Blaming self for others' pain

Workaholic

Chronic fear, anxiety, dread

Feeling overworked, overburdened

Low self-esteem and self-confidence

Damage from incest, sexual abuse

Inner child-inner parent dysfunctions

Depression and phobias

Withdrawal from people

Impaired immune function

Pyschosomatic illness

Appendix IV

Personal Growth Workshops With Ken Keyes, Jr.

In his Caring Rapid Counseling Center in Coos Bay, Oregon, Ken personally leads workshops that are outstanding in their ability to heal childhood wounds and help reclaim the beautiful true-self. In a group setting, they are designed to produce a remarkable healing of childhood false-self injuries in six days—provided one is ready to do the intensive inner work needed for rapid healing.

From time to time, workshops for singles or couples are offered to assist people in their journey from the romantic phase through the power struggle—and then to healing and re-romanticizing. This is usually a six-day workshop that can show you what you need to understand, and how to do the inner work needed to create the marriage of your dreams.

The Caring Rapid Counseling Center is operated by The Vision Foundation, a non-profit corporation dedicated to helping us build a better world for ourselves and our children. For brochures, schedules, and costs, please write to Workshop Registrar, The Vision Foundation, Inc., 1620 Thompson Road, Coos Bay, OR 97420. Phone (503) 267-6412. Fax (503) 269-2388.

Caring Rapid Counseling Center
Coos Bay, Oregon

Appendix V

Acknowledgments

The author wishes to acknowledge his debt to countless sages, scientists, and therapists who have discovered the principles that have acted as a lighthouse to guide humanity in its quest for a better future. Some of them are acknowledged in the text when I have quoted from them or used their material.

I have especially benefited from the work of John Bradshaw, Harville Hendrix, Ron Kurtz, Alice Miller, Robert Ornstein, and John Pollard, III. I am greatly indebted to Harville Hendrix for checking Part V and to John Pollard, III for reading Part IV and offering suggestions. Both have given their permission to use their material. I deeply appreciate the contribution of Wes Hiler, whose scholarship and experience in psychotherapy led to many insightful suggestions. Ron Kurtz has most generously given permission to use his material on childhood character strategies.

Many people have helped in the preparation of this book. Scott Balius and Lee McFadden helped in proofreading and offered helpful corrections. The typesetter who contributed the most was Rosalie Wray. The cartoons on each chapter page were drawn by John Mecozzi. The three road maps and some of the other graphics were prepared by Ann Hauser. Marjorie Tully gave the manuscript the benefit of her professional proofreading.

I am indebted to those who have generously read all or part of the manuscript and have given me the benefit of their suggestions. These include John Andrews-Labenski, Tolly Burkan, Jim Ponsart, Angela Wesley, Lenore Schuh, Harry Klopf, Tim Krug, and Lowell Kobrin, M.D.

Special appreciation is due to Lydia, my wife, who has helped in countless ways, including getting up at 3:30 a.m. so I could use the early morning hours to work on the manuscript.

Appendix VI

Ken's Books

Handbook to Higher Consciousness
Ken Keyes, Jr.

Why are our lives filled with turmoil and worry? The *Handbook to Higher Consciousness* presents practical methods that can help you create unconditional love and happiness in your life. Countless people have experienced a dramatic change in their lives from the time they began applying the effective techniques explained in the *Handbook*. There are over one million in print worldwide.

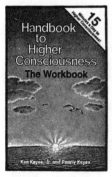

Handbook to Higher Consciousness: The Workbook
Ken Keyes, Jr. and Penny Gillespie

Filled with three months of worksheets, this workbook is geared for the busy person. In 15 to 20 minutes a day, you can begin to apply the methods presented in the *Handbook to Higher Consciousness* in your day-to-day interactions with yourself and others. Each day you are gently guided to uncover the roadblocks that are keeping you from experiencing the most enjoyable life possible. Based on years of practice by thousands of "living lovers," this workbook offers the daily practice you need to get results.

The Power of Unconditional Love: 21 Guidelines for Beginning, Improving, and Changing Your Most Meaningful Relationships
Ken Keyes, Jr.

You are shown how the enormous power of unconditional love can enable you to create a wonderful trust and comfort with the diverse issues, different backgrounds, and changing wants and interests of your partner. It contains guidelines to help you prepare yourself for a relationship that can fulfill your heart's desire for love and intimacy. Additional guidelines help make your relationship richer and more delightful. Also offered are guidelines for how you can let go of a relationship with love and compassion.

Gathering Power Through Insight and Love
Ken Keyes, Jr. and Penny Gillespie

Here's how to do it! This outstanding book gives you detailed instructions on exactly how to develop the love inside you. It has practical, how-to-do-it techniques you can use to handle upsetting situations in your life. It describes the 2-4-4 System for going from the separate-self to the unified-self: 2 Wisdom Principles, 4 Living Love Methods, and 4 Dynamic Processes. These skills are essential for those who want the most rapid rate of personal growth using the Science of Happiness.

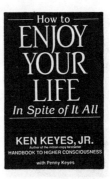

How to Enjoy Your Life in Spite of It All
Ken Keyes, Jr.

Learn to enjoy your life, no matter what others say or do! The Twelve Pathways explained in this book are a modern, practical condensation of thousands of years of accumulated wisdom. They help us remember when our egos blind us. Using these proven pathways will help you change your mental habits from separating, ineffective reactions to practical, loving ways for making your life work better. They promote deeper levels of insight and help increase your energy, inner peace, love, and perceptiveness in your moment-by-moment living. A must for people who are sincerely interested in their personal growth.

Your Life Is a Gift
Ken Keyes, Jr.

Presented in a lighthearted and delightful fashion, here is a wonderful introduction to ways you can use to create more happiness. This charming book is fun to read. It shows how simple it is to experience life with joy and purpose by insightfully guiding your thoughts and actions. Every other page has an amusing and endearing drawing. The reading time is about one hour. It makes a great gift for someone you care about.

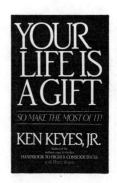

**All of these books are available in bookstores,
or see page 295 for order form.**

Prescriptions for Happiness
Ken Keyes, Jr.

Use these easy-to-remember "secrets" of happiness that work for both children and adults. Designed for busy people, this book can be absorbed in about an hour. These three simple prescriptions can work wonders in your life. They help you put more fun and aliveness into your interactions with people. They help you learn to ask for what you want with love in your heart. These three prescriptions can show you how to increase your insight, love, and enjoyment in everyday situations in your life.

Discovering the Secrets of Happiness:
My Intimate Story
Ken Keyes, Jr.

In this inspiring story, Ken shares his own journey of inner growth from being an unfulfilled man seeking happiness through money and sex to becoming a respected teacher of personal growth and world peace. Ken candidly describes his successes and failures as he recounts how he gave up a lucrative business to dedicate his life to serving others. He shows how you can enormously benefit from applying the methods he discovered.

PlanetHood
Benjamin B. Ferencz and Ken Keyes, Jr.

This important book, which is the sequel to *The Hundredth Monkey*, explains what must be done to give ourselves and our families a future on Planet Earth. It tells how we can replace the *law of force* with the *force of law*. It explains eight ways you can personally help the world settle disputes *legally*—instead of *lethally!* Discover this workable, practical way you can play your part in bringing prosperity and permanent peace to our planet.

All of these books are available in bookstores,
or see page 295 for order form.

ORDERING KEN'S BOOKS

Books	Price	Qty.	Amt.
Your Road Map to Lifelong Happiness	$19.95		
Handbook to Higher Consciousness	$9.95		
Handbook to Higher Consciousness: The Workbook	$8.95		
The Power of Unconditional Love	$9.95		
Gathering Power Through Insight and Love	$9.95		
How to Enjoy Your Life in Spite of It All	$8.95		
Your Life is a Gift	$7.95		
Prescriptions for Happiness	$7.95		
Discovering the Secrets of Happiness	$9.95		
PlanetHood	$9.95		

Shipping ($3.00 first item; 50¢ each add'l item) _____

TOTAL _____

For credit card payment

Visa ❑   MasterCard ❑   Discover ❑   Exp. Date _____

Card # _____ Day Phone _____

Signature _____

Name _____

Address _____

City _____ State _____ ZIP _____

❑   YES! Please put me on your mailing list.

Ken Keyes' books may be purchased through any bookstore. For mail order, send your check in U.S. funds or credit card information to Love Line Bookroom, 1620 Thompson Road, Coos Bay, OR 97420. To order by phone with VISA, MasterCard, or Discover, call (800) 545-7810. In Oregon (503) 267-6412, Monday through Friday, 9:00 a.m. to 4:30 p.m. Pacific time.

Footnotes

Bold type indicates recommended reading.

Introduction:

1. The quote from *Merriam-Webster's Collegiate Dictionary* (10th Edition) is under "they" on pages 1224–1225.

Chapter 1:

1. *New World New Mind: Moving Toward Conscious Evolution* by Robert Ornstein and Paul Ehrlich, page 23. (Doubleday, 1989.)
2. Ibid., page 6.
3. *The Three-Pound Universe* by Judith Hooper and Dick Teresi, page 3. (Macmillan Publishing Company, 1986.)
4. Ibid., page 2.
5. Ibid., page 30.
6. The figure of 100 billion is a personal communication from the Population Reference Bureau, October, 1994.

Chapter 2:

1. ***The Evolution of Consciousness: Of Darwin, Freud, and Cranial Fire: The Origins of the Way We Think* by Robert Ornstein, page 2. (Prentice Hall Press/a division of Simon and Schuster, 1991.)**
2. *The Amazing Brain* by Robert Ornstein and Richard F. Thompson, page 159. (Houghton Mifflin Company, 1984.)
3. *The Three-Pound Universe* by Judith Hooper and Dick Teresi, page 59. (Macmillan Publishing Company, 1986.)
4. ***For Your Own Good: Hidden Cruelty in Child-Rearing and the Roots of Violence* by Alice Miller, page 118. (The Noonday Press, Farrar, Straus and Giroux, 1983.)**

Chapter 3:

1. *The Three-Pound Universe* by Judith Hooper and Dick Teresi, pages 48–49. (Macmillan Publishing Company, 1986.)
2. *The Evolution of Consciousness: Of Darwin, Freud, and Cranial Fire: The Origins of the Way We Think* by Robert Ornstein, page 80. (Prentice Hall Press/a division of Simon and Schuster, 1991.)
3. ***Getting the Love You Want* by Harville Hendrix, Ph.D., page 11. Copyright 1988 by Harville Hendrix. (Reprinted by permission of Henry Holt & Company.)**

Chapter 4:
1. *Beyond the Brain: Birth, Death, and Transcendence in Psychotherapy* by Stanislav Grof, page 25. (State University of New York, 1985.)

Chapter 5:
1. *Homecoming: Reclaiming and Championing Your Inner Child* by John Bradshaw, page 39. (Bantam Books, 1990.)
2. *Facing Codependence: What It Is, Where It Comes From, How it Sabotages Our Lives* by Pia Mellody, page 61. (Harper & Row, Perennial Library, 1989.)
3. *The Drama of the Gifted Child* by Alice Miller, page 16. (Basic Books, a division of Harper Collins, 1990.)

Chapter 6:
1. Ibid., page xx.
2. Taken from the pamphlet entitled *The Negative Love Syndrome* by Bob Hoffman, Hoffman Institute International, 2861 Chelsea Drive, Oakland, CA., 94611. Phone (510) 482-4040.

Chapter 7:
1. *The Inner Child Workbook: What to Do With Your Past When It Just Won't Go Away* by Cathryn L. Taylor, page 13. (Jeremy P. Tarcher, Inc., 1991.)
2. *Homecoming: Reclaiming and Championing Your Inner Child* by John Bradshaw, page 24. (Bantam Books, 1990.)
3. *Embracing Our Selves: The Voice Dialogue Manual* by Hal Stone and Sidra Stone, pages 226–227. (Nataraj Publishing, 1989.)
4. *For Your Own Good; Hidden Cruelty in Child–Rearing and the Roots of Violence* by Alice Miller, page 271. (The Noonday Press, Farrar, Straus and Giroux, 1983.)

Chapter 8:
1. *Homecoming: Reclaiming and Championing Your Inner Child* by John Bradshaw, page 40. (Bantam Books, 1990.)
2. *For Your Own Good: Hidden Cruelty in Child-Rearing and the Roots of Violence* by Alice Miller, pages 6-7. (The Noonday Press, Farrar, Straus and Giroux, 1983.)
3. Ibid., pages 14–15.
4. Ibid., page 16.
5. Ibid., page 118.
6. *When I Say No, I Feel Guilty* by Manuel Smith. (Bantam Books, 1985.)

Chapter 9:
1. *The Drama of the Gifted Child* by Alice Miller, page 69. (Basic Books, a division of Harper Collins, 1990.)
2. *For Your Own Good; Hidden Cruelty in Child-Rearing and the Roots of Violence* by Alice Miller, page 249. (The Noonday Press,

Farrar, Straus and Giroux, 1983.)
3. Ibid., page 97.

Chapter 12:
1. *Supermind: The Ultimate Energy* by Barbara B. Brown, page 74. (Harper and Row, 1980.)
2. *Healthy Pleasures* by Robert Ornstein and David Sobel, page 4. (Addison-Wesley Publishing Company, 1989.)
3. *Embracing Our Selves: The Voice Dialogue Manual* by Hal Stone and Sidra Stone, page 170. (Nataraj Publishing, 1989.)

Chapter 13:
1. *Self-Parenting: The Complete Guide to Your Inner Conversations* by John Pollard, III. (Generic Human Studies Publishing, 1987.) To tune-in to Pollard's Self-Parenting Program, or get a free information packet, or order his books, write to the Self-Parenting Program, P.O. Box 6535, Malibu, CA 90265. Call toll free (800) 458-0091.

Chapter 14:
1. Bradshaw's audio and videocassettes, and workshop schedules are available from Bradshaw Cassettes, P.O. Box 720947, Houston, TX 77272. Phone local (713) 771-1300 or toll free (800) 627-2374.
2. *Self-Parenting: The Complete Guide to Your Inner Conversations* by John Pollard, III. (Generic Human Studies Publishing, 1987.)

Chapter 15:
1. *Embracing Our Selves: The Voice Dialogue Manual* by Hal Stone and Sidra Stone, pages 226–227. (Nataraj Publishing, 1989.)
2. *Getting the Love You Want* by Harville Hendrix, Ph.D., page 193. (Henry Holt & Company, 1988.)
3. *Keeping the Love You Find: A Personal Guide* by Harville Hendrix, Ph.D. (Pocket Books, a division of Simon and Schuster, 1992.)
4. Taken from a "Getting the Love You Want (Couples Workshop)" led by Harville Hendrix, Ph.D. This is available in four audio cassettes from the Institute of Relationship Therapy. You can phone (800) 729-1121 for a catalog and workshop information.

Chapter 16:
1. *Embracing Our Selves: The Voice Dialogue Manual* by Hal Stone and Sidra Stone, page 32. (Nataraj Publishing, 1989.)

Chapter 17:
1. Taken from a "Getting the Love You Want (Couples Workshop)" led by Harville Hendrix, Ph.D. This is available in four audio cassettes from the Institute of Relationship Therapy. You can phone (800) 729-1121 for a catalog and workshop information.

2. Information on the "Homevideo Workshop for Couples" is available from the Institute for Relationship Therapy, 1255 Fifth Avenue, Suite C-2, New York, NY 10029. Phone (800) 729-1121. In New York City, phone (212) 410-7752.

Chapter 18:
1. *Joy Words: An Invitation to Happiness Through an Introduction to the Option Method* by Frank Mosca, Ph.D. (Options for Living Press, 1994.) This book may be obtained by contacting Frank Mosca, Ph.D., Options for Living Press, 762 Warren Avenue, Thornwood, NY 10594. Phone (914) 769-1503. This is a gem for anyone who wants to get free from the illusions that keep us from *naturally and effortlessly* living a happy life.
2. Material in Chapters 18 and 19 has been taken from *Gathering Power Through Insight and Love* by Ken Keyes, Jr. and Penny Gillespie, (Love Line Books, 1987) and *Handbook to Higher Consciousness: The Workbook* by Ken Keyes, Jr. and Penny Gillespie. (Love Line Books, 1989.)

Chapter 20:
1. *New World New Mind: Moving Toward Conscious Evolution* by Robert Ornstein and Paul Ehrlich, page 98. (Doubleday, 1989.)
2. *For Your Own Good; Hidden Cruelty in Child-Rearing and the Roots of Violence* by Alice Miller, page 251. (The Noonday Press, Farrar, Straus and Giroux, 1983.)
3. *Reinventing Your Life: Smart Moves for Escaping Negative Life Patterns* by Jeffrey E. Young, Ph.D. and Janet Klosko. (Dutton, 1993.)
4. Wayne Dyer's audio and videotapes are available through Nightingale-Conant Corp., Chicago, Illinois. Phone (800) 323-5552.

Chapter 21:
1. Anyone seriously interested in maintaining vigor, improving memory, and living longer should subscribe to "Smart Drug News: The Newsletter of the Cognitive Enhancement Research Institute," P.O. Box 4029, Menlo Park, CA 94026. Phone (415) 321-2374. This journal can keep you up-to-date on the latest findings—and how to do it to enhance your life.

   The following books can introduce you to this exciting field: *Mind Food and Smart Pills: A Sourcebook for the Vitamins, Herbs, and Drugs That Can Increase Intelligence, Improve Memory, and Prevent Brain Aging* by Ross Pelton with Taffy Clarke Pelton, (Doubleday, 1989.); *Deprenyl: The Anti-Aging Drug* by Allister Dow, (Hallberg Corp., Publishing, 1993.); *How to Buy Almost*

Any Drug Legally Without A Prescription by James H. Johnston, (Avon, 1990.); *Smart Drugs II: The Next Generation* by Ward Dean, M.D. (B and J Publishing, 1994.); *Life Extension: A Practical Scientific Approach* by Durk Pearson and Sandy Shaw. (Warner Books, 1982.)
2. *The Holy Bible, King James Version*, I Timothy 6:10.

Chapter 22:
1. *Homecoming: Reclaiming and Championing Your Inner Child* by John Bradshaw, page 88. (Bantam Books, 1990.)
2. Ibid., page 156.
3. *For Your Own Good: Hidden Cruelty in Child-Rearing and the Roots of Violence* by Alice Miller, page viii. (The Noonday Press, Farrar, Straus and Giroux, 1983.)
4. Ibid., page 196.
5. Ibid., pages 65–66.

Chapter 23:
1. Association to Unite the Democracies, 1506 Pennsylvania Avenue, S.E., Washington, DC 20003. Phone (800) AT-UNITE.
World Federalist Association, 418 7th Street, S.E., Washington, DC 20003. Phone (800) HATE-WAR.
2. *Planethood: The Key to Your Future* by Benjamin Ferencz and Ken Keyes, Jr., page 22. (Love Line Books, 1991.)

Appendix I:
1. A great debt is acknowledged to Ron Kurtz, author of *Body-Centered Psychotherapy: The Hakomi Method*, Chapter 3 (Life Rhythm, 1990), for the basic data used to construct this inventory. Appreciation is also due to Pat Ogden, who compiled and edited "The Chart" in *Supplementary Readings for Students and Graduates of Hakomi Trainings*, Hakomi Institute, Boulder, CO 80306. Material describing the eight strategies is reprinted with permission.

Index

306

Smart Drug News: The Newsletter of
the Cognitive Enhancement
Research Institute, 226
Smith, Manuel, 92
Some Thoughts on the Education of
Children, 89
Stone, Hal and Sidra, 74, 128, 132,
137, 158, 165, 220
Stress
    See Quirk, time
    threats, real or imagined, 18
Subconscious mind, 28
    See Mind, unconscious
Supermind: The Ultimate Energy, 128
Supplementary Readings for Students
    and Graduates of Hakomi
    Trainings, 264-281
Suppression
    naturally self-healing, 16-17
    need for expression, 16-17, 149

T

Taylor, Cathryn, 71
Teresi, Dick, 8, 28
"Terrible Two's," 52, 71
Thompson, Richard F., 13
Thoreau, Henry David, 188
Three-Pound Universe, The, 8-9, 28
True-Self, 59-68, 228
    attitudes of, 60-61
    beyond recall, 86
    definition of, 59
    disowned parts, 71-75
    hidden, 67
    journey of, 48-57
        graph of, 48
    path of ideal growth, 72
    perfection, original, 65
    reclaiming, 209-222, 260
    See Healing
    shadow of, 63-64
    splitting of, 62-64, 66, 71-75
    wholeness, feeling of, 67
Truman, Harry, 250
Trummelschlager, Johann, 235

U

United Methodist Church, 247
University of Life, 52, 115, 211,
    225, 259

V

Voice Dialogue Method, 137, 165
    166, 220

W

Webster's Collegiate Dictionary,
    Merriam, xv
When I Say No, I Feel Guilty, 92
Whitehead, Alfred North, 22
Wisdom principle, first, 187-199,
    225-226
    changing demands to preferences,
    196-199
    changing our perception, 195-199
        we're not our programming, 197-
        198
    demands cause unhappiness, 188-
    194
        pinpointing form, 190
    preferences, key to happiness,
    189, 194, 198
        characteristics of, 197
    responsible for your experience,
    187-190
Wisdom principle, second, 201-206,
    225-226
    misusing, 204-206
    people basically good, 201-202,
    205
    positive intention, beneficial, 202
        behind harmful actions, 204
        formulating, 202-204
        list of, 203
    unskillful acts and goals, 202, 204-
    205
Workshops, personal growth, 290
World anarchy, 250
World Federalist Association, 246,
    248
World republic, 250
World War II, 237

Y

Young, Jeffrey E., 210, 221
Your Life Is a Gift, 293

307